6

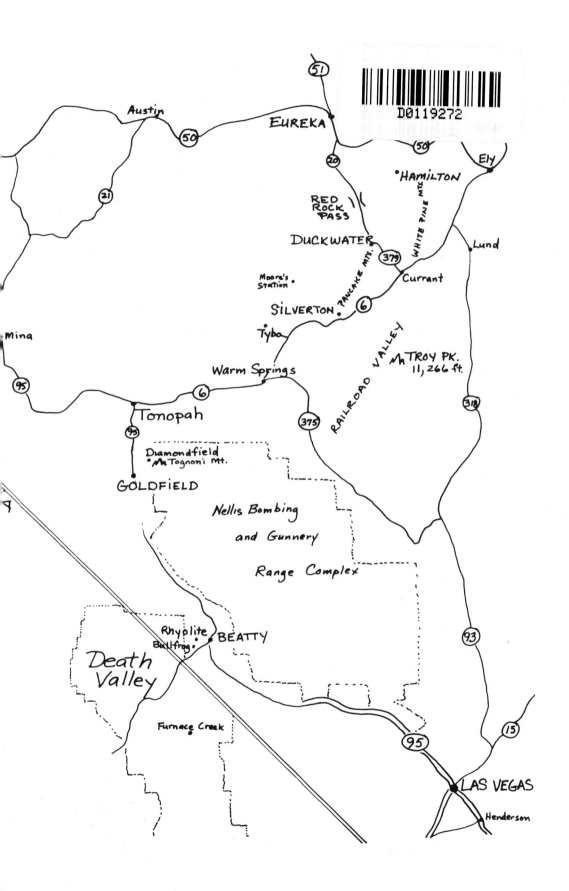

TREASURE IN THE DUST

Enduring Gold and Silver's
Century of Divorce

TREASURE IN THE DUST

Enduring Gold and Silver's Century of Divorce

Becky Boudway

Library of Congress Catalog Card Number 85-063261
ISBN 0-914330-86-1

Published by Panorama West Books, Fresno, California

This book available from:
Mineral Economics Publications
1525 West Northern Avenue
Phoenix, Arizona 85021

Manufactured in the United States of America

Contents

Table of Photographs VII

Introduction IX

Chapter 1
Whispers of the Gold Rush 1

Chapter 2
Abandonment 11

Chapter 3
Echoes from Walls of Time 19

Chapter 4
Up Against the Sierra 27

Chapter 5
Chant of the Survivors 35

Chapter 6
Legend of the Family Mine 45

Chapter 7
Moon on the Sagebrush 55

Chapter 8
Journey into Silence 63

Chapter 9
People's Silver 73

Chapter 10
Blood to a Metal Heart 85

Chapter 11
Defiant Dreamers 93

Chapter 12
Red Rock Pass 109

Chapter 13
Mountain Link to the Past 117

Chapter 14
Miner's Destiny 125

Chapter 15
Beneath the Wounds of Greed 135

Chapter 16
Water from the Rock 147

Endnotes 159

Bibliography 167

Index 175

Photographs

Hale Tognoni, author's father, at a "brass cap" XVII

Maria Cross, author's great-great grandmother, with her third husband,
   John Cross, in Duckwater Valley, Nevada XVIII

Dr. Vincent Gianella and the author...................................10

W. C. Ralston, banker that helped finance Virginia City.................18

Harry Stimler, Goldfield promoter, photo and cartoon 26

Senator Key Pittman, photo and cartoon...............................33

J. C. Tognoni, cartoon...37

The surviving locator on the Black Oil claims, Frank V. Collins, with
   his young family 44

Richard P. Haskins, Jr., driving his father's Ford truck, c. 1925...........44

J. C. Tognoni and George Wingfield in the lobby of the Mizpah Hotel,
   Tonopah, Nevada 54

George Wingfield 54

Silverton about 1921. J. C. Tognoni holding pick 62

Silverton mining camp, c. 1930 69

Myrtle Jacques with her second husband, J. C. Tognoni.................69

Hale Tognoni, 16 years old, packing ore car up Elephant Mountain 72

Bronze sculpture by George-Ann Tognoni 72

"Puck" magazine cartoon, March 2, 1892, Nevada Historical Society......74

Joseph Russell Tognoni, author's grandfather, c. 1920 86

Children in Duckwater's School with teacher, 1903 92

Water-master Nye Tognoni at work in Duckwater Valley, c. 1930 95

Men of Duckwater in the lane along one of the Valley's irrigation ditches,
   1903 95

J. C. Tognoni on his Silverton claims, c. 1915 110

Eureka, Nevada, looking west 116

Hale Tognoni and brothers with garbage collecting wagon, c. 1929.......124

Wagons hauling wood to make charcoal for smelters...................124

Goldfield, Nevada, 1981 137

Diamondfield, c. 1905. J. C. Tognoni on horse 137

George Wingfield, cartoon 146

J. C. Tognoni with claim monument 158

J. C. Tognoni, c. 1915 158

Introduction

*. . . who can fail to realize that mining is
a calling of peculiar dignity?*
Agricola[1]

Literature about mining seldom seems to capture popular imagination with the full force of its potential. Certainly, the controversy that surrounds mining in our times attracts the popular journalist, but so much misinformation and mythology pre-exists about mining that no matter how responsible modern newspaper and television news may be, it usually only ripples the slew of ignorance. As for the fine literature of mining, it has been abandoned amid the dusty tomes of historical science; and most modern attempts to bring light to mining are marred either with unresolved shame or romantic nostalgia.

Herbert Hoover, perhaps the most successful mining engineer of all time, pointed out that among the professions, mine engineering has "more romance, wonder, excitement, success and failure,"[2] than any other calling. His own career in mining was to take him out of the Sierra Nevada to Australia, China, India, South Africa and Russia. Before the age of thirty, he was a celebrated "doctor of mines,"[3] and despite political slander directed against him in later years, Herbert Hoover was to maintain a fellowship with the communist and non-communist peoples of many nations giving a transcendency to the engineering that he practiced.

Apart from the compelling qualities which Hoover found in the profession of mine engineering, mining itself is brimming with literary devices which ought to make informative stories of mines very popular:[4]

> . . . a magic world, where men with lamps on their heads, speaking a strange language, move about confidently in dark passages . . . miniature railroads . . . elevators that put one down and whisk one up many times the height of tall buildings . . . underground streams that gurgle in

> channels along the passageways . . . near or far, explosions of dynamite
> . . . always the sight of ore, red or black or bronze or yellow . . . object of
> the men's search. The child . . . senses that here man has achieved con-
> quest of an alien world, in which he belongs no more than upon the sea or
> in the air. Like the conquest of these other two . . . exciting when seen
> with fresh eyes.

Naturally, when poets have explored the underground, even meta-
phorically, as did Dante in the *Inferno*, the inner forces of the earth seem to
have fused the poet's words with greater passion, just as those same forces
have metamorphosed quiet sediment from the planet's surface into aston-
ishingly beautiful maps of strength and weakness, stress and ease. But
mining repels with the same prodigious power with which it fascinates
because, like sex, sin and death, it is on the darker and more private side of
our human condition; and many shrink from dark realities. Mining is
stamped in man's psyche on the side of evil; and it is not surprising that in
polite society the true mining men among us remain like diamonds in the
rough, holding to superficial appearance, silent as to inner visions.

Literary men do not frequently give their talents to the subject of
mining, and even when they do, as with Mark Twain, they often reveal
themselves to be indisposed either to the idea or to the work:[5]

> . . . We judged that we had learned the real secret of success in silver-
> mining—which was not to mine the silver ourselves by the sweat of our
> brows and the labor of our hands, but to sell the ledges to the dull slaves
> of toil and let them do the mining.

Where the mining company has cooperated with the writer for public
relations purposes, the engaging details of human interest too often have
been an evasion of difficult questions. As for mining men themselves, their
ability to communicate has frequently decreased in an inverse relationship
with their technical knowledge.[6] Lately this phenomenon has been due, in
part, to the defensive position from which most "dull slaves of toil" speak.

It was inevitable that mining should become a villainous activity to
those who have rejected the values of an industrialized society. Industrialization has made great demands on Earth's mineral resources at a greater
rate than ever before. Still, censure of mining is not new. In the mid-six-
teenth century, Georgius Agricola felt compelled to defend mining in an
essay separate from his technical treatise, *De Re Metallica*. In the essay, he
"refuted the charges which have been made against metals and against
miners."[7] Moreover, the first book of *De Re Metallica* is much the same in
tone and substance as the introduction to *Treasure in the Dust* which you
now read:[8]

Several good men have been so perturbed by (the harmful and destructive events in which metals have played a part) that they wish absolutely that metals had never been created, or being created, that no one had ever dug them out. The more I commend the singular honesty, innocence, and goodness of such men, the more anxious shall I be to remove utterly and eradicate all error from their minds and to reveal the sound view, which is that metals are most useful to mankind.

Is is among the most inscrutable of human paradoxes that this science for which man has had such recurring repugnance is at the very foundation of our ascent from primitive cultures. Even the period of that ascent and of human history are designated by metals. The discovery of how to roast lustrous, black cassiterite to release tin and then to alloy it with copper to make bronze began centuries of human existence that we call the Bronze Age. Holding its edge, bronze offered to human life a stability which had been observed by man during the Stone Age only in simple rock.

Supreme among man's elemental blessings, however, must be gold. Found like copper uncompounded in nature, gold is scarce but widely distributed, heavy but not bulky, indestructible but easily worked, and so beautiful as to be of great difficulty to imitate,[9] all of which has made gold a fitting measure of human energy and the medium for earthly intercourse between men. Commerce and peace have worn a golden face universally, and gold has been produced extensively on every continent and by almost every nation.

But mining has also been intimate with war: mining is a Janus. Among those gods invented by the practical Romans to give dignity to simple acts of everyday life, Janus was personified in his chief temple in the city of Rome by a two-faced statue. The younger of the faces looked to the eastern door of the temple or to the sunrise; and the older face looked to the western opening. The fact about Janus which is most worthy of pondering is the Roman ritual of leaving the doors of his temple open wide only during war. Since the Romans maintained the longest period of world prosperity in human history—the Pax Romana—Janus' temple doors were not thrown open lightly. In peace the Romans must have felt that Janus, and for our purposes, mining, required reverent study by the glow of a cautious torch, if men were to find the wisdom to perpetuate themselves harmoniously. In war the civility of protecting Janus' four eyes was abandoned, and man's ignorance lost its privacy.

The 200 years of peace known as the Pax Romana coincided approximately with the Roman conquest of ancient and rich mines of Spain; and in Spain the peace was to last an incredible 600 years. But the Romans developed mines all over their empire, the Cornish tin mines being an important example. Although the mining was done by slaves, the slave-miners were not unattracted to their work. The worst punishment prescribed in the laws governing the miner was to be sold with the provision that he could never again work in the mines.[10] The miner's physical living standards were pre-scribed by Roman law and may have been better than the standards for slaves in other occupations. No doubt, however, even as slaves men felt a fascination for mining.

Sadly, the popular image of mining men today holds little more public respect than slavery. Worse, the history of the event from which the mining industry in the United States took root—the gold rush—is viewed from the smug vantage point of recent historians as basically a phenomenon of "greed, waste, hardship, social breakdown and environmental butchery."[11] Few voices are heard which have both an appreciation for mining and an understanding of economics. Few voices are heard like that of U.S. Senator William Morris Stewart, "Father of the Federal Mining Law."[12] Haunting the brittle pages of the *Congressional Globe* is a remarkable speech which the senator from Nevada intoned in 1866:[13]

> The failure of the metal crop taxed every energy and resource of the financier and provoked inordinate issue of bills of exchange and paper money . . . The nations of Europe, heavily encumbered with debt, were exhausting their ingenuity to relieve the people from oppressive and ruinous taxation . . . It was reserved for California to awaken the latent energies of the entire mining world. This youthful and proud and vigorous state is already enrolled in the history of the monetary world as the valorous leader that headed the forlornest of hopes and rescued the drooping nations of Europe from pecuniary ruin and national dissolu-tion; for I need not assure the Senate that money is the sinew and safety of modern government.

In Senator Stewart's day mining men were not pathetic, backward characters. They were more like heroes battling nature for the wealth of a nation. The esteem in which they were held was not due solely to the magni-tude of the riches which they uncovered. The laws by which the miners governed their work and guaranteed to themselves the fruits of their labor were an embodiment of human dignity. Senator Stewart:

> The miner's law is a part of the miner's nature. He made it. It is his own . . . he loves it, trusts it, and obeys it. He has given the honest toil of his life to discover wealth which, when found, is protected by no higher law than that enacted by himself under the implied sanction of a just and generous government.

In 1866 the United States Congress adopted the miner's laws as the first body of federal mining law. Historically, the laws were akin to free mining of medieval Germany. But the gold rush miners brought the seeds of it, not from Germany alone, but from Ireland, England, Wales, France, Spain, and Mexico. They first planted those seeds in a lawless California territory, and a proud species of common law grew along the "mother lode." Although fathered in Europe, free mining behaved as if native to the Sierra Nevada and quickly bore fruit.

As it turned out, the government's generosity, necessary for the survival of free mining, did not last. After all, Senator Stewart had used no small measure of sagacity to garner the Senate's trust in 1866. The federal government's Civil War debt eventually was to have repercussions in the monetary system of the United States antipathetic to gold and silver mining. Consequently, the first federal mining laws were as concealed as the minerals for which they legislated ownership. They were a rider on "An Act Granting the Right of Way to Ditch and Canal Owners through the Public Lands, and Other Purposes."

The European forefathers of the United States had not foreseen that the federal government, which they so carefully crafted, would one day hold millions of acres of land, much of it rich in minerals. So the "sanction of just and generous government" of which Senator Stewart spoke had no direct Constitutional guarantees. When it came to mines, even Benjamin Franklin lacked vision; but in his day the science of geology did not even have a name. So Franklin felt free to say in arguing for paper currency, "Gold and silver are not the produce of North America, which has no mines."[14] The awakening of a nation to the power of its natural resources would take place after the death of its founders; and after the gold rush, the story of government's struggle over the ownership of those resources has escaped popular recognition.

Hale Christopher Tognoni, my father, seems to have been educating me in that story ever since I was old enough to serve in any capacity whatsoever in his mineral development corporation and mining law practice. I've been throwing rocks out of old mine roads one way or another for a very long time. My father comes from a Nevada mining family. He has been a miner; he became a geological and a mining engineer; and as a mining lawyer, he has fought for the dignity of the American mining laws and for the rights of the prospectors and small mine operators who have trusted those laws. Much of Hale Tognoni's experience epitomizes the modern struggle of mining people with self-righteous, governmental greed. In the 1960s federal agents loosely accused a mining company by whom Tognoni had been retained of salting desert land with gold. The charges were left innuendo and never made formally, but the Bureau of Land Management succeeded in bringing a contest in the federal district court of Arizona wherein the company's mineral patent was revoked.

In the transcript of that trial exists a seemingly inconsequential exchange between the U.S. attorney and gold miner Daugherty. In this short excerpt is the heart of the frustration which has been oppressing small miners in the United States too long. The U.S. attorney's sensibilities were so foreign to Daugherty's that communication between them became hopeless and even pathetic in the confines of courtroom formality:[15]

Attorney Ross:	"If I walked out on this Desert Gold . . . it would be pretty barren and empty, wouldn't it?"
Daugherty:	"Well, there is a portion of this land that is really well mineralized. Some will run a little lighter than others."
Attorney Ross:	"I move to strike that as being unresponsive."
The Judge:	"Possibly he didn't understand your question."

"Barren and empty" was not descriptive of the land Daugherty knew and on which he had been living and mining for over a decade. Furthermore, Daugherty's vision of the land had no more to do with greed than a farmer's love for the soil of his fields. How else should we interpret Daugherty's frank admission that his mining work on the Desert Gold property often had been "an expensive living."[16] Mining men like Daugherty are not detractors from the value of the land by any true human perspective. Daugherty loved the land and stayed with it the only way he knew how. The dry, hot, rocky hills of the old San Domingo gold placers north of Phoenix, Arizona, hold little attraction for most men, and most men will never share Daugherty's visions nor marvel as did Senator William Morris Stewart that the "Great American Desert" was "revealed to the startled world . . . to be laden with purer and more abundant ores than . . . ancient Ophir." Perhaps the United States government is currently experiencing some disbelief that it spent so great an effort in keeping its citizens from the ownership of "barren and empty" land. Or maybe those government men who have clung to their jobs through the unreasonable embroilments of this policy have stoically adopted the suicidal philosophy of John Charles Van Dyke. In a book written about his wanderings in the American desert at the turn of the century, Van Dyke, the art historian and critic, wrote:[17]

After the making of Eden came a serpent and after the glorious furnishing of the world, a human being. Why the existence of the destroyer? What monstrous folly, think you, ever led Nature to create her one great enemy—man!

This pessimism seems to have underlaid federal land policies for a very long time, breeding utter disregard for the health of the nation's mineral industry. Frequently public communications do not list mining among the "multiple uses" which the government sees fit for its more than 375 million acres of public land; and the budgets which state departments of mineral resources keep are so low as to relegate them to rock and mineral museums with little say in public policy. Meanwhile we trade invaluable nitrates to Russia in exchange for commodities for which we have no great need,[18] and we sell our gold and silver reserves with abandon to bring down the prices. Furthermore, we rely upon imports for at least half of twenty major mineral commodities and live with a rapidly growing trade deficit in imported minerals, leaping from two billion dollars in 1973 to eight billion in 1978.[19] This insanity has its roots in economic policies which would deny that a nation's wealth, as measured by its money, must be of substance, must be of something besides trust in an undisciplined government. Money still must represent human energy as measured for centuries by that amount of labor required to mine the precious metals which have been at the foundation of our earthly money systems. When money ceases to measure labor, government has lost its only enduring power.

In war, governments pay for their destruction with devalued money, sharing the responsibility for war's devastation with some degree of equity. After World War II, however, when the nation's leadership, Republican and then Democrat, was faced with making the necessary devaluation in U.S. currency by raising the price of gold, it continued instead on the artless path of least resistance. War followed war, hot and cold—and no serious attempt to return to sparser peace-time economy was made. The lesson of history which we must take most seriously is that a strong mining industry can be as important to peace as it is to victory in war. We must not fall to a way of thinking against which Agricola warned in the sixteenth century:[20]

> ... the products of the mines are not themselves the cause of war. Thus, for example, when a tyrant, inflamed with passion for a woman of great beauty, makes war on the inhabitants of her city, the fault lies in the unbridled lust of the tyrant and not in the beauty of the woman. Likewise, when another man, blinded by a passion for gold and silver, makes war upon a wealthy people, we ought not to blame the metals but transfer all blame to avarice. For frenzied deeds and disgraceful actions, which are wont to weaken and dishonor natural and civil laws, originate from our own vices.

According to powerful economists, gold, the touchstone for the condition of the mineral industry in the United States, has long been and will always be in hopelessly short supply. The economic scientists have told us since the first days of this nation's history that gold is deplorably scarce due to the nature of the earth. Although the fear that no more gold exists has again and again proven a false one, this fear continues to contribute to bad economic management and self-fulfilling economic prophecy. There is no lack of gold mines, only a general ignorance of the fact that gold ore, like every other mineral, comes in low-grade and high-grade varieties. Whether there is gold has not depended on its actual existence but on those economic factors determining whether the gold may be mined. If cared for, gold and mining remain adequate tools of earthly prosperity, and there is hope that even if we manage to mine all the metals of the earth, those metals will endure and continue to measure human labor in a manner necessary to lasting peace.

With the chapters to follow, we will examine the concerns of one mining man, Hale Tognoni. By telling the story of his mining family, it is my hope to cut a diamond in the rough and to slow the light falling upon its facets, that mining and some harmonies of truth may be illuminated. We will travel to California and Nevada and into the past, on a pilgrimage to mining country where man first awakened to the vast quantity of natural resources in what has become the United States.

Hale Tognoni at a "brass cap," the object of many a surveyor's search when marking mining claims on public lands.

Hale Tognoni's great-grandmother, Maria Cross, stands with her husband John Cross and unidentified traveler in Duckwater, Nevada. Born Maria Usher in 1820 in Ohio, she married gold-rusher Ernest Jesse Jacques and came west.

1   Whispers of the Gold Rush

And lay thou thy treasure in the dust, and the
gold of Ophir among the stones of the brooks.
Job 22:24

At Sutter's Fort in late summer, August 13, 1981, our journey begins, but in a sense, it began a year earlier when I undertook to write *Treasure in the Dust* for my father. I quickly discovered that he would not be satisfied with a technical or academic treatise. The stories of his mining family were ever ready for repetition when he spoke to me, and his mind worked eagerly to find the metaphors in his family's history for all that he knew and wanted to say about mining in the United States.

Our journey begins in the 1980s, but it will take me into the past as much as into the countryside where in about 1880 my Italian great-grandfather, Guiseppe Cristofo di Tognoni, arrived in Nevada to become a U.S. citizen. Further back into the past in 1858, my great-grandmother, Jesse Myrtle Jacques, was born, reputedly at Sutter's Fort. She, like much of which I will write, was conceived in California's gold rush, and my father's memory of her is steadfast, practically a refrain to his stories of growing up in mining camps and towns of the American West. Otherwise, Hale Tognoni and my brothers—geological engineer, mining engineer, landman and mining lawyer amongst them—have given the continuity of their vision little poetry. As for myself, my heritage has guided me only intuitively until my pilgrimage into the past to the "mother lode" and the basins and ranges of central and western Nevada where at least four generations of my father's family have mined and ranched.

In the family's Bible, my father remembers seeing the words "first white child born at Sutter's Fort" printed after his grandmother's name.

Further particulars of Myrtle's birth to Mary Usher of Ohio and Ernest Jesse Jacques of Delhi, New York, are neither etched in known memory nor in Duckwater, Nevada's cemetery marble. Myrtle spent her last eight years in a county hospital in Tonopah, Nevada, where just after midnight in the January darkness of 1954, she showed no vital signs for the attending physician to measure. Dr. Russell A. Joy wrote the single word "senility" on Myrtle's death certificate in the blank for "condition directly leading to death." Since she died without her family, much on the certificate was left "unknown" and much is in error, even her name. If a chorus of small clouds danced across the full moon the night she died, no one took note on the numerous blank lines of her last documentation. Her death remains as silent and obscure in historical record as her birth; and in this as in many other aspects of her life, she is the perfect metaphor for the silver half of the precious metal standard of monetary value so widely held to be antiquated today.

Still, in hope of finding some clue to the "first white child's" circumstances, I ask the young man raising the American flag out in front of Sacramento's Fort Sutter if any records are kept inside. He replies that he knows of none; and while I wait with a band of tourists outside the heavy, rough-hewn doors of the fort, he inquires within as to where I should go. Around the fort the buildings of the city press close where once there was nothing but dust and far-reaching fields of wild oat grass, dried yellow as are the meadows now beyond Sacramento's asphalt. From here Captain Sutter probably could see the green horizons of the Sacramento and American rivers which converge to the northwest. Today the sunlight glares from the white-washed walls of the fort, and the unshaded concrete walkway up from busy "M" Street is already hot when the fort's flag-raiser sends me to the California State Library.

Along Sacramento's Capitol Park the streets are shaded, and at the roots of the trees squirrels cunningly perform for appreciative visitors to the capitol's flower gardens. The flowers are as fanatically manicured and as colorful as in the royal gardens of London, and I try again to imagine the field of oat grass where now stand the heavy stone palaces of government for the most powerful state in these United States. Sutter's Fort, behind me, is only the abandoned shell of this imposing beast of State from which I hope to pluck clues for my story. Was Myrtle's father one of those who found good fortune here, and did Mary find a birthing bed at Sutter's Fort for the first white child? I will probe only gently for answers in Sacramento, but I *am* driving a car, and traces of parking aggravation in my face arouse the state's librarian at the outset of my brief investigation: "We do try to serve people here."

She does try. From the card catalog she helps me to glean a diary kept by four men at Fort Sutter,[1] including the raucous Captain himself. Many days carry lone entries testifying to little more than that the sun rose in a clear sky; but on Wednesday, October 1, 1845, I find: "Today the party left for the Mountains. Harry's wife was delivered with a girl." I will discover in searching for the identity of Harry and his wife that "white child" is not easily defined in the crude, male society of Sutter's "New Helvetia." Harry's wife was an Indian named Manawitte, formerly in the possession of Captain Sutter until his loan of her to a second man excited ill feeling. She was awarded to Captain Sutter's Sandwich Island ward, Harry, as either compromise or revenge. Needless to say, Harry's daughter was probably not white, but I do find a white child in Heinrich Lienhard's diary.[2] Amid further evidence that I will have no trouble bringing a little intrigue to the shadows of my story is the following:

> " . . . among Sutter's employees was an Indian vaquero whose wife had a white child whom she exhibited with considerable pride. One day I asked the woman if Sutter was the father of the boy; and she laughed with delight . . . "

The name Jesse Jacques, father of the white child for whom I search, does not appear in the state's pioneer index, and I resign myself to no quick confirmation of my great-grandmother's skin-color claim to fame at Sutter's Fort. Meanwhile I have been perusing the *Fort Sutter Papers* wherein John C. Fremont is struggling for power with the Mexican command in northern California. It is likely that women of all shades were making themselves scarce at that time, while the men threw up their battlements and issued their edicts. The gold rush would eventually bring white women to California, but only after the rush had demolished Sutter's empire would a certifiable white child be born at the old fort, no longer a bastion for hardy white trappers, woodsmen and explorers with their native wives.

First white child or not, Jesse Myrtle Jacques came from gold country to Duckwater Valley, Nevada. More than likely her father was among the prospectors who rushed into the Reese River district of central Nevada in the early 1860s. From one rush or another, Jacques probably brought wealth as well as beautiful daughters with him to Duckwater. Perhaps he and his wife heard of Duckwater's thick, wild hay when they hastily made their way through Nevada to California in the 1850s. On the Oregon-California trail, they would have passed far to the north of the high Nevada valley where their bones finally came to rest. They may have stopped at an Overland Trail station owned by James O. Williams, whose progeny would have control of one of the large ranches at Duckwater and into whose family

Myrtle Jacques would marry. After two children, however, she ended that marriage to John Williams with a Declaration of Annulity from the Catholic Church, maybe the first such declaration in Nevada. Her second marriage, to my great-grandfather, Joe Christopher (Guiseppe Cristoforo) Tognoni, would last until his death in the 1930s.

With Tognoni as with Williams, Myrtle clung steadfastly to her ambitions, or illusions of grandeur as some would have it—ambitions and illusions which came naturally to a child of the California gold rush. She kept in her own name a good part of the land which she and J. C. Tognoni purchased from the State of Nevada to build their Monte Carlo Stock Farm; and after they lost Monte Carlo to the bank, she jumped J. C.'s mining claims at Silverton to make her home in isolation from troubled Duckwater, where she and her family had repeatedly fought for water rights. Atop the tongue of black lava, near which J. C. found water and silver, Myrtle's rocking chair looked out onto the broad, white salt flats of Railroad Valley. She squarely faced the blue, granite mountain range rising steeply out of the sagebrush to wall the valley. The constancy of her vigil in that chair rivaled the geologic formations around her. The clouds clung above the dark face of the mountains beyond according to natural laws as faithful as Myrtle's rocking, and in the black ridge of volcanic rock beneath her, she would bury her husband and their son, my grandfather.

On our journey into the past, I will visit Myrtle's forsaken perch and the silver deposits which my grandmother, Ina Belle, believed would be the making of her children. But I am still in Sacramento where I will make one more stop at Argus Books before heading east into the foothills of the Sierra and beyond. The state's librarian has told me that I will find some of the books that I want at this unique bookstore, but I cannot stay long in Mr. Kaplan's store. I want to get to the Searls Historical Library in Nevada City, California, before it closes. Both Kaplan and the state's librarian seem puzzled as to why I should want to use precious time in the tiny, antique law office which serves as a library for the Nevada County Historical Society. Maybe my Sacramento informants do not know or are too cautious to imagine that in the little library across from the Nevada County Courthouse, power once grew with all the ferment supposed for life's origin by spontaneous generation in mud. Men with property met between the high, book-lined walls of the Searls' law office to sign deeds and rights-of-way which would allow frontier enterprises like South Yuba Canal Water Company to grow into Pacific Gas and Electric, and Searls' mining efforts to grow into Newmont Mining Company.

My immediate justification for opening the library's door on Church Street in Nevada City is to investigate the transcript of *Edward Woodruff vs. North Bloomfield Gravel Mining Co.*[3] A kind woman of the Nevada County Historical Landmarks Commission has written me that the Searls Historical Library holds a copy of the transcript. In *Woodruff vs. North Bloomfield*, the decision by Judge Lorenzo Sawyer culminated efforts by Sacramento Valley farmers and railroad powers to shut down hydraulic mines in California. The gold rush, hydraulic mining, and my great-grandmother were at the root of growth in the American West, and all three, like breeding itself, have been regarded with disdain and pity, as well as with wonder. Hydraulic mining gave birth to the forerunners of California's major utility company: the first canals and aqueducts in Northern California were constructed to serve hydraulic miners. Now, like a trophy on a handy, low shelf in the library, a row of slick white boxes contain the microfilmed details of death for North Bloomfield Gravel Mining Company. In 1893, the California legislature would try to revive hydraulic mining with a "Debris Commission" created by the Caminetti Act,[4] but California's sin was not to be so easily redeemed.

I have only one hour until the Nevada County Historical Library closes for the day, so I do not even try to begin reading the testimony presented to Lorenzo Sawyer in the Debris Case. Instead, I content myself with questioning the man who sits reading at a desk by the library's only memorable window. He slides a loose-leaf notebook from an upper shelf and hands it to me. In the notebook, members of the historical society have collected articles about prominent personages of Nevada County. Among them are Aaron Sargent and William Morris Stewart, western champions of democracy. If clarity of thought and strength of expression were the primary measure of fame, Sargent and Stewart would be as popularly known as Jefferson and Hamilton. My interest in the miner, lawyer, newspaperman, U.S. senator and ambassador, Aaron Sargent, brings color to the face of the librarian, and the cool library air billows almost visibly when he tells me that Ambassador Sargent insulted Prince Otto Von Bismark so bluntly as to have himself expelled from the emperor's realm.

"You have, of course, read William Morris Stewart's biography?" he asks, and he greets my surprise with uneasy control. Proudly he informs me that Ruth Hermann, the biography's author, is a resident of Nevada City. Although Hermann copyrighted her Stewart biography in 1975, I had failed to turn it up in any of my Arizona libraries. Instead, I had read, re-read, cited and quoted Senator Stewart's 1866 speech urging the adoption of the laws of the gold rush by the federal government. I had gleaned biographical facts from an early history of Nevada and from an obituary in the *Mining and Scientific Press*. I am, of course, ecstatic to have before me, even if only briefly, a full length biography and several photographs of William Morris

Stewart, the "Silver Senator." Between my rapture and the librarian's fleeting enthusiasm before returning to his book by the window, the dark library warms a little before closing time. After dinner, I quickly check for a copy of Hermann's book about Stewart in a Nevada City book store, but my questions dumbfound the clerk. In her bookstore Carlos Casteneda, the pseudo-cowboys, drug culture and self-improvement seem to have wiped history from the shelves. Criticism of Ms. Hermann's book as hero-worship, in this desert of learning, would seem petty. I smile to allay apprehension which my historical concerns may be causing, and to extricate myself gracefully, I tell the bookstore clerk that the author reportedly lives in Nevada City.

The town is a relic on a scenic loop of the highway to Lake Tahoe and Reno, Nevada. Surrounding its winding streets are the magical Sierra foothills where men came from around our planet to become kings. Like the legendary rivers of the ancient world and the illusive land of Ophir from which came the gold which contributed to King Solomon's great power, rivers of the western Sierra watershed—the Feather, the Yuba, the American, the Mokelumne and others—gave up fortunes along their forks and gulches to an eager world. What Captain Sutter's millman on the north fork of the American River discovered in the tail race of his mill wheel was a kind of gold which could be had with little work, little capital investment and little regard for a man's race, color or creed because the land had no iron-clad property rights. As one chronicler of the gold rush, J. D. Borthwick, wrote: "The habitual veil of imposition and humbug, under which men usually disguised themselves from the rest of the world, was thrown aside as a useless inconvenience."[5]

The rebel British colonies, which had become the United States and which had reached the point of civil war with their attempts to transplant European forms of hierarchy, needed a lesson in the law of the land. When the gold rushers reached California, there was no written code to keep one man from taking the discovery of another. Human dignity was in the balance but the gold rushers, who are glibly slandered today, did not forsake the spirit of law. They created a set of rules by which a man's discovery could be protected by his peers, and a respectable number of them proved to be among a class of men who cared little for that which the gold was or what it gave to them, but more for the good which gold has long symbolized.[6] Mining men know well that men who are prospectors by nature frequently do not stay with one mine or know its profits; they are seekers as fond of the solitary life as monks, but they discerned that there can be no freedom without law. They made law to suit their ideas of justice and to suit the ore deposits and land on which they worked.

The common mining laws which arose in the mother lode and found acceptance throughout the western territories were literally the laws of the land. Gold rush miners, like Aaron Sargent in Nevada City, helped their fellows to form a type of community they called a mining district, wherein they agreed upon simple rules for the size and maintenance of a mining claim; how to mark it on the land; and how to record it with the clerk of the district so that prior rights to a claim could be verified. The numbers and other particulars of the rules would vary district to district, but the principles and manner of enforcement were so alike that a common law evolved which the federal government would eventually codify. Even today, in the absence of pertinent state or federal law, the custom of the mining district prevails.

The size of claim that a man could have was a major problem. At first, on rich deposits in the stream, a man could establish his place as fifty foot square. Elsewhere, in less prosperous diggings, he might be allowed as much as a mile along the dry gulch or stream where water had deposited gold with the gravel. So America's first mining claims were stream or gulch placers, the consensus of the mining districts being that a prospector could have one claim 300 feet on each side of the gold bearing waterway for a distance of 1,500 feet along the course, slightly more than twenty acres. The gulch placer, in particular, lent itself to adaptation for hard rock mining, since a gulch is by definition confined by hard rock whereas a stream may meander variously through its gravels. The hard rock mining adaptation of the gulch placer would become the "lode" claim allowing 1,500 feet along the course of an ore vein. The more widely disseminated gravels of the less restricted stream would be brought into line with surveyed land sections which governed other real estate. Commonly known as a placer claim, it was 1,320 feet by 660 feet or exactly twenty acres.

In California and elsewhere, when panning the loose gold from gravels became tedious, the prospectors moved up into the mountains to the source of the auriferous gravels. They followed the "lead," the "lode," the "ledge" of rock in which the gold was most frequently deposited. Although this deposit in solid rock is also called a vein, the gold is usually found along a plane rather than a line. Furthermore, this gold ledge often does not descend into the ground vertically but at a "dip" or angle, creating the need for a right unique to mining claims—the extralateral right allowing a miner to follow his dipping vein under and beyond the side lines of his claim. As Aaron Sargent, once U.S. senator from California, tried to explain to the 1880 Public Land Commission:[7]

> "The old miner's law . . . gave a locator so many feet from his starting
> point, in either direction, 'following the ledge, with its spurs, dips, angles

and variations.' This is common sense. It secured to the discoverer or developer of a ledge the full . . . claim . . . Only claims of extraordinary richness could be worked when the possessors were confined within perpendicular side lines."

In the federal codification and modification of the mining laws, this unpredictable right and masterful piece of common sense would become infamous as the cause of lengthy, bankrupting litigations. I am inclined to draw parallels between this unfortunate development and the behavior of another child of the gold rush, my great-grandmother. Although she staked her ranching claim in Duckwater by marriage, she was not afraid to break the boundaries of marriage when Williams grew abusive. As Tognoni's partner, she accepted the consequences of her errors and of misfortune alike, to raise her two families and the families of two daughters. After J. C. Tognoni died, she clung to her Silverton mining claims, just as the miner's three dimensional property right, the extralateral right, remains part of mining law despite misinterpretation.

My great-grandmother and others, like William Morris Stewart, carried the laws that governed the gold rush and the mining districts of California back over the Sierra into Nevada and beyond. Using what they had learned in California, these gold rushers discovered new lands of Ophir in the western territories and Alaska and as far away as Australia. Those prospectors who stayed in California found extensive gold deposits underground, three hundred million in gold from the deep mines of Grass Valley district alone.[8] Those who stayed in California also found a kind of gold deposit to which they would respond with unsurpassed resourcefulness. Millions of years ago on this part of the continent, gold-bearing rivers flowed to the south along what is now the western Sierra foothills. The new watershed created by the uplift of the Sierra Nevada mountains would cut across the old riverbeds to carve mountain banks of ancient river sediment. The difficulties of burrowing into these high gold-bearing walls generated a type of earth-moving and mining which made even a few cents in gold per ton profitable—hydraulic mining. Like mining the quartz veins, however, hydraulic mining required a good deal more labor and capital investment than panning on a gulch placer.

Furthermore, by the hydraulic miner's time, an old problem had arisen. Out of the gold rush a new social order grew. Farmers had moved into the Sacramento River Valley and begun to complain of the miners' debris. Only the wisest of men who created the engineering marvels of the high California gold counties found ways to compromise. Most were slaves to their rebellious spirits, and eventually, the farmers, the railroads, the newspapers and the complexities of state politics shut the hydraulic mines down.[9] By that time my father's family had transplanted itself in Nevada. My great-grandmother's birthplace in gold-rush California would not be a home for her, just as mining would become increasingly less important to the state's economy. Tomorrow I will travel the old diggings of the proud hydraulic miners with Dr. Vincent P. Gianella, author and professor of mining and geology who grew up in this countryside.

Dr. Vincent Gianella and the author, Empire Mine, Grass Valley, California
(Photo by Sandra Hewitt)

2   Abandonment

"I believe in time . . . and in the life chronological
rather than the life existential. We live in time and
through it, we build our huts in its ruins, or used to,
and we cannot afford all these abandonings."
Wallace Stegner

"The Malakoff pit," explains Dr. Gianella, "is famous in the textbooks partially because foreign names make better reading." He believes the name "Malakoff" must have come from the Crimean Wars during which, in fact, Russia won a decisive battle in 1855 at Malakoff Fort on the Black Sea. Many of the names we will encounter on this day's journey through California's gold mining country will receive Gianella's careful deliberation. I could not have hoped for a better guide. Dr. Vincent Gianella was once my father's professor at the University of Nevada's School of Mines, and he examines names and words with the same circumspection that he uses in analyzing rock. His influence is particularly beneficial on a journey propelled by the power of a name—Tognoni, my father's family name. "Tognoni" is on my maps to name a Nevada mountain and a spring which are our final destination.

Like other Italian immigrants to America, my great-grandfather translated the name of the village where he was raised into a surname for his family. J. C. Tognoni's intimate knowledge of a Nevada mountain and its spring of water would return the name to geography once again. I have never been to Italy, just as I have never been to Tognoni Mountain, but I suspect that geological similarities between Nevada and northern Italy where my great-grandfather herded goats with his father may have given J. C. the instincts of a native in Nevada. I am on my way to find Tognoni Mountain, but like any good pilgrim, I am attentive to the lessons of my journey and pleased that my traveling companion's name has been given to a rock, the mercury mineral Gianellite.

Dr. Gianella is a retired professor of mining and geology, and at the entrance to the mineral museum at the Mackay School of Mines, a bronze bust of Dr. Vincent Gianella greets you. The full figure of John W. Mackay stands outside the entrance to the mining school. Like J. C. Tognoni, Mackay was a European immigrant mining man. Educated in Europe before coming to the eastern United States, Mackay pushed out to California and then Nevada and the Comstock, "country of boundless possibilities, where habit and thoughts had not petrified into a social bedrock which could not be penetrated with shaft or tunnel, or blown up with giant powder."[1] Among the schools which grew out of America's bursting on the scene as a major mining power would be the Mackay School of Mines at the University of Nevada, established in 1886. In the gold rush years, mining engineers came from the Royal Mining Academy of Freiburg, Germany. The oldest advanced technical institute in the world, it was founded more than 100 years earlier than the Mackay School of Mines. When the need arose dramatically in the nineteenth century, America had no major institutes for mining. Mackay School of Mines was one of the first, and among the staff of mining men who would gain respect for the school was Dr. Vincent Gianella. He has titled his autobiography, "From Mule Skinner to Professor Emeritus."

Early on this Friday morning, Dr. Gianella drives from his home in Auburn to our appointed meeting place in Grass Valley. Over a cup of coffee, we decide that I should see the Malakoff pit. While the Old World was fighting in the Crimean to decide control of the Black Sea, the gold bearing sediments of an even older water body were being excavated in tremendous quantities in California's new world. I can't be certain what effect this mining had on the gold rushers of my father's family, but in 1858 when my great-grandmother was born, hydraulic mining was a growing and important industry. At some point her parents took her and her unmarried sisters to Nevada. If they left to escape conflict, they could have chosen a more peaceful valley than Duckwater, Nevada, where they settled. In Duckwater the battle for water rights flared endlessly, and the nearest mining town, Hamilton, teemed with deposed southern gentlemen of the Civil War.

Dr. Gianella, like my great-grandmother, Myrtle Jacques Tognoni, was born in the Sierra Nevada foothills where he and I will travel today. I tell him that I am interested in seeing the mines named in the Debris Case, *Woodruff vs. North Bloomfield*, but I am also interested in seeing Spring Valley's mine. Dr. Gianella does not recognize the latter but wants me to see one of his favorite mining towns, Cherokee. As it turns out, they are the same. Cherokee, named for a party of Cherokee Indian miners, is the major townsite of Spring Valley mining district which yielded approximately fifteen million dollars, mainly to the single large hydraulic mine of Spring Valley Mining Company.[2] This company responded with positive action to complaints that its debris was destroying land downstream. The company constructed a long ditch, the Cherokee Canal, to carry its debris to Butte Creek and 21,000 acres of swamp purchased along the Sacramento River for a settlage basin. The company surrounded the basin with a double line of levees.[3] Even so, the town of Cherokee began to diminish in population before the Debris Case struck its fatal blow to hydraulic mining. Maybe the conflict between California farmers and miners, like so many battles, was just a display hiding some deeper, economic problem—an overabundance of gold. Regardless, it is frequently the philosophy of California history books that the decline in mining population is due to some inherent weakness in mining people—characterized as a sort of nervous disease rendering the mind powerless.

From our meeting place in Grass Valley, Dr. Gianella and I drive north. Five years ago we drove farther east on a tour of the grounds at Grass Valley mining district's most famous mine. When the Empire-Star Mine shut down in 1957, it ended nearly 106 years of gold mining in California's richest mining district. On the earlier tour, my sister and I followed Dr. Gianella to the vine-covered president's mansion, to the engineer's club, to the mine offices and the mill, to the mouth of the inclined shaft—4,000 feet long. As we walked, Dr. Gianella pointed with a wide gesture of his arm to the dismantled grandeur that he once knew here—the riggings and tramways which hoisted and carried the rock from mine to crusher, from mill to tailings dump. We climbed and walked out on one ridge of discarded rock to where the frame of a grand hoist rose like a dinosaur above the tall pines. The tramway connecting the top of the hoist to the upper story of the mill was gone, yet with Dr. Gianella at our side, it was easy to imagine the bygone tramway and to envision gravity's cooperation inside the mill. From the rocks at his feet, he picked out two round quartz stones. He scraped the pink stone against the white one, back and forth until they smelled of sulphur. He told us that they would glow green in the dark. "Tribo-luminescence," he called it; and with a good deal of delight added, "There is no scientific explanation for that."

During the first tour with Dr. Gianella, my memories of a trip to the old hydraulic mines with my father were strong, so I asked Dr. Gianella about his friend Blanche Brown, at whose Joubert workings on Depot Hill we had camped. Mrs. Brown's husband, a retired mining engineer, had hoped to revive the old mine. Joseph F. Brown and my father would talk for hours in the old man's study from which I still remember a warm glow and imagine the smell of paper and books. My father was evaluating another gold property in the area for a client who had come into possession through a default unrelated to mining. Hale Tognoni's report would call for the association of claims in the district for cooperative diversion of Indian Creek via the old "Brown Ditch." Today a group of men are working with the title information and with the water plan which took shape in that week of 1965, and according to Dr. Gianella, Blanche Brown still lives in the hills despite the death of Joe and the frailties of her old age.

North out of Grass Valley, Dr. Gianella and I cross the South Fork of the Yuba River. We stop at the crossing to photograph the thin white lines of rock radiating from a fault in the granite. These aplites date to a time when this gorge had its slow beginning in the breaking, shifting and uplifting of the rock faces which surround us. More than once Dr. Gianella has served as a guide to this spot, but one story is underlined in his memory, so he tells it twice on the steep banks of the South Yuba. Many years ago he showed the aplites to Dr. Hans Kloez, a respected expert on granite intrusives. Granite formed the rock banks of the concentration camp in which the Nazis imprisoned Dr. Kloez during the Second World War. Kloez had a tragically intimate understanding of granite, and he voiced his respect for the native geologist, Vincent Gianella, who had made free observations as sharply drawn as his own.

Near where we are stopped a pick-up truck pulls over and lets out a dark, hulking hitchhiker who approaches us for something to drink. In the wake of his expansive gratitude after he has refreshed himself, I introduce Dr. Gianella as a man brought up in this countryside; but Dr. Gianella takes his perpetual inquirer's stance and says that he is sure that this young "Indian" knows more about the country than himself. So I ask the beaming hitchhiker about his home. He replies, "Wisconsin" and informs us that he makes jewelry. The polished stones that he peddles capture Dr. Gianella's interest. Meanwhile I take pictures and speculate about the geology. In my informal studies of this science, I take very seriously the principle that *the present is a key to the past.* While dedicated earth scientists are making measurements at active volcanoes, I must be content with applying to rock my observations of physical phenomenon in my kitchen. While cooking family meals, I have seen surfaces of hot liquid like one preserved here in granite. Dr. Gianella has been introducing his guest to metamorphics despite the fact that the young man wants only to make a sale. He has a pair of feather earrings which I want, and for my cash, I am clutched to his bullish breast. I would like to think that this Indian brave took the feathers

from one of his grandfather's molting birds just as Dr. Gianella hoped that
the young jeweler would take an interest in the identity of his polished
stones. "He only learns what he needs to know—an uneducated man,"
concludes Dr. Gianella as we wind our way up to North Bloomfield mining
district.

We never reach the Malakoff pit, but the hydraulic diggings along the
road are spectacular, and we stop to take more pictures. Dr. Gianella tells
me that three quarters of a cubic mile of triassic river bed gravels were
moved in the western Sierra foothills by high pressure hoses known as
monitors. In 1853 a man named Edward E. Matteson suggested to his
partners that they break down a cut they had made into American Hill with
a stream of water rather than with a pick. By 1855 hydraulic mining had
become the major industry of North Bloomfield. As we look out over the
blond cones and ridges that surround us, I try to shape a cubic mile in my
mind. Standing here, we are very small, like ants on a path through water
beaten sand castles. An exceptionally large wave has altered the transient
architecture here, and the numbers that normally give man his bearing in
situations like these are too large to help me. The soft banks I touch were
laid down two hundred million years ago; the Malakoff pit alone yielded
three and a half million dollars in gold with an estimated hundred million
yards of gravel left to be mined or not to be mined.

My anchor in this sea of numbers and time is Dr. Gianella. Ninety-five
years have weathered him, but I have begun to understand ninety-five
years, and Gianella seems an ageless man in these hills where even the
miner's brief history here brings a sense of eternity. Once again Dr. Gianella
picks up two smooth quartz stones to demonstrate tribo-luminescence. This
time he explains that "tribo" means friction. But even after I tell him that I
remember his lesson from my last tour, he takes fresh delight in telling me of
the inability of science to explain the phenomenon of this rock friction.
Oblivious to the mysteries of these hills, double trailer dump trucks whiz by
us and make it hard to linger. In the hazy distance are the destinations of our
day including my guide's birthplace in the ranching and gold dredging
districts below here.

We drive west across a long, narrow bridge over the gravel bed of the
Yuba River proper. We motor peacefully through pine forests that were
non-existent in Dr. Gianella's youth; through dormant olive groves planted
at the behest of a confederation of college professors in the 1890s; along side
of fire-blackened stretches where motorists have carelessly altered the
vegetation; next to red banks where exposure over hundreds of thousands
of years has oxidized the iron-rich earth. The blond mounds of North
Bloomfield, if left unmined, will be pink in another hundred thousand

years. Back there, Dr. Gianella pointed to the red layer of earth which covers the triassic river beds and recounted its probable age. He seems to take comfort in the age of the rocks.

As my guide, he continues to demonstrate his appreciation for the careful use of words and names as he answers my questions about the rock banks we pass. In making the distinction between the varieties of granite— the andesites, the rhyolites, the granodiorites—he tells me that he never liked the term "acidic" as applied to rocks. The word "ancient" is too mild for rock and the word "acidic" is too strong. He explains that if you powdered the most acidic of rocks, mixed it with water and drank it, your stomach would produce much stronger acids just to digest the rock. Acidity and non-acidity in rocks hover so close to the neutral point that Dr. Gianella has often struggled with finding another word for use in earth science.

I am engrossed by his musing. I have been puzzled by the word he ponders, and I recognize the idea of his objections in my own struggle to write about the mining law which came out of California. The law was truly *the law of the land*, yet today educated men flail at this native common law and call rock "acidic" never wondering that it does not burn their skin and that our country has never applied the law of free mining to provide for extended peace rather than war. The first gold rush into California and then into the Comstock were violently linked to the bloody Civil War; the gold rush in which my great-grandfather participated at the turn of the century preceded World War I; and in the late 1930s the gold dredges, the hand made gravity separators and the quartz stamp mills rumbled anew in mining country until President Roosevelt ordered a halt to the gold mining so that its men and machinery could be used for strategic minerals and World War II.

In Brown's Valley we turn north near a quartz mill and the tailings from one of the several rich mines in the gold-bearing quartz rock which laces the countryside. The tailings look curiously fresh. Brown, after whom the valley is named, recovered $12,000 from his mining claim in a matter of weeks back in 1850. Here, as back in Grass Valley during volcanic ages, the primal forces of water mobilized, deposited, remobilized and concentrated gold and other precious metals fluxing in the hot magma at inner depths of the earth. Past the site of an old school house which Vincent Gianella attended and beyond Sugarloaf Mountain, so named for the blocks of sugar which my companion remembers from his childhood, a dirt road steeply rises into the black rocks. Illustrious mining engineer Waldemar Lindgren, who studied this region and who estimated the amount of still unmined gravels back at the abandoned Malakoff pit, wrote about an ore deposit in these black hills which beckon Dr. Gianella every time he passes.

We only pass again. Lindgren, Swedish-born and educated at the Freiburg Institute, was associated for over thirty-one years with the United States Geological Survey. Early in Lindgren's career, he wrote a series of economic geology reports that remain unequalled in their energy and breadth of view.

The U.S.G.S. would become the greatest geological organization in the world due, in part, to Lindgren's work, but the science of geology owed an even greater debt to the grand underground mines of the far west. Lindgren made important observations in the shafts of Grass Valley and Nevada City mines. S. F. Emmons, another eminent scholar of American ore bodies, would study in the deep mines of Leadville, Colorado. With his observations, he would re-shape the mining world's ideas of how minerals are deposited in the earth's crust. According to Emmons, "The study of a single group of mines which have been opened to a great depth affords more valuable information than many districts where workings have penetrated but a few feet below the surface.[4]

When Waldemar Lindgren joined the United States Geological Survey in 1884, the mines were in hard times. By the *Fifth Annual Report* of the U.S.G.S., the government's grand ambitions of aiding and cooperating with the mining industry seemed to have been quietly shelved. Topography replaced deeper concerns of geology, and Emmons turned his talents to problems of water supply for Denver. Lindgren would have to found his own publication, "Economic Geology," to continue his design of furnishing the mining industry with useful scientific conclusions. So, in the 1930s, Vincent Gianella directed the digging of water wells in these hills for President Franklin Roosevelt's Work Project arm of economic recovery; and he continued to pass by the ore deposits in Lindgren's report of the geology along our road. Domestic production of precious minerals has held low priority in the United States for a long time.

At Bangor, little of what the good professor remembers is left to see. This mining town, named after the home in Maine of the two founding brothers, once had a blacksmith shop and markets on the corners to which Dr. Gianella points. Now ponies graze in loosely fenced, irregularly furrowed plots of land and overgrown rubble. Beyond Bangor is a hazy lowland and a view of Table Mountain rising north of Oroville. On the other side of the majestic alignment on our horizon is our destination—Cherokee.

W. C. Ralston, California banker who helped finance the Comstock
(Courtesy Nevada Historical Society)

3 Echoes from Walls of Time

*Harmony with land is like harmony with a
friend; you cannot cherish his right hand and
chop off his left . . . you cannot love game and
hate predators . . . The land is one organism.*
Aldo Leopold

The afternoon of my day in California gold country with Dr. Vincent Gianella begins in Oroville. We eat lunch, and Dr. Gianella successfully engages me as a listener for a very unusual account of the Battle of New Orleans, about which he reads at home. His delight in irony is served well by histories of war. Shellacked to a piece of knotted wood on the wall beside our lunch table are old magazine photographs of mining operations on the Feather River and in Oroville mining district. Dr. Gianella remembers a mine in one of the pictures because he used to drive cattle and horses past the wall constructed to send the Feather River out of its bed and around a mountain. With the river diverted, the gravels, old and new, could be shoveled into long sluice boxes designed to catch heavy, free gold behind an obstacle course of low riffles in the bottom of the boxes. The caption beneath the magazine photo says that McLaughlin dynamited his wall and returned the river to its stream when his mine closed. Now the site of the wall and the mine are beneath the waters of Oroville Lake created by a government dam.

I make a note of McLaughlin, but I will find no more about him or the mine. I like to think that he may have been making a statement with his explosives about the wastefulness of sentiments which vilified and economically frustrated the maintenance of mines in California,[1] sentiments of persons either fearful or skeptical of the immense achievements and aims of the mining industry in the Sierra:[2]

...The mining reservoirs,...already constructed for hydraulic purposes, can store at least 10,000,000,000 cubic feet of water, which is
utilized during the summer or dry season through long lines of canals or
ditches....The amount of money expended in construction of these
reservoirs and canals exceeds $20,000,000. In the future, when the gravel
mines which these works were constructed to supply are exhausted, they
will serve to irrigate all the lower slopes of the Sierras for cultivation.

It should be remembered that the gold, which men like McLaughlin
dug out of this country, bought cannons and bayonets for a bloody civil war.
More important, the United States government chose to rebuild after the
war by printing greenbacks rather than by raising the price of gold to allow
more gold to be mined by more free men. Prior to the Emancipation
Proclamation, the eastern states had produced gold by using slave labor,
almost twenty million dollars worth from the Appalachian gold fields.[3] In
the far western states, the diggers kept the mining for free men through a
combination of regulation and prejudice, the latter receiving the most
modern publicity. When an estimated three-fifths of the one thousand
miners in California were Chinese, devoted to working and re-working
abandoned placers,[4] the white men were moving east across the Sierra into
new western territories where their mining knowledge and experience
would become important.

My great-great-grandfather, Ernest Jesse Jacques, left California sometime after 1862 when the last of his daughters was born. Before our journey
is ended, I will stand at Jacques' headstone in Duckwater cemetery. Now I
sit with a man who knew McLaughlin's wall. The brevity of the caption
under the picture decorating the wall behind our napkin dispenser gives me
no other choice of name for the ramification. Surely, however, McLaughlin's
wall was financed and built by an association of men on the Feather River.
From the first years of the gold rush, men formed unions to dam California
rivers and to turn the water into artificial channels. Hired labor was too
expensive and interest rates on borrowed finance too high[5]; so joint stock
associations were created in which a man's labor gained shares. Out of the
need for organization, the miners developed a type of mining claim known
as the association placer, allowing eight locators to claim 160 acres of
mineral land. The law bound the locators to supply labor or capital to the
maintenance of the claim or to lose their right to title and to a share of the
earnings. This larger claim allowed for cooperation instead of competition
and valuated capital with labor. Under the miner's law a man kept his claim
by doing so much work annually or, in an association of men, by providing
capital in an amount agreed upon with those who had only labor to contribute.

In this context, it is little wonder that the Soviet leader, Stalin, fanatically studied the laws of the gold rush in California for purposes of developing
the frontiers and gold mines of his own country. He sent agents to California
and hired American mining engineers to serve in his Gold Trust. Under the
Soviet Gold Trust, no single mine would be abandoned so long as the gold
mines, as a whole, remained profitable.[6] Economic security became envi-
able in the gold mining districts of Siberia. Although he was responsible for
the death of millions of miners in Siberia, Stalin grasped the fundamental
principle of the California gold rush—government encouragement of miners. Ironically, it is known as "free mining." In medieval Germany in such
mining regions as Freiburg, Goslar, and Joachimstal, miners were exempt
from military service and from taxation. They were not necessarily employees of a feudal lord but formed free associations like craftsmen.[7] The "free
tinner" of Cornwall would mark out his claim or "bound" with stones, where
he would search for and extract ore, and then pay a royalty, not to the
Crown, but to the owner of the soil. Like these earlier systems, Stalin's Gold
Trust sanctioned mining, and he built a major mining industry in the Soviet
Union.

Meanwhile, the United States trusted increasingly to paper currency,
kept the price of gold low, turned mineral lands over to the Department of
Agriculture, and produced 50 percent of its new gold from one mine—the
Homestake in Lead, South Dakota. A growing percentage of new gold, as
much as 40 percent,[8] would be the by-product of mining copper and other
metals. As quickly after the Civil War as the government could pass greenbacks or otherwise jeopardize the government's ability to redeem its notes
in gold, mining law in the far west fell into disfavor. Most good mining
claims in the far west struggled to develop, or they lay fallow. Men to whom
the earth spoke of minerals became intruders on government land and
government agents began to seize mining claims with no compensation to
claimants. During the 1930s when gold mining became widely possible due
to President Franklin Roosevelt's decision to raise the price of gold from
$20.64 an ounce to $35, mines like the Max Delta in the South Mountains of
Phoenix, Arizona, resumed production. In the style of California gold rush
associations, men with a variety of skills and education took a chance with
their labor on the Max Delta's returns. But today the mine is a city park just
as placer mining claims along Lynx Creek, one of Arizona's richest gold
regions, have been supplanted by government maintained playgrounds.[9]

To help my father, Hale C. Tognoni, defend the old mining claims and
the stubborn prospectors and miners who try to develop them, I learned the
mining law; and I have discovered above all else that "law of the land" is
a complex idea with which our awkward federal government has been

unsteady and impulsive. Thus, mining law, like the land, has been manipulated to conform to realms of greed which succeeded in entangling even Abraham Lincoln. In 1863, President Lincoln was persuaded briefly by a political associate and agent of Quicksilver Mining Company of New York that the title to the lands of the oldest mine in California, the New Almaden quicksilver mine, represented a Spanish land grab. Lincoln briefly authorized the Quicksilver Mining Company of New York to operate the mine on behalf of the U.S. government until legal issues could be settled. Quickly, the mining people of California convinced Lincoln to reverse himself and leave the mines in the hands of its owners by local custom and law.[10]

The law which grew out of the California gold rush was "an indigenous product, the legitimate offspring of our institutions and the peculiar circumstances of our miners."[11] It is truly law of the land like the common law which evolved with the equity courts of England in the Middle Ages. English common law represented a revolution against established order and codes of law associated mainly with monarchies and religion, and from it came important elements of American law, including trial by jury and the doctrines of case precedent and supremacy of law.[12] The miners' law grew and changed outside of legislative edict. Like the new equipment being invented, discovered and imported for gold mining, the mining law adjusted to a variety of conditions. One important condition was the high cost of time. Where imported devices proved too slow, though more thorough, the American gold rusher opted for a less gentle, steeper slant to his gold-gravel washers.[13] The pan and rocker were supplemented by the "long tom" allowing two men to continuously shovel dirt into the rocker while a third stirred the gravel over a screen. Likewise, where the men, the mineral, the land, and the economy allowed, the single twenty-acre placer mining claim grew to be an association placer. The law in those days was more like the word "placer" itself—indebted to the Spanish and the Sonorans for elements of its origin, admitting of many interpretations, rich in meaning. Spanish speaking people preceded the Americans in California and provided sound mining technique and knowledge. The miners adapted the Spanish word "placer" to their claims partly because it had significance in English. It suited the indefinite expanse which is the reality of a gold discovery, and in its verb form, "placer" was descriptive of gravity's somewhat orderly concentration or placement of the gold in river gravels.

Under the old town of Oroville, the gravels of the ancient flood plain of the Feather River are so valuable that the citizens once had to pass an ordinance to keep miners from tunneling under Oroville's establishments. Years ago gold dredging companies tried to buy the old townsite, according to Dr. Gianella, but the residents made the prices of their lots too high. Now dust lies unscuffed on the cement walkways along the river and the windows of the old buildings are uniformly murky and empty. Dr. Gianella and I speculate that the price of the old town may be low enough now and the price of gold high enough to bring the gold miners back. Would men like J. C. Tognoni be among them? Have I learned enough to recognize a man like him?

Table Mountain sits above Oroville like a lid containing us to these flatter lands. Up Table Mountain the road is narrow and shady, and deep red bushes dot the yellow hills through which we rise. "Poison oak," Dr. Gianella tells me when I ask, and he points out the tell-tale contours of landslides from beneath the basalt which crowns the soft sediments of the mountain's lower formations. The table top cuts the sky so sharply as we ride out onto it that we seem to be entering a nether region where the yellow grass blankets the black rock so softly as to transform the harsh surface into a dream-like meadow. We drive across it and over the edge beyond to Cherokee, where I walk out to a mound of boulders in a dry channel. From the foot of a peculiar, dark peak I hear a loud rumbling which makes it easier to envision the boulders under my feet being lifted by powerful jets of water and dropped here via the heavy guide shoots that Dr. Gianella describes. A modern Spring Valley Mining Company is at work, but trees and a gate hide it from our investigation. The original Spring Valley Company was begun by a man of means, Egbert Judson, in 1870, who made admirable attempts to appease farmers in the area of his debris drainage,[14] but in 1887, after the Spring Valley Mining Company had washed ten million dollars in gold, the mine closed. Only a few houses remain of old Cherokee. Most of it was lost to fire. Now the greenery is thick along our road.

Back to the highway, we wind down through some rolling hills along which narrow canals carry water. As early as 1857, thousands of miles of ditches and flumes ran through Sierra foothills to provide the water upon which placer gold mining depended so heavily. As we near Oroville again, gravel ridges flank us on both sides. Dr. Gianella waves his hand upward and leans forward, heightening his view and inviting heroic dimensions to the scene which he recreates beyond the confines of our car. He remembers this road when it was a gravel banked channel in which every pebble hummed to the roar of the dredges. W. P. Hammon and others introduced dredges to the Oroville mining district in 1898. Here and there in the omnipresent raw oats, a row of trees follows a furrow dug by small dragline dredges of the 1930s. Much of the water coming out of the hills still pools in this grass land or tules where California farmers are beginning to cultivate rice fields. The sale of these swamp lands primarily to men of wealth back in the nineteenth century caused a great deal of accusation and suspicion against the buyers and against the mining men who were proposing projects to make these tules into productive farm land using their mine debris.[15] Huge earth-movers work now to level great square rice paddies bermed on all four sides for flooding the seed. By 1966, the last underground mine in this country had closed and the last dredge lay rotting in the Yuba River.[16]

To get to Honcut and the ranch land that once belonged to Dr. Gianella's family, we turn off the highway to drive a road cutting across fields where Gianella once baled hay and ate the tastiest watermelon of his ninety-five years. He tells me that there is no gold in these fields and goes on to talk about how his grandfather and father bought their ranch for $500 and an unsecured note which they paid off after only one season of raising and selling hay. "No such opportunity now," he grants. Dr. Gianella's grandfather and his opportunity were of an age when "wild-cat banks" in the eastern United States had swallowed the fortunes of their depositors, creating a distrust of banking corporations or (as they were popularly regarded in the far west) of "association(s) of capital to war against labor."[17]

People had lost their faith in the integrity of banking to perform the service of transferring capital from hands where it lay idle into hands by which it would be usefully employed. Accordingly, early legislators of California wrote into the state's constitution prohibitions against "any act granting any charter for banking purposes."[18] Not until 1864 were commercial banks allowed, and in that same year W. C. Ralston, the most colorful of the California mining financiers, organized the Bank of California, which became intimately involved with the Comstock mines of Nevada. Ralston and other San Francisco lords of capital would enable mining to take a strong hold in the west. Investment in mining required creative men for whom security held little attraction: men who hoped to develop a mining property from a prospect by intelligence, daring and stamina; men who knew that the large mining corporations in California had spent many years and millions of dollars before they could return dividends on their capital; men who understood that in a country where mining was not the government concern which it had been throughout history, capitalists were, in effect, the nation's mine commissioners.

Dr. Gianella and I have been riding since Cherokee when, just two miles out of Honcut, we stop across the road from a house where my companion spent his early childhood. I take his picture beside a a majestic oak tree that he knew when it was only thirty feet tall and still could be completely embraced at the trunk by a man. He points to the level of the road where it was when he traveled it horseback, almost two feet higher and at the same level as the fence posts on the embankment. He is showing me the erosion of a lifetime. He tells me of discussing with a local storekeeper the names of Honcut's water channels and being disregarded when he tried to explain the old natural channels before gold dredging. Now Dr. Gianella mostly just listens to those who shuffle in Honcut's dust and is amused by their ideas about the nature of the land's past. He does not offer himself up to their incredulity as often as he once did. It is late in the afternoon.

Traveling south out of Honcut, we reach red banks of soil beyond which the crests of old dredge tailings rise, and an active gravel dredge rumbles from amid them. In the field of wild oats above and beside the road, Dr. Gianella's trained eye picks out the gentle, regular mounds where placer miners worked in the 1930s. I have seen mounds like these before in the western Humboldt mountain range of Nevada, where between 1884 and 1895 3,000 Chinese miners dug out the "largest placer output in the state during any period."[19] In an empty grocery bag we collect a little of the red dirt, which Dr. Gianella encourages me to pan when I get home. We near the end of our day's journey, and the road is growing shady again in the canyons. Once again Dr. Gianella begins to indulge his fascination with names. We pass above Indian Springs Valley, and he explains the impudence of such a name. "The Indians came to the valley to live because there were springs. The springs are not of the Indians' doing, as the name unforgivably implies to Dr. Gianella. I think of Tognoni Spring, and wonder if my great-grandfather only chanced upon the water or whether he dug into Nevada volcanics and struck water like a driller striking oil.

Back in Grass Valley, Dr. Gianella kisses me goodbye, and I promise to return soon. "You like this country, don't you," he summarizes hopefully. "I do," I tell him, but I admit a longing for my home and the dry, open spaces on the other side of the Sierra. When I reach Donner Pass on my way to Reno in the dusk, the traffic is so unforgiving that I manage to pull over to take pictures and use my binoculars only twice. The barren opalescent granites are other-worldly, and the ranches tucked up against the hills are like jewels. A curious structure notched into one wall of Donner Pass is so magical that it seems natural, like rock urged into an impossibly horizontal crack by inner pressures of the Earth, but it is wood, metal and maybe concrete, clamped to the cliff by an act of human will. Like Reno's imposing MGM Grand Hotel, rising out of the basin into which I descend, the cliff structure will not last in this majestic mountain range for any significant period of geological time, but I admire the courage.

Harry C. Stimler

"He struck it rich." What other calling than mining evokes such an expression in reference to its successful members? To Harry Stimler is due the credit of the discovery of Goldfield. At that time but a boy of 22 years, he is still called "The Father of Goldfield." It was in November, 1902, that he and his brother left Tonopah in shattered rig, drawn by a horse and mule, and camped near Rabbit Springs. He took surface samples on what are now the richest mines of the district and hurried back to Tonopah to have them tested and to report to the men who had staked him. The results were good, and Dec. 4, 1902, found him back again in the Goldfield district, where he located the Sandstorm, May Queen, Nevada Boy and Columbia Mountain Groups. Even a brief sketch of this young man's adventures seems almost improbable.

Harry Stimler was born in Belmont, Nev., twenty-six years ago, and is now one of the wealthiest men in the State. With his partner, C. B. Higginson, he conducts a vast brokerage and promotion business in their elegantly appointed offices in the Nixon block. He is a hard and industrious worker, because he loves it. By nature Mr. Stimler is of (?) disposition, unassuming, somewhat reserved, but his exceptional character and ability have made him one of the foremost mining men of Nevada.

Harry Stimler

4 Up Against the Sierra

*I remember well how slow, simple and methodical
was this old American silver freighter, patiently
plodding back and forth over a land of desolation,
placidly sorting out his ideas until they were as sweet
and real as winds from Sierra pine forests...*
Charles Howard Shinn[1]

It is a clear Saturday in Reno and the third day of my pilgrimage. The casinos have opened their ground levels to Virginia Street and laid claim to the asphalt for the hordes of weekenders who aim their paths as if through tunnels between the colorful concrete caverns on Reno's main strip. Amidst these purposeful merrymakers I take my own pleasure. I breathe deeply of the dry air and allow the sunshine to cleanse my vision. I have spent the last two days and three chapters in northern California where my great-great-grandfather, Ernest Jesse Jacques, Quaker gold-rusher, spent several years before crossing back over the mountains to Nevada with his family. The Reno into which he descended had grown from a ferry crossing on the Truckee River to little more than a toll bridge. The changes which white men brought were not so plentiful in Reno as to the south on the Comstock. Nearby in the state capital, Carson City, the first United States senators from Nevada had persuaded the federal government to build a mint in 1870,[2] and more than forty thousand people populated the Comstock town of Virginia City. Maybe Jesse Jacques came from California on the train which first crossed the mountains from Sacramento in 1868.

Unlike northern California, the foothills on the Nevada side of the Sierra Nevadas do not rise so gently into the granite face of the magnificent mountain wall. Here there are no winds off the Pacific Ocean to drive clouds against the cliffs where the pounding force of water could be released above the high thrusting volcanics and all that rests on them. Here the great upheaval of the Triassic age, sixty million years ago, is fresh and has not retrograded to gravel and dust. In Nevada, mountains are enduring and ripple sharply across the expanses of the state in over 160 ranges[3] which rise like tense sinews between the Sierra and that other great ramification of North America, the Rocky Mountains. Mineral ledges bristle in Nevada; and hidden in places beneath only a very thin skin, water runs in arteries to the hot depths of the earth. North and south of Nevada, ancient seas found outlet in the Columbia and Colorado rivers, square miles of sea which have been slowly disappearing into the ground and into the air, leaving behind salt and sulphur and a thousand other bitter chemicals on the floors of Nevada's valleys. Alkali dust has infected and toughened my father's skin. A person does not grow up in this countryside without being shaped by it. Only to a map-maker or geographer are these mountains an "army of cater-pillars crawling toward Mexico."[4] The people who live in these mountains comprehend them only through a sense of poetry about which maps do not usually speak.

Human history in Nevada is almost void of monument.[5] It is as scat-tered and disarranged as the sagebrush on this virtually naked record of the formation of Earth's crust. The only real monuments here pre-date man and relentlessly remind him of life's transience and frailty. Supreme among these reminders is Pyramid Lake, north of Reno. Driftwood paves the mud flats of the lake's west bank like bones, and the rock hills at the lake's edge crawl with dead form, the encrustations of a retreating sea. The intrepid explorer, J. C. Fremont, gave the lake its English name from the barren, pointed islands out to which the pelican population of Pyramid Lake bliss-fully floats. There is no white-man myth of human security here[6]; and near here in 1860, the Pah-Utes would make their most absolute statement of broken sufferance—the Ormsby Massacre. Almost one hundred deluded Americans died in that Indian ambush of their disorganized vigilance committee.[7]

To a white man survivor of that tragic affair, my father's grandmother would make her first marriage. Myrtle was ample of figure, even lush, and with the layers of long calico skirts which she liked to wear, she created the illusion of a harbor for the men who married her, John Williams and J. C. Tognoni. Some claim that moral codes were transformed on Nevada's sea of land by elemental struggles between good and evil.[8] Certainly harsh ethics prevailed, humbling the greatest of men and women and dissipating memory of them with equanimity as sure as the waves of an ocean. When I listen to tales of J. C. Tognoni and Myrtle Jacques, the struggle and harsh-ness manifest themselves in the desire either to heroize or villainize the gold rushers including relative unknowns like J. C. and Myrtle. My aunt, who has written unpublished historical novels about her Nevada mining family, tells me anecdotes of how widely admired was J. C. and how treacherous was Myrtle. My uncle's memory retains only J. C.'s drunkenness, and from inside his cheek he spits out the label "promoter" with his tobacco juice. I suspect that Myrtle has too many likenesses to a brass spittoon for him, although he chuckles charmingly and cooperates, despite himself, with my queries. Both aunt and uncle regard my father's admiration and respect for his grandparents as naivete, but like my father, others of the many grand-children and old people who knew J. C., Myrtle and their times, transcend personal rivalries to convey to me a sense of urgency that memory of these two lives be preserved.

I find the same sense of urgency and lack of mercy in literature about the history of silver or the abandonment of precious metal standards for paper money. Authors rush to expletives or forsake logic, leaving the gold standard and bimetallism a haven for the smoothest deceits. J. C. may have had a heart of gold, as those who experienced his generosity believed, but Myrtle was the silver. Today the trading between them, their marriage, is no more commonly appreciated than the peculiar dignity of mining. The laws which had served mining began to serve lawyers. This was so of not only the mining laws, but of laws such as the six week Nevada citizenship law suited to transient mining populations. Upon this law Nevada would build its divorce industry, a fitting parallel to the dissolution of the monetary wed-lock of gold and silver.

Bimetallism, the use of both silver and gold to measure value, was for centuries the unnamed tradition of the trading world. In the United States, establishing the initial value of silver in relation to gold has been a major concern of Alexander Hamilton and others who set up the United States Treasury.[9] Thomas Jefferson in 1792: "I concur with you [Mr. Hamilton] that the unit must stand on both metals."[10] The silver in the unit or dollar had to be very close to the same value on the open market as the gold in a dollar; or whichever dollar was worth more would disappear from circulation following a long accepted law of money and greed. Nevertheless, the ratio would adjust itself over long periods of time by a natural process. Accord-ing to promotional material for the precious metal market, strategy for investing in both gold and silver requires "no special knowledge, no split-second timing and no complex charting techniques."[11] Using the ratio history of gold and silver market values, a man can profit from the buying and selling of gold and silver by manuevers very much like riding on a see-saw. As long as the party on the other end of the see-saw does not climb off as the U.S. government has done, bimetallism can keep any one class of people from securing their money by monopolizing money supply. If the rich hoard the gold, the more numerous poor use the more plentiful metal—silver. The demand for silver increases as well as its price relative to gold until the see-saw tips gold up into curculation again—up and down, ad infinitum, so long as gold or silver will pay the bill.

Despite the pessimism of numerous commissions which have been appointed to study the question of whether there is enough gold and silver,[12] when the price goes up, mineral prospects are developed into mines and lower grade ores in old mines become profitable. Partially because of the self-depreciating nature of mining, gold and silver have what the economists call a very "inelastic supply curve." This inelasticity is what makes gold and silver ideal for a monetary standard. Over the long run the quantity of precious metals in circulation expands at a steady rate and tends to parallel the rate of population and economic growth through an underlying economic reality unsurpassed by the artifice of bankers.[13]

After the gold rush, the United States became the world's leading silver producer. In the first report of the United States Geological Survey by Director John Wesley Powell in 1881, Powell could report that "one-third of the gold and one-half of the silver yearly produced in the world are mined within our borders."[14] The breathtaking quickness with which the United States achieved this world mining status suited the radical nature of the state which was at the heart of U.S. mining—Nevada. Mines and mills on the mighty Comstock Lode were producing millions of dollars of silver and gold only a matter of a few years after a motley crew of gold prospectors became aware that the black scum which had been frustrating their retrieval of gold from the canyons of the Washoe Mountains was the richest discovery of silver in the history of the world. Suddenly, thousands of fortune seekers were converging, not far from where a group of Mormons had made the first white settlement in western Utah Territory less than ten years previous.

The discovery of the Comstock Lode contributed to an abundance of coining metal which would free the people of the world to find wider circles of trade, but the silver mines of the United States would be short-lived in comparison with the great mines of Germany and Mexico. When the U.S. stopped coining silver, it struck a staggering blow to its mining regions. Then with the harnessing of electricity, copper deposits began to draw hard-rock mining men, silver and gold would become by-products of copper, but while silver briefly enjoyed the political support and attention which was to be copper's, the Comstock attracted the European continent's educated mining men.

Baron Richthofen would write the first geological description of the Comstock's "porphyry horse"—that animal or wall of rock which reared up and fell into a chasm opened by the volcanic upheaval of the Washoe Mountains where hot water from beneath would impregnate the shattered body with nodes and veins of silver and gold under the sustained pressure of thousands of years. The hot water which Baron Richthofen identified as the agent of riches in the Comstock would necessitate an engineering marvel by another German mining engineer, Adolph Heinrich Joseph Sutro. He would leave gold rush California in 1860 for Nevada and the Comstock, there to advocate and plan a drainage tunnel for developing and exploring the ore body. By 1865 Sutro's vision would gain approval of state and federal legislation, but construction would not begin until 1869, when mine workers initially financed the tunnel. Funds would come eventually from international bankers, but not until 1878, after $5 million had been expended, would the tunnel be completed, but development of the ore body had ceased. Like the Comstock's ore, the tunnel quietly endured beneath the Washoe Mountains oblivious to plummeting silver prices. Then, 100 years after its completion, a modern mining company would find the tunnel worthy of shoring up to revive the Comstock.

Houston Oil and Minerals Company, responding to soaring prices for gold, began in 1978 to prepare the Comstock for another round of production. Twentieth century mining men proudly walked the Sutro tunnel before Houston Oil was halted on the Comstock by concerns unencountered in the nineteenth century. According to Nevada State Archivist Guy Louis Rocha, he and his group acted to protect the historic townsite of Gold Hill. Houston Oil Company was buying Gold Hill through eminent domain laws peculiar to mining states of the far west.[15] The mining company offered to transfer the buildings to a park area away from the site of their planned open pit, but according to Mr. Rocha, his organization feared that the mining operation threatened other Comstock townsites. When vociferous citizens succeeded in getting the state legislature to modify its 1872 eminent domain law to express non-cooperation with mining, Houston Oil had already begun building a mill. Mr. Rocha and others presented evidence to the lawmakers that mining was no longer an important industry in Nevada, that gambling and tourism had long ago outstripped the mines.

My father's mother, Ina Belle Conway, served as postmistress in Gold Hill during World War II, although she did not have the higher education normally required. Her long experience delivering mail on contract to mountain ranches around Eureka, Nevada, persuaded the U.S. Postal Service to make an exception in Gold Hill, but most likely no one with a higher degree would have considered isolating herself in the dilapidation that we revere today as an "historic site." Still it is heartening that during the crusade to preserve some sign of human history in the state, the technology which is necessary to retrieve "no see-um" or microscopic gold has put Nevada back on top of United States gold production.[16] Newmont Mining Corporation pioneered this type of mining at its Carlin Mine north of Eureka. Near Eureka members of my father's mining family spent years struggling through the depression in precious metals which was their fate after the gold rush.

Despite a U.S. silver purchase act in Senator William Morris Stewart's day and a U.S. agreement after World War I to mine the silver for British war debts to India; despite Nevada Senator Key Pittman's and President Franklin Roosevelt's attempts to bolster silver prices, most U.S. silver mines could not overcome the glut of silver on the world market. In the twentieth century, industrial use of silver increased, but when the market price of silver began to approach a level at which widespread silver mining could redevelop, fresh stockpiles of silver in world treasuries would be dumped on the market. Presently silver is the only mineral being used at a greater rate than it is being mined.

The tools by which capitalists financed the Comstock had fallen into abuse. The assessable stock corporation, for instance, no longer had the trust of investors. As a member of this early form of corporation, the stockholder was liable to share more directly in the company's needs and future. If profits were made, he shared in them, but he also could be asked to contribute working capital in lean years or early years of development. Experience soon taught the courageous investor in assessable mining corporations that stockholder assessments frequently did not reach the developers of the mines. With the assessable stocks, brokers who held shares for their clients had ways of selling to two owners, collecting the annual assessment twice and paying the mining company only once. No matter how unwisely the corporations were being directed, the brokers stood to gain, and since the brokers, with proxies from their clients, were voting on corporate policy, it was a disinterested group that considered the future of the mines. They contributed like a cancer to the failure of many mining corporations to pay legitimate investors.[17]

Many a mining company would be started on the strength of strong surface deposits, but the greater amounts of money and time needed for development of the deeper ore bodies became harder to acquire. At Silverton, Nevada, the forgotten mining camp where J. C. Tognoni and Harry Stimler began Treasure Hill Mining Company, they would mine $50,000 in silver shortly after 1910. Funds for deep development never materialized, and silver prices were never lower. At Silverton my father's heritage became one peculiar to the far west and to mining. He holds his family's mining claims by doing the necessary annual assessment and by

Senator Key Pittman
(Courtesy Nevada Historical Society)

Key Pittman
(Courtesy Nevada Historical Society)

managing leases to companies rich enough to command exploration capital. The Silverton mining claims may not become a fully developed ore body in his lifetime, but like others who maintain mining claims on the public lands, he has attempted with limited means to contribute to the slow exploration and development of this country's natural resources. Despite public confusion as to the value of natural resources and who should develop them, he has kept faith with his forefathers, ignoring accusations of greed. He has preserved man's knowledge of an ore body until such time as mining is no longer the nation's scapegoat for the excesses of its past.

During my Saturday morning in Reno, I visit the University of Nevada and the Mackay School of Mines, where my father became the first geological engineering graduate, but the libraries are closed for the day. The only sign of life on the campus is a gathering of 4-H Club dog trainers and their green-vested canines. A boy named Mitch poses for my camera with his dog. I wish to tell him how my father and his brothers once trained dogs in Eureka, Nevada, to pull a wagon and collect the town's garbage to feed their pigs, how they marketed the pigs on the roulette wheel in one of Eureka's taverns; but I allow my interest in taking Mitch's picture to speak my respect for his labors with his dog. Before I finally meet my father at the Reno airport later in this day, I have a task to perform at Schurz on the Shoshone Indian Reservation south of here.

5   Chant of the Survivors

We sit and talk and the silence speaks of the giants
who have died in the past and have returned to those
scenes unsatisfied and who is not unsatisfied, the
silent, Singac the rock shoulder emerging from the
rocks—and the giants live again in your silence
and unacknowledged desire . . .
William Carlos Williams

After a brief visit to the Carson City mint which now serves as a museum, I am on my way in the unclouded noonday sun to the Walker River Indian Reservation and the town of Schurz. There I hope to find the predecessors of the many Collins family members who, in 1919 with my grandfather and my great-grandfather, located a group of mining claims called the Black Oils. More than the predecessors, I will find one of the original locators, Frank V. Collins, now ninety-three years of age, and I will hear the poetry and silence of the Shoshone language as he speaks of the land and mutual history of our families.

The highway takes me through Dayton and past the historical marker which points out the mouth of Sutro tunnel, barely visible in the Washoe Mountains to the northwest. Southeast of my route is the Carson River, whose waters meander between the remains of many old Comstock mills. Rising beyond this canyon are the Pine Nut Mountains in which miners founded the town of Como, naming it after Lake Como in northern Italy near the town of Tognoni from whence came J. C. as a very young man. Flat and straight, the highway through this mining history of Nevada gives no intimation of the excitement of the century past.

I soon turn off the pavement onto a graded gravel road heading southeast along a bend in the Carson River. I will not intersect with black-top again until I reach the ruins of the United States government's first, largest, and most important military post in Nevada—Fort Churchill. The 1860

Ormsby Massacre and Indian raids on stations along the emigrant routes moved the government to build Fort Churchill and garrison 600 men there in 1861. By 1869 Indian trouble had ceased, and the fort became a privately owned traveler's station.[1] The hills rise bare and sharp off the road that I travel with only the treeline along the river and an occasional ranch to break the stark geology. The road seems in precarious agreement with time as the cracked and tumbling rocks on overhanging mountains insist that I go here in the grace of God or not at all. Occasionally, a wide draw moves back into the mountains exercising a magnetism on my spirit as if by wandering between the rock shoulders I would somehow reach the head and mind of this landscape.

Finally the narrow canyon of the Carson opens out into a wide plain where sprawl the dissipated adobe walls of old Fort Churchill. My road, a passage now entrenched in the blond sediment of ancient Lake Lahontan, meets the pavement at a painted arrow, pointed on both ends and anchored in the bank directly ahead of me. There is no instruction, not even a stop sign, only affirmation of the obvious; I must turn one way or another. Beyond the bank in which the arrow is posted stretch alkali flats, dry lake beds and occasional patches of land surrounded with a red dotted line on my map and labeled: "Danger area (travel restricted)." I am now directly east of Carson City with the Pine Nut Mountains between. To the south in the Singatse Mountains, Anaconda Copper Company developed a mine in the early twentieth century. The name Singatse was probably transplanted from China like Como from Italy. There was such a large population of Chinese placer gold miners in this vicinity that Dayton on the other side of the Pine Nut Range was originally called Chinatown.[2] The closest name that I can find on a map of China is Singtze, a town on a south fork of the Yangtze River. Perhaps the Chinese mined in the mountains to the west of Singtze just as the Italians mined lead and zinc in the mountains above Como Lake.

I am told that my grandfather spoke several languages. It is not an impossiblity. The Nevada into which he was born held pockets of many nationalities within the limits of his travel by horseback. In Duckwater Valley, where he was raised, there were at least four languages other than English to be learned from native speakers—Italian, Basque, Spanish and Shoshone. Among my grandfather's papers I find a picture of a Greek funeral procession in Ely, Nevada; and in Eureka my grandfather could have learned Chinese, although it is unlikely. The surviving Black Oil claim locator, Frank V. Collins, tells me that my grandfather spoke the Shoshone language so well that the Indians thought he was one of them. If the name of the outpost, Wabuska, through which I pass south on Interstate Highway Alternative 95, is any indication of the nature of the Shoshone tongue, there

J. C. Tognoni
(Courtesy Nevada Historical Society)

may be some primal forces of language at work in Nevada. Wabuska means white grass. Wabuska. The grass on the desert often huddles in bunches— little bushes. White bushes. Wabuska. Language here is in the wind, which rises with the sound of an ocean wave and overtakes human beings. In Nevada the "Washoe zephyr" spoke to every man and combed the needles of the pine nut trees, important native source of sustenance, like the ocean's kelp. Maybe here as on the sea, international word and law are as basic to survival as nutrients.

The men who could have affirmed my words, the men who knew the wind and its home in the mountains, fueled the mills and smelters for the "Silver State." In groups the Indians, the Chinese and the Italians cut the trees and sagebrush to burn for Nevada's mining. The most highly skilled of these groups were the Carbonari, or the Italian and Swiss-Italian charcoal makers. These men carefully calculated moisture content of the wood, size of logs, and kiln temperature to regulate the rate of combustion in their rock charcoal ovens. Carbonari could increase the number of British thermal units to be gotten from a pound of pine wood by almost 63 percent.[3] The Carbonari were imported mainly for the smelters in Eureka, Nevada. There the silver-lead ore was of a complicated variety requiring advanced smelting techniques and large amounts of fuel. Around Eureka, the wood-cutters would clear a fifty mile circumference before the railroad brought fuel to the smelters. As a young man my father hauled wood from the old Carbonari cut-sites, and he would harvest the pine nuts in the same mountains. He believes the Carbonari may have spared the pine nut trees and cut a larger type of pine.

Cutting in the precious Nevada woodlands would be a source of conflict not only between the Indians and the white men, but in 1879 a skirmish between the smelter operators and the striking Charcoal Burners' Association left five men dead. It was not long after this Fish Creek War that my great-grandfather arrived from Italy, sponsored like many others by his older brother, known as Big Louie. Frank V. Collins will speak to my father about Big Louie's death: "I saw the spoons with the salt still on them lying on the table. He had eaten a bad piece of jerked meat and the salt was to make him throw it up." The dream slowly changes and a laugh enters Frank Collins' voice as he tells us that "the old man" (meaning J. C. Tognoni) dug up all around Big Louie's place looking for Louie's money.

Frank Collins is not the only man from whom I will hear versions of this story. When a published story mixed Big Louie with old man Pogue, whose roadhouse was near Big Louie Spring, fortune-seekers descended upon Pogue's Station looking for Louie's treasure. Frank Collins lightly scoffs at the idea that Louie was rich. I find among my grandfather's papers the final account and report of Agostine Luigi Tognoni's estate, dated 1909, four years after Louie's death. In it, my great-grandfather, as administrator of the estate, recorded that Big Louie had only $3.50 on hand at the time of his death. Of the appraised value of Louie's estate, J. C. managed to pay Louie's debts, his funeral expenses, and a small inheritance to their brother, Giacomo.

From Frank Collins' story I begin to understand that he harbors some resentment toward J. C. Tognoni. His ninety-three-year-old eyes are as young as in the picture I later recognize of him and his family in my grand-father's photo album. They are blue, gay and thoughtful and meet mine with a wide openness; yet there is something being left unsaid. My road has taken me to Frank Collins unexpectedly. I thought I would find a son or daughter in the town of Schurz on the Walker River, but in the home of his niece, Florence Brown, a woman of my father's age, I meet Frank Collins himself. He is much more deaf during this first meeting than on a subse-quent visit that I will make with my father and my brother months later. On the second visit he will speak untiringly as his daughter, Evalyn Martinez, his niece and her daughter, Linda Brown, record him on tape.

Frank Collins is reticent on my first visit partially, I suspect, because I confuse him with my pronunciation of my family name—Tognoni. I had not yet learned that the people of Duckwater pronounce it "tie-oh-nee." I grew up calling myself "Tog-no-nee" with all the correctness of English phonetics. My father had grown up believing that the Duckwater pronun-ciation was a slur on Italians, and my college professors informed me that proper Roman Italian would have it "Tone-yo-nee." Now my Uncle Nye tells me that the Duckwater pronunciation is the way the Italian immigrants themselves said the name Tognoni in their own peculiar dialect, Pied-montese. But never having heard "Tie-oh-nee," I am puzzling the ears of Mr. Collins with my English and Roman variations. They fail to strike a chord of recognition.

On my second visit I am with my father, and Frank Collins tells him, "Joe Tognoni and I grew up side by side." To illustrate, Collins straightens the index finger of each hand and holds them together. Still there is some-thing not being said. There is resistance to my father's skillful tugs at this man's venerable "veil of tears." Finally, at a point in the casual cross-exam-ination where my father is silently searching for another question, Mr. Col-lins volunteers, "Joe Tognoni took everything I had." My father disguises his surprise by shifting slowly in his chair before asking, "How?" I steal a glance at Evelyn, Linda and Florence, who give their steadfast attention to the elder's words. I ask myself if what I am about to hear for the first time is an old story for them. "Joe Tognoni and I bought a herd of sheep together.

I put in sixteen hundred dollars. He put in the same. We were partners, but when the bank took the Tognoni place they took my sheep too. That's when I came here to Schurz. All I got out of it was a car they gave me." As with the story of Big Louie, Mr. Collins ends this one on a note of sonorous contentment by telling stories of the car given to him by my family as if it were a mustang to be tamed.

During my first encounter with Mr. Collins, when I despair of getting any information from him regarding the Tognoni family, I doggedly refer to the location notice which I lay out before him on Florence Brown's dining room table. Beside it I have displayed my grandparents' marriage license on which Adams Franklin Brown, Adeline Collins and J. L. Collins signed as witnesses. The location notice is for a group of association placer claims called the Black Oils in "an unknown mining district about half way between Portuguese Springs and Ike Springs." Mr. Collins does not seem to understand that I am showing him an oil claim. He answers my inquiries with a Shoshone rhapsody about a copper "prospect" in the vicinity of the Black Oil claims. I will follow the mustang trails between the pine nut trees in the very mountains about which Mr. Collins speaks, and his words will come back to me like poetry. He remembers a white mountain and three little red hills with little chips of copper on the ground. He recalls a one-and-a-half inch streak of copper in a ten-foot-deep prospect hole which assayed at 49 percent copper, "key to the whole layout." He describes a big ledge above the diggings and more streaks of copper to the north of the hole. On the white mountain's west side, there are hundreds of acres of shale: "Some people said it would burn. Vegetable matter," says Collins, "left in the rock by an ocean." One mile from the shale he has found old sea shells embedded in slabs of rock.

The location notices for the Black Oil claims were turned up by my brother Brian while searching the Nye County records to make sure that all of the family claims in the Pancake Range were recorded with the federal government under a 1979 program for eliminating mining claims from government lands. Any later than 1919 and my father's family and the other locators of the Black Oil claims would have been prevented from locating an oil claim. In 1920, the United States government made oil and other fuel and fertilizer minerals leasable and not locatable under the mining laws.[4] Not since the early nineteenth century, when Congress acted to lease lead deposits on the public lands, had the Department of the Interior experimented in mineral leasing. The first attempt had been economically disastrous. By 1844, the cost of administering the lead mine leasing program exceeded the amount collected in rentals by more than four times for a four year period. So, in 1845, with President Polk's recommendation, the legislature provided for the sale of the lead mines.[5]

In the vicinity of the Black Oil claims my father's family and the Collins family had long gathered wood for fuel. Oil prospecting was to replace wood gathering and become a sign of the times. If one element were selected as most characteristic of modern times, it probably would be the use of minerals as sources of energy. Beyond doubt, J. C. Tognoni was a man of vision. Few, including Mr. Collins, would understand why "he ran all over locating claims." More important than his prophecy of oil's growing importance was J. C.'s comprehension of politics. He knew that if free men did not take the initiative in using their land, the government and those who had secured fortunes were about to take the land away from free men. Memory of fighting for liberty flowed in him like blood: the Carbonari were more than woodcutters and charcoal burners. They were a secret political society organized in the early nineteenth century to resist misgovernment by the Bourbons and Austrians and to secure Italian freedom and unity. So Guiseppe Cristofo di Tognoni, seeing the signs of the times, located an association placer claim for oil, and attempted to share it with his unconvinced friends.

No sooner did petroleum become valuable than the secretary of the interior in 1896 acted to take oil out from under the mining laws. Congress responded by reasserting the mining laws in 1897 with the Oil Placer Act.[6] As a placer, the oil claim gave up the extralateral rights conferred by a lode claim under the location system. If more had been known about oil deposits, the extralateral right to the entirety of a deposit conferred by a lode discovery could have served conservation. By limiting an oil claimant to vertical side lines drawn down through pools of oil, an estimated 75 to 90 percent of oil deposits was being left underground. Each of those who had a pump on the deposit reduced the pressure needed to extract the entirety of the pool.[7] Competing operators were drilling with such density that the "legs of the derricks [interlocked],"[8] and, at one point, oil was selling for the ridiculously wasteful price of five cents a barrel.[9]

Instead of recognizing the basic error in thinking with regard to the reality of oil deposits and mining, we Americans found men to blame instead of a false idea. Thus the greedy oil man became a fabled villain, and in 1909 the Department of the Interior succeeded in temporarily foiling him by withdrawing approximately three million acres of land in California and Wyoming from mineral entry. The department proposed that it would be an injustice for the government to purchase needed oil from citizenry.[10] Yet it had no alternative plan for finding and pumping the oil itself. Furthermore, the Department did not have the power without an act of Congress, to make the withdrawal other than what the Supreme Court would urge as tacit consent in *U.S. vs. Midwest Oil Co.*[11] In 1920 when Congress created the Mineral Leasing Act to resolve the problem of oil on public lands, Teapot Dome ensued. Becoming a popular synonym for graft and malfeasance in public office, Teapot Dome would rarely be interpreted as a natural result of government leasing. To complicate matters, the mineral leasing act had pledged over 50 percent of its proceeds to reclamation projects in arid lands. Billions of dollars worth of development throughout the West were envisioned.[12] The purpose of the federal reclamation program passed by Congress in 1902 was to provide national assistance to develop the water resources of the West for homesteading purposes.[13] But according to the 1931 Report on Conservation and Administration of Public Lands, only three-fourths of 1 percent of the total crop value of the nation could be attributed to irrigated western lands. Mineral leasing had failed in its basic intentions, but this time its failure had been accompanied by growth of power in the Forest Service and the Bureau of Land Management. The citizenry of the far west was slowly giving up any real sovereignty over its land.

To return to my great-grandfather and Frank Collins, and to the mountains and valleys of Nevada, my great-grandfather over-extended himself in legal battles for his water rights at Duckwater and lost his ranch to the bank. In failing health, his son, my grandfather, moved with his young family to Eureka, Nevada, where the smelters had shut down, and Frank Collins moved his family to the U.S. government's Walker River Indian Reservation. The copper and oil industries, heavily dependent on government and eastern capital took over the basins and ranges of Nevada, and the ranchers traded off millions of acres in military reservations for expensive government programs designed to increase the range value of leased land. Where the Indians sparingly burned the juniper to keep its deep root from robbing the pine nut tree and the sweet white sage, the government would drag battleship anchor chains between crawler tractors to uproot all trees on land classified as range.[14]

The complexities of administering the public lands without living on them proliferated government agents and hastened the circumvention of law created when people, not the government, owned the land. Law no longer guided these agents. Policy—mercurial, vague and ridden by "euphemisms that abdicate all real power"[15]—became their most cogent concern. Finally any pretense that the government administration of public lands resulted in revenue for reclamation projects was no longer necessary. The national forests had long operated in the red.[16] The idea that the people of the west would destroy their own land had become institutionalized. With regard to our mineral resources, the *Western Rebel* draws the gloomy situation with some humor.[17]

> Back in the 1800s Mark Twain said a mine was a hole in the ground with a liar standing beside it. Times have changed. Today, a mine is still a hole in the ground but now there are a herd of bureaucrats looking at it. None of them know what it is, but they are in common agreement that it has to be regulated and controlled.

Little wonder that Mr. Collins seems disinterested in his locator's rights to the Black Oil claims. Despite the encouragement of the women in his family, he resists negotiating a grubstake agreement with my father's corporation, Mineral Economics. The Hualapais and Navajo Indians in northen Arizona so distrust the government and the American mining industry that they negotiate with Arab and Mexican exploration companies to find the oil on their land.[18] Although Frank Collins' niece, Linda Brown, is a strong minded woman who has been very cautious from the start with me, I share with her the same refusal to sit quietly while frightened government agents with university degrees speak about land which they normally cannot know from either experience or culture. With respect I listen to Frank Collins sing the Shoshone song to which the tribe's women seasonally dance, and it is with hope that I regard Florence, Linda and her daughter Shoshone (meaning Star), for they seem anxious to be proud of their choices for the future. Even if we drill dry holes in the Black Oil claims, there is hope that we may renew the spirit of our mutual heritage in the land. If we can find oil, then maybe we will have the financial independence to live on the land with pride again and build for ourselves and our children.

Back in Reno my father awaits me at a car rental desk in the airport where he is conducting business by telephone and putting himself on familiar terms with the Hertz girls. My great-grandfather probably would have negotiated sale of at least one share of Treasure Hill Mining Company by now, but Mineral Economics and my father are kept to innocent flirtation by the Securities Exchange Commission.

Richard P. Haskins, Jr., driving his father's Ford truck without truck box and the double set of wheels which could be bolted on to haul rock at the family's quarry. The fugitive Irishman on the far left made a lasting impression on young Haskins, c. 1925.

The surviving locator on the Black Oil claims, Frank V. Collins, with his young family.

6 Legend of the Family Mine

Riding beside my father while stretches of desert and mountains moved at their separate paces around us and past the window frames of the truck, I have listened for many years to a refrain of stories about our mining family. Now, at long last, my father, Hale Tognoni, and I are about to embark together on a search for the facts, and the pilgrimage which I started three days ago becomes more difficult. I will struggle to draw answers from my father to verify the tales about places through which we will pass, places he keeps in his heart. During Hale Tognoni's career as a mining lawyer, the role he has played with many a grizzled philosopher from the hills is now mine with him. It is I who must cross-examine the wanderings of his mind, and as I remain one of his five children, whom he raised by a good number of military methods, I must walk carefully the thin line between doing my job and insubordination. He is unaccustomed to trusting to someone else's purpose and is bound up in vigilance, but for good reason. The struggle of another man, Richard P. Haskins, Jr., and his mining family should illustrate.

Mr. Haskins' quarry is being threatened by government agents anxious to erase all trace of the Haskins family mining activities during the past ninety years. Even as I help my father load into the trunk of our rented car his bags, briefcase and one constant tool peculiar to his practice of law—a prospector's hand pick—Haskins' claims pend adjudication. I began writing Mr. Haskins' story ten years ago when my father harnessed my over-developed skills as a student to the tedious work of picking through transcripts and engineering reports and the voluminous files of memorandums, appeal briefs and decisions in *U.S. vs. Haskins*. Simply stated, Mr. Haskins wanted to patent his quarry. The government did not want to recognize Haskins' rights to the land, and Hale Tognoni had filed a complaint in the federal district court on behalf of Mr. Haskins. I was to help write a memorandum to the court.

I first met Mr. Haskins about four years earlier when my father took me from my college dormitory into the mountains east of Los Angeles on an unexpected tromp in the rocks and bushes. In my school sketch book I drew Mr. Haskins' old hard hat as it lay in his mobile home. I was yet too young to see behind the thick lenses of his peculiarly cocked eyeglasses to find the plenitude of intelligence and passion which are his. Ten years later, aided by old photographs, I began to understand how we came to have a second meeting. A picture of Richard Haskins as a young man confirmed the spirit which is still strong in his abused and worn body, and I was able to draw the links between his family and mine.

In one photo taken in 1925 of "Junior," as Mr. Haskins was called, he sat proudly at the wheel of a 1914 Ford truck which he modernized with sleeker fenders. Richard P. Haskins, Sr., originally purchased it for his mining claims in Limerock Canyon. The truck box was removable, and a second set of wheels could be bolted on to make wider tires. Thus, young Haskins and his brother could haul heavy loads of rock over sand from their father's quarry. But the photo holds much more than a predecessor to the sand buggies that careen for thrills on southern California sand dunes. Sitting in young Haskins' buggy were two men, one of whom the British exiled to Australia for his Irish patriotism. Like the Carbonari in the Tognoni family, this man represented Mr. Haskins' early awareness that in the country from which his father came, men still had to fight for the dignity which law has attempted to give to human affairs in the United States. "Trust only the words from a man's mouth," Chinese businessmen in Los Angeles would later tell Richard Haskins, but his strong Irish heritage implored him to seek justice in the conscience of his culture, in written word, in law. My father, a rare practitioner of "common law" or the "law of the land," is one of Mr. Haskins' ties to his principles. Common law has a concern for justice which the tyranny of legal codes would abandon.

When Mr. Haskins' father ran away from Ireland with a friend at the age of ten, they worked in a Chicago brick yard for five years until Haskins, Sr., struck out for California. From there he followed the gold rushes and set up saloons in Cripple Creek, Colorado; Nome, Alaska; and Rhyolite, Nevada. Frequently, it was in his saloons that prospectors kept their records of mining claims in a new mining district, and in the saloons prospectors often found the men to grubstake them. Tramp Consolidated Mining Company in Rhyolite made the senior Haskins a small fortune, allowing him to marry in 1904 and travel to Europe with his wife, Tessie Cooke, and their first son, Bartholomew. In Paris, Mrs. Haskins studied the harp, later to become a member of the Los Angeles symphony orchestra.

Prior to his marriage, the history of Haskins, Sr., on his mining claims in California's Little Tujunga Mining District, began. In 1894 he gained a third interest in the Lone Jack mining claim by grubstaking two of the patrons of his Los Angeles drinking establishment, F. A. Lovell and Francis Clark. Ore from the Lone Jack showed significant quantities of gold, silver, vanadium and uranium. On and around the Lone Jack the limestone had been mined by a German mining company in the 1880s. The Germans had loaded the limestone or "carbonate rock" into kilns and "dead burned" it. The disintegrated limestone or lime could be shoveled from the kiln's bottom to be sold for plaster. Remnants of three of these rock kilns, similar in size and shape to the charcoal kilns of the Carbonari, still exist at Haskins' quarry. An earthquake in 1971 and subsequent fire and flood summarily demolished a fourth kiln.

F. A. Lovell's discovery monument on the Lone Jack, however, still stands at the mouth of an eighty-five-foot tunnel into the mountain. The tunnel follows a seam between the limestone and granite on the Lone Jack where precious metals accumulated that once flowed in the hot magma where it intruded the limestone and slowly cooled to granite. Mr. Haskins says that John Hays Hammond's Colorado group ended a lease on the Lone Jack consequent to the silver panic of 1893. In that year the bimetallic standard for money, had its silver crutch yanked. The crutch or the Sherman Silver Purchase Act of 1890 was revoked in 1893, and a new one-legged measure of value—the gold standard—was asked to hop along until banking interests could craft an artifical limb. Meanwhile Hammond left the United States for South Africa, like many other celebrated mining men who went abroad in the final years of the nineteenth century. Mining claims like the Lone Jack were able to continue the development of their precious metal deposits only if other mineral assets of the property could help support the miners. Stone or "cobble rock" which had broken loose from the walls of Limerock Canyon and adjacent ravines provided just such a bumper against the fall of precious metal prices. Before the turn of the century loads of stone were being hauled from the area of the claim for building projects in Los Angeles; and from 1894 until 1908, as many as six men were working to drive tunnels in pursuit of an ore body rich enough for the failing metals market.

In 1907, upon the return of Haskins, Sr., from Europe, he acquired the entirety of the Lone Jack, and located a second claim, the Lap Wing, in Tessie Cooke-Haskins' name. The Lap Wing extended from the south end of the Lone Jack down into the canyon and alluvial beds where drainage merged with Little Tujunga Creek. Location notices for two more lode claims adjacent to the Lone Jack on the west and reaching across the steep walls of the canyon date to 1908. Lovell and Clark joined Haskins, Sr., in locating the Lady Helen and the Roger Williams, but later in 1908, they sold their interests to Haskins. Lovell would live and work on the claims until the early 1920s along with another man, Cy Overman, hired to do maintenance.

In 1908 and 1909 Haskins, Sr., located two millsites in his wife's name to straddle Little Tujunga Creek where a blacksmith shop, three bunkhouses, stables and a cook shack formed what became known on government maps as Sycamore Camp. Also in 1908 Haskins, Sr., filed a water claim on the creek where he built a dam and a diversion ditch to process rock and raise vegetables. Water from a tunnel on the Lone Jack also supplied the camp. With prohibition in 1918, Haskins, Sr., bought property including a general store and dance hall in Pacoima, where he moved from Los Angeles with his family. His wife was making musicians of their children, Bartholomew, Maude, and young Richard. She taught Richard to play the piano and violin and wanted him to pursue a career in music as Maude would do, but the Haskins brothers were wedded to mining. Although Bartholomew would finish law school, he lived and worked on his family's mining claim rather than take the bar exam.

From Pacoima, the claims were only six miles away. Haskins, Sr., made agreements with rock companies who were hauling and crushing rock on his claims for his sons to bring the rock out of difficult ravines and to stack it where it could be more easily loaded onto large trucks. Maude Haskins participated by cooking for "the boys," as I have done for my father's Mineral Economics Corporation. Haskins, Jr., even took out a special driving permit at the age of twelve enabling him to drive the Ford truck legally on the mine roads. With his brother he learned to "pop boulders" which had descended and continued to cascade from the walls of the canyon and ravines. Limestone is soft among rocks, so that there usually existed a crevice in the white boulders. Into this likely opening the brothers would insert dynamite and a fuse, packing a barnacle of mud over them to direct the explosive forces down into the boulder, breaking it into sizes which could be lifted. Mr. Haskins grasps his softly swollen torso to tell me about his desire as a boy to lift the heaviest rock possible, which he believes did damage to his internal organs.

"Popping boulders," Mr. Haskins told me, was child's play compared with what skilled mining men must know, and he began to explain how carefully placed smaller explosions can direct the force of a larger blast. Like my Uncle Nye when telling his favorite stories from several years as an explosives salesman, Mr. Haskins seems far away, examining the magical rubble at the end of a burned fuse. In the same trance, Uncle Nye describes one occasion when he created a water ditch by fixing long rows of dynamite—a stick every so many inches in the ground. Two or three days he worked digging the explosives into the ground so that the first blast set off the whole series, lifting a wave of dirt and dropping it in a neat berm alongside the new ditch. My uncle's elation at the very memory of that trick may be as close as I'll ever see him come to singing praises to the Lord.

Natural forces at the Haskins quarry long ago heaved the limestone and other peaceful sediments, displacing, crushing and re-cementing them into harder stone valuable for building. During the 1920s the whiter rock or altered limestone was being sold for stucco dash, mosaic terrazzo and for flux in the purification of iron ore. Large quantities of granite were also crushed for chicken grits, an aid to many a Los Angeles layer's digestion. Mineral Products Inc. even constructed a short railway in one ravine below two of the larger white outcroppings. In ore cars the rock could be rolled to loading bunkers at the mouth of the ravine. Prospecting the granite and limestone contacts also continued by tunneling. In 1920 Mr. and Mrs. Haskins, Sr., had signed a mine option with Captain Jesse A. Tiffany, who attempted to develop a vanadium mine on the claims.

In 1929 Haskins, Sr., died, and the men who had associated themselves with his mining disappeared from the scene, so that in 1930 Mrs. Haskins made an agreement with a Mr. O'Leary to quarry 200 tons of rock on her Lady Helen claim. Mr. O'Leary, however, was not to be trusted. He may have counted on the emotions of a new widow to dismiss his illegal fumbling of the quarry enterprise, but Tessie Cooke-Haskins took quick and forceful recognition of her mistake and sued for breach of contract. At this point a number of affidavits in the lawsuit provide a suddenly detailed record of mining activity on the claims.

While living in a tunnel on the Lap Wing, Carl Taux and his son, hired by O'Leary in March of 1930, piled up "a lot of stones in the creek below Lady Helen," about fifteen or twenty tons, and they took rock already piled on the Lap Wing. Mrs. Haskins had intended that O'Leary should blast from the deposits still on the walls of Limerock Canyon, and Carl Taux, his son, a third worker and a grocer had intended that O'Leary should pay them. O'Leary did none of the above, so that when another of the affiants, L. E. Wood, dealer in all kinds of rock, sand and gravel, came out to the quarry in July of 1930 to get the rock for which he had already made a down payment to O'Leary, Mrs. Haskins and her son Richard met him. She explained her complaint with O'Leary and ordered Wood to stay away. After talking to O'Leary, Wood returned to pay Mrs. Haskins for rock from the Lap Wing. In response, O'Leary broke the lock on the gate into the quarry and blasted on the Lady Helen for three or four days in July, presumably trying to redeem himself. In August of 1930, Wood signed a contract with Mrs. Haskins to remove stone boulders and "lime rock."

Meanwhile Mrs. Haskins had initiated a patent application for two of her lode claims and one millsite, claiming the presence of valuable gold and vanadium. The Forest Service challenged the application, but on April 25, 1931, the land office registrar issued this decision:

> In view of applicant being in actual physical possession and occupancy of the lands for a period of nearly a quarter of a century, and the extensive improvements made thereon, it is clearly manifest that applicant has been acting in the utmost good faith, which is an essential element worthy of consideration when the character of the land is questioned; and it appearing by preponderance of the evidence that said land is mineral in character containing appreciable values of the precious minerals, and that the showing of such minerals upon said lands would warrant a prudent man in expending his time and money thereupon in the reasonable expectation of success in developing a paying mine, I would recommend that the charges be dismissed and the three claims in question be passed to patent.

But the patent would have gone against a trend in land policy—keeping the public lands out of private hands. In fact the land of Mrs. Haskins' claims had been removed from further entry for mineral by a watershed withdrawal act in 1928. Such withdrawals and the increased reluctance of land officials to release land to miners represent a complete reversal of earlier land policy and law designed to give land title to people who would produce. So the commissioner of the land office and the secretary of the interior went about overturning the registrar's decision with regard to the Haskins patent application.

While the patent pended, Bartholomew Haskins began to run the quarry. Also during this time Los Angeles County condemned a right-of-way for a road across the southern end of the millsites breaking up Sycamore Camp. The County paid Mrs. Haskins $1,000 and paved her road, extending it through the mountains to intersect the Antelope Valley Freeway, east out of Los Angeles. The old road had been built and maintained by ranching and by mining interests like the Haskins' and had once served horse-drawn wagons.

Giving up hope for her patent application in the Department of the Interior, on July 23, 1935, Mrs. Haskins sought a reprieve from President

Roosevelt, whose concern sent a Forest Service mineral examiner to the claims. In his report he observed that Bartholomew Haskins "works alone, breaking down, 'cobbing' and sorting, loading and hauling the material to the chemical company's plant." The examiner concluded that the claims which contained dolomite, a limestone with magnesium carbonates, were "unquestionably patentable." But the lode claim from which Bartholomew was mining dolomite was not part of the 1930 patent application. The registrar rejected the application, and Mrs. Haskins gave up her pursuit of a secured property title to her claims.

The Forest Service was much more passive then than it would become in later years, and the written rejection of the patent application did not declare the claims to be "null and void" as is federal policy today. On the contrary, the secretary of the interior stipulated that there being no "suggestion that the claims are not maintained in good faith," nor that the land is valuable for timber or other forest use, nor that the continuance of mining exploration would be harmful to government interests, "the proper action seems to be to merely reject the patent application and leave the mineral claimant free to pursue exploration under her locations."[1]

In the late 1930s and early 1940s, the war in Europe was creating demand for steel. Kenney Iron Works, Long Beach Foundries, Alhambra Foundries and Bethlehem Steel Company began buying from the Haskins quarry, and a new product, rock wool insulation, was using rock from the claims. Previous to this period of heavy production, natural forces had done the breaking of the dolomite from its source. The cracked and tumbling surface limestone had been sufficient to supply buyers, but now cuts were made into what the geologists call "dolomitic lenses" and the lawyers term "lode formations." Surface mining continued, however, and the Haskins brothers repaired part of the old Mineral Products tramway. Their newly acquired tractor made the lower part of the tramway obsolete. Rock slides have again covered the upper tramway and the crushers and bins for the war steel and chemical companies have been removed to avoid the natural demolition in Limerock Canyon.

Between 1923 and 1940, the Haskins brothers sold an estimated fifteen to eighteen thousand tons of rock. In 1941 Bartholomew joined the army. Richard, whom the armed services rated "4-F," had a young family to care for, so mining at the quarry slacked off until Bartholomew returned in 1948. He hauled rock regularly to M. Tregoe Foundry Supply and various masonry contractors in Los Angeles until his death in 1962 on the road from the quarry. Although Richard Haskins would visit the quarry on weekends with his son Patrick, he contributed mostly capital to the mining operation in the years after the war when Bartholomew mined. Haskins purchased a diesel skip loader, core driller, dump truck, a mobile home, and during the uranium rush of 1955, a steel fence and gate at the request of the Forest Service. The hoards with geiger counters were creating a fire hazard in the quarry, according to officials.

Around this same time, the government began to actively eliminate mining claims from the public lands. Their encouragement for doing so had come by way of the Act of July 23, 1955 (Public Law 167), which sought to curb the use of mining claims in bad faith for purposes other than mining. The program initiated under this act in the Los Angeles National Forest required persons holding valid mining claims to register with the Forest Service. So on June 1, 1962, the Haskins brothers submitted a verification of the four lodes and two millsites under which their parents had originated title to the quarry. In the next two years Forest Service mineral examiner Emmett Ball visited the claims twice. Seeing Richard Haskins removing stones from the creek bed and selling them, Ball told Haskins that he couldn't do that on a *lode* claim and in due course, the Forest Service made complaint against the lode claims and millsites.

In the early 1930s during Tessie Cooke-Haskins' five-year struggle to obtain patent, she won a hearing at which government experts avowed that the dolomite was "insufficient to be valuable and could not be mined economically." In the 1962 Forest Service contest against the lode claims, government experts, recognizing the war production of dolomite for the manufacture of steel, declared that the mineral deposit had been "mined out." An expert testifying for Haskins estimated that there were at least 200,000 tons more of dolomite on the claims and perhaps as much as 400,000 tons. Haskins notified the Department of the Interior that he would appeal the nullification of his lode claims, but he filed late with the office of appeals, and the department promptly dismissed his right to appeal. At this point, Hale Tognoni, who was working on a patent application for the quarry, won a reversal from the Ninth Circuit Court of Appeals. That court said that so long as Haskins' right to the land of his quarry was of substance, the claims and the appeal could not be dismissed on a technicality. The words were that the department should "exercise discretion" with regard to the appeal.[2] Narrowly interpreting this order, the department issued a new decision against Haskins. It argued that discretion had already been exercised and with its heavy hand, the department pressed a new wrinkle into Mr. Haskins' struggle.

Haskins had decided not to appeal the lode claims and millsites. Rather, he would pursue a patent on the property under a more proper legal classification. He made a *placer* patent application following mineral examiner Ball's definition of his mining, but the mineral survey required with such an application was waylaid by the California State Director of Land Management. He believed that the nullification of Mr. Haskins' lode claims and millsites voided the placer operation as well. He cancelled the survey and declared Haskins to be in trespass. Remaining in possession of his quarry, Haskins defied the land bureaus, and the state director brought a suit to eject Haskins from the property. But the federal district court in Los Angeles would not force Haskins to vacate his mining claims, and it ordered the department to hear the facts of a placer discovery. Incredulous, the U.S. attorney motioned immediately for a re-trial and submitted affidavits from various Forest Service employees stating that they had not seen any significant mining on the claims and implying that Mr. Haskins kept the land purely for recreational purposes. Mr. Haskins remembers an apology after the re-trial from one of the affiants who had complied with his superiors out of fear for his job.

Again, however, the federal district court decided that the placer discovery should be heard. The department then appealed its case to the Ninth Circuit Court, where again the judge ordered the department to hear Mr. Haskins' placer patent application.[3] Finally, nine years after submittal of the patent application for the Haskins Quarries Placer Mining Claim, the department's hearing examiner, or administrative law judge, found for Haskins and recommended issuance of patent. The Interior Board of Land Appeals stepped into *U.S. vs. Haskins* here, and in October of 1981 nullified the placer claim. In the past year the government has begun serving notice on Mr. Haskins that he must move his equipment and housing or it will be burned; so Mr. Haskins has filed a complaint in the federal district court and once again I am helping to write a Motion for Summary Judgment.

In the years during which the most recent patent application has pended Mr. Haskins has mined the quarry with his son and kept the claims largely out of love. The quarry has given the members of his family a substance to their lives denied to those who will never know and care for a mountain, a creek or a canyon the way a person who has mined or farmed them does. Now Mr. Haskins is alone, seventy years old and visibly weary. He has defended his rights to mine on the public lands where others have and would have succumbed to government policies which no longer protect and encourage lawful and productive investments of human energy. Unless young Patrick Haskins sees a value in enduring the heavy tolls of government, or the government finally issues patent, the Haskins quarry will return to the quaked, flood-worn brush country that the Haskins family mined and cared for in times when acquittals may have been more than just legend and private ownership of land was the bedrock of the United States Constitution.

George Wingfield
(Courtesy Nevada Historical Society)

*J. C. Tognoni and George Wingfield in the lobby of the Mizpah Hotel,
Tonopah, Nevada*

7   Moon on the Sagebrush

*"The past changes as we change ... only
the present is knowable" ...* [1]

After our meeting at the Reno airport, my father, Hale Tognoni, and I
planned to drive southerly 215 miles to Tonopah. A full moon will keep the
night hours of our drive from darkness and inspire the landscape. To reflect
the light of my father's past in Nevada and in mining with the acknowledg-
ment of subtle changes like the moonlight on resplendent countryside
would be a worthwhile achievement, but with my father this trip and our
book must answer those who would apologize for Nevada's mining past.
Mining people are receiving so little compassion from historians that a
smaller man than my father might be embittered. He is not tall, but he
carries himself on his toes, eager to express his own view of history. He
presupposes only ignorance, not malice, in those who seem to prefer in-
gratitude over recognition of greatness in Nevada's mining men.

We will drive to Tonopah tonight where we have guaranteed reservations. Accommodations are scarce in Tonopah. MX missile reconnaissance
crews of the United States government have virtually laid siege. Fortunate-
ly, the Mizpah, once a stylish meeting place of mining men during Nevada's
twentieth century mining boom, has already done its duty as a military
barracks. During World War II construction workers used it while laying
out a "heavy bombardment base"[2] or nuclear test site in desert flats for
which Tonopah was the closest outpost of civilization. Now the old hotel
stands reinforced, reupholstered and lavishly draped to befit the sancti-
mony of historical significance.

The town of Tonopah did not exist in 1900 when Jim Butler, a prospector and rancher, brought rich ore out of the Tonopah hills. Butler did not

have to unearth his mineral ledges. They sat open to the sky, contemptuous-
ly visible alongside the faded paths of previous prospectors. One of the
more worn trails, probably the route of mustangs, ran through the center of
property which would belong to Tonopah's largest mining company.[3] Just
as the California gold-rushers who were working in the vicinity of the
Comstock did not recognize the silver at first, early prospectors in the
Tonopah and Goldfield mining districts may have been looking for silver-
bearing formations like the ones they had seen in the Washoe mountains of
the Comstock. The valuable hills of Tonopah and of Goldfield, to the south,
were lighter in color, and accelerated erosion had both disguised and
enriched the mineralized regions over which black malapais flowed to
form mesas and cover soft iron-stained ash.

Theories regarding the deposition of precious metals would develop
after American geologists had studied deep mines like the Comstock. Still
the ideas of these educated men would not replace the personal observations and experience of those who tromped the Nevada deserts and
mountains in pursuit of mineral fortune. The Indians, whose way of life had
demanded intimate knowledge of the land, often guided the prospectors.
So long as surface outcroppings existed, the largely inarticulate intelligence
of the Indian, and the prospector's "nose for ore" were still guiding the picks
and shovels of Nevada's mineral industry. The story goes that Jim Butler
picked up Tonopah's first ore sample to throw at a wayward burro. The
extraordinary weight of the rock made him pause. When my great-grandfather, J. C. Tognoni, staked his first claims in nearby Goldfield mining
district, he was probably seeking asylum more than gold or silver. If a burro
is to claim credit for development of mines at Tonopah, then I am properly
within the twisting path of acknowledged mining fortune when I point out
that one of Goldfield's pioneer prospectors was cooling his heels after
having his irrigation dam attacked in a distant valley. Nobody brought
Butler's burro to trial where a transcript might confirm his unintentional
contribution to mining. As for my great-grandfather, his testimony in *State
of Nevada vs. Joseph Tognoni* is that in May of 1903 he fired his gun at the
ground around neighboring ranches who were destroying his irrigation
dam. Two weeks after his trial, records in the Nye County recorder's office
show that J. C. was staking mining claims in Goldfield district. Otherwise,
the verdict in *Nevada vs. Tognoni* is lost to record.

In 1903, when J. C. entered Goldfield, it was still only the mining camp
of a few hardy prospectors. The winters in Goldfield's high plain, its
remoteness, and the scarcity of water had thinned out the first rush of men.
Four miles distant from the trompled and dusty sagebrush that would
become the largest city in Nevada in 1907, J. C. Tognoni found water

flowing from beneath the volcanic rock of an eminence to be named Tognoni Mountain.[4] On his location notices he described his mining claim in Gold Flat by their distance from Tognoni Spring.

I have a photograph of J. C. Tognoni taken around 1917 in the lobby of the Mizpah. His contemplative stance and starched formal collar suggest to me that he may have been preparing to talk about money with the man who is signing in at the hotel desk. From the casual leaning of this second guest, I suspect that he is accustomed to signing papers, and I go to my books to study his resemblance to the wealthy men who made fortunes in Tonopah and Goldfield, someone whose registration at the Mizpah might be worthy of a photograph. I am partial to believing that it may be George Wingfield. In the years after his Tonopah gambling success Wingfield's footsteps across Nevada beckoned the hordes like water filling tracks on a beach. Wherever Wingfield took even the slightest interest a mining district flourished: Goldfield, 1902; Silverbow, 1905; Fairview, 1906; Bellehelen, 1907; Buckhorn, 1908; Terrill, 1911; Quartz Mountain, 1925; Weepah, 1927; and Wahmonie, 1928.[5] From fact, J. C.'s relationship with Wingfield can only be sketched. Wingfield's papers have been sealed until 1997, and current accounts of Goldfield leave J. C. out of the picture.

Tognoni Mountain and Tognoni Springs are just across a county line in the obscurity of western Nye County while most of Goldfield District is in Esmeralda County. A "protracted illness at Tonopah,"[6] which forced J. C. to lose many of his locations through lack of assessment work, also faded his image in Goldfield's early history. When George Wingfield and George Nixon were consolidating mining rights at Goldfield, J. C. was again locating claims. Reportedly he located almost one quarter of the valuable portion of the district, so some of his old claims were probably included in the Wingfield empire; and as J. C.'s enthusiastic biographer deduced, most of the claims located by him are famous throughout the mine interested world."[7]

In August of 1905, Tognoni Mining, Milling and Reduction Company would win a court injunction against Diamondfield Jack Davis, after whom a townsite near Tognoni Spring had been named. The injunction also thwarted Diamondfield Development Company, presided over by Tasker L. Oddie, one of Jim Butler's cohorts in Tonopah. (Oddie would become governor and U.S. senator.) Oddie's Diamondfield Company and Diamondfield Jack Davis, who would become a guard for Wingfield's Goldfield Consolidated Mining Company had begun to sell water from Tognoni Spring against the will of Tognoni. J. C. had held the spring open to the public until he sold four of his most developed claims to a New Yorker in 1905, and returned to Duckwater. In the latter part of 1905, the railroad reached Goldfield, and I suspect that the place was growing too crowded for a man like my great-grandfather who gave mining claims to people who had shown him kindness as a farmer might do with the vegetables from his garden.

Continuing to trace the ties between George Wingfield and J. C. Tognoni takes us to 1917 when J. C. mortgaged his Duckworth ranch to one of Wingfield's banks. During the period J. C. located the Black Oil claims. In 1921, however, the Monte Carlo Stock Farm, as J. C. called his Duckwater spread, would become the Bank Ranch. Wingfield foreclosed the mortgage.

My father's birth coincided with the foreclosure. His older brother Nye, born into the thick of J. C.'s financial strivings, does not remember his grandfather fondly. Being the oldest child, Nye Woodrow Tognoni, from a very young age, was his ailing father's muscle as they eked out a living from Nevada. Hale Christopher, too young and small to work, sometimes stayed with his grandparents on the rock crest of Silverton mining camp. In those kind afternoons, J. C.'s warmth and laughter instilled heart, courage and dreams in his grandson. But unlike J. C. and his son, the grandson's enthusiasm would have the benefit of formal education. Overcoming poverty to do so, Hale Tognoni would enroll in the Mackay School of Mines at the Universtiy of Nevada, and as a geological engineer, he would help move his mining family into a new era.

As my father drives with me south out of Reno, he pounds his memory to reconstruct the town he knew as a university student forty years ago. He likes to laugh at the swagger with which he proudly strode Reno streets in the early 1940s, but he remembers fondly the girls it impressed, one whose family-home faced out onto the grassy bank of the Truckee River where a casino now anchors its wall at the water's edge. My father's brother Nye would precede him to the university, and Nye would be elected to the state assembly and senate of Nevada while still a university student. Hale Tognoni would distinguish himself as a long-distance runner for the university's championship track team, and together Nye and Hale won debating contests. Twice my father would leave Reno and his college career to work in the quicksilver mines of New Idria in the Diablo Mountains of California. The Indians had used quicksilver or mercury in its red compound, cinnabar, for pigment; the gold rushers carried quicksilver to separate gold from less valuable dust; but when my father worked at New Idria in the 1940s, one of quicksilver's primary uses was for explosives detonation. Old Idria in Europe had already become the booty of conflicts preliminary to World War II.

War brought a prolonged interruption to Hale Tognoni's university schooling, but in 1946, after his duty with the Army Corps of Engineers, he returned to his home in Eureka and then to Reno and the university. In 1947, my mother, George-Ann Neudeck, would come to Reno from her family's Iowa farm to marry the insistent young lieutenant whom she had met while serving in the Red Cross in the Philippine Islands. Together they would work for the United States Geological Survey while Hale finished school. He had begun as a student of mine engineering, but he would graduate as a geological engineer. To her husband's studies George-Ann would make an extraordinary contribution. She applied her training in drawing and sculpture to geology and awakened in Hale what he describes as a third dimensional vision of the earth. When George-Ann looked at the landscape, she wanted to know what each change in line and color represented. To answer her questions, Hale had to visualize the structure beneath.

This ability had become very important to the mining industry as surface deposits of mineral disappeared. When Hale Tognoni began to study geological engineering rather than mine engineering, he learned to know the age and order of the sediments above and below the horizon so he could determine whether the mineral bearing sediments existed on a mining property or whether the ore had been eroded away. He trained in the science of geology to know whether eruptive rocks were in a dike cutting up across sedimentary beds or whether they were once part of a flow on the surface. If he could decide the origin of precious metals on a mining claim, whether they precipitated from above or arose from some deeper source, he could help to avoid at least some of the costly shafts and tunnels undertaken mistakenly in the great lottery of mining.

The U.S. Geological Survey had once shared this aim. Hale and his wife would work for the survey at Steamboat Springs, through which he and I drive on the highway out of Reno. Steam continues to rise here from the soft slopes where the earth's volcanic crust has intersected the water table. Most of the crevices and pools where my parents studied in 1946 and 1947 lie beneath a heavy layer of white sediment (sinter) carried to the leaks from below. Steam, gases and acqueous solutions broke the surface, brightly colored the rock with chemical activity and marked the air with the stench of sulphur. A rumble beneath the slopes gave witness to deep water channels carrying water to the surface after its journey down through the Sierra. The U.S.G.S. wanted to determine where the silica and calcium carbonate solutions in the earth's hidden plumbing had most likely deposited minerals such as gold, antimony and mercury. My parents were measuring and mapping a system of disseminated gold deposition like that being most profitably mined in Nevada today. The information gathered at Steamboat Springs would have economic import just as the founders of the geological survey in 1879 had hoped.

In the 1860s Clarence King, the daring young mining engineer who, at the age of twenty-five years, led the Fortieth Parallel Survey between the Missouri River and the Sierra Nevada, became the first director of the United States Geological Survey. He had made men believe that "the mountains of our great interior are not barren, but full of wealth; the deserts are not all desert; . . . All that is needed is to explore and declare the nature of the national domain."[8] Pre-Incan prospectors of 40,000 years ago may have preceded King in his ambitious exploration. Some believe that the ancient prospectors gathered gems, gold and platinum from the surface in North America. King and his associates decided that the survey should make detailed monographs of particular mining districts where deep mines allowed them to see beneath the surface. The men employed by the U.S.G.S. would become revered fathers of economic geology, but the noble ambition that their work might aid in the mining of the nation's resources was to be dashed by popular fear. Just as scientists who developed the atomic bomb to end World War II were accused of leaking information to enemies, so U.S.G.S. employees were accused in earlier times of giving information to friends and profiteers. If mines were found rather than developed, there might have been some basis to the fear, but information from the U.S.G.S. has never been a key to a safe deposit box of mineral.

Not the U.S.G.S. nor all the new tools available to twentieth century prospectors have eliminated the ultimate gamble. The search for uranium is a good example. Government geologists working with the Atomic Energy Commission in the early and mid-1950s made airborne surveys of the United States using Geiger counters and scintillators to map radioactive areas called "anomalies." These radioactivity surveys would set off a rush of treasure hunters. One technique of the uranium-rushers was to drop sacks of flour from the air to mark their uranium claims for ground crews. After the anomalies had been generously dusted with flour, marked and recorded with the rhythmic certitude of a patty-cake game, most of the uranium-rushers made their only real find. They discovered that costly drilling would be necessary to determine whether economic quantities of uranium existed. Most A.E.C. anomalies did not yield proof to the drills.

After Steamboat Springs, our route along the eastern foot of the Sierra is banked on the east by the Washoe Mountains and their Comstock promontory, Mount Davidson, once called Sun Peak. In 1859, Mr. Davidson, a San Francisco banker, bought ore being hauled to San Francisco by James Walsh and Henry Comstock.[9] It is difficult to imagine ore and bullion pouring from the opposite side of Mount Davidson through rail tunnels into this pastoral landscape which is quietly reflecting the lavendars of dusk. It is as difficult as imagining Judge Terry and his party of Southern gentlemen attempting to hold the Comstock in 1860 for the Confederacy by surrounding it with three forts.[10] Much about this adolescent region of American mining history—the Comstock—has lapsed into realms of incredulity which remind me of Dr. Gianella's story about the promoter who bought the Comstock railroad tunnels and sold them for post holes in Los Angeles. Historians seem to have forgotten that without the Comstock, all the care, patience and ingenuity that the mightiest of mortals could have mustered might not have availed against the raging winds and blistering droughts that plagued Carson Valley pioneers. This "oasis of fragrant, green fields, poplar-lined lanes, commodious barns and white, Victorian farmhouses"[11] has made the region's mining history very difficult to imagine.

In Minden, my father and I stop at a Basque "family style" restaurant. Nothing about the cool, dark barroom through which a diner must pass would prefigure the warm, bright and noisy dining room. It is common for restaurants in Nevada to have entrances through the bar as if Nevadans take pleasure in defying appearances and reminding themselves that life for the faithful and fearless, like water in Nevada, runs behind the facade and beneath the surface. In Minden the restaurant's long tables are crowded, and the folding doors which separate the raucous diners from the kitchen and its one heavy, smiling cook are open wide.

As we drive away from the feast, the full orb of the moon is still only a glow emanating from behind the horizon's mountain silhouette. By the time we reach Walker Lake, the water is luminescent below us like a high lake in the Alps as Hemingway described it. Maybe Hemingway saw Lake Como near which J. C. Tognoni grew up. Como was used to name an early Comstock mining camp, and the oldest white settlement in the Carson Valley bears a place-name from Italy—Genoa. Maybe a grand spirit alive in this countryside suggested the Italian Renaissance or Roman antiquity to Nevada pioneers, or maybe the geography and geology of Italy are similar. Like a wedge driven under the continent of Europe, Italy lifts the brittle outer layer of earth to form the highest and most rugged mountains of Europe. So the Great Basin of Nevada digs under some of North America's loftiest peaks to form niches where Italians feel at home like the Basque sheepherders who came here from the foothills of the Pyrenees.

Not until one o'clock in the morning do my father and I press our way through the aisles of shiny slot machines and people in the Mizpah's lobby. Heavily laden with my bags, I feel like an intrusive making its way to the fault line where an elevator will speed the path out of the sediment that has gathered on the Mizpah's ground floor to drink and gamble through the night.

J. C. Tognoni holding pick at bottom, beside ore car

8　Journey into Silence

Here I possessed nothing in the world. I was no more than a mortal strayed between sand and stars, conscious of the single blessing of breathing. And yet I discovered myself filled with dreams.

They came to me soundlessly, like the waters of a spring . . .

Antoine de Saint-Exupery
Wind, Sand and Stars, 1939

Now begin the three days which are the heart of our trip. In these long days, we will pass where J. C. Tognoni rode, first horseback then in his motor car, "lonesome as a jackrabbit":[1] through Tonopah, Warm Springs, Silverton mining camp, Railroad Valley, Duckwater, Eureka and back again to Goldfield, and Tognoni Spring. My father, Hale C. Tognoni, and I will work to discover along this route what is left of his family in the memories and lives of those who still abide in these places. We will walk on the desolate ridge at Silverton mining camp where J. C. died and is buried with my grandparents, Joe and Ina Tognoni. In Tonopah, J. C.'s wife, my great-grandmother Myrtle, was laid to rest by the County, but I cannot find her grave. Most likely her bones are beneath the cemetery's field of tin plackets and paper on which the sun has created anonymity. But before our journey's end, I will walk where Myrtle walked, and I will touch the cool walls of the stone and earth houses where she lived and helped raise many children.

The morning in Tonopah is warm and clear. By afternoon clouds will cap the mountain ridges and dress the sky in a moody wardrobe of whisps, billows and stripes as we travel the Grand Army of the Republic Highway out of the hills of Tonopah. This highway crosses the entire state connecting Tonopah and Ely, the two major Nevada mining regions of the twentieth century, and linking the last of the large, old Nevada mines for gold and silver with the first of the new mines for copper. When the railroad companies were busily making tracks to Tonopah and Goldfield from three directions and from Ely north to the transcontinental Central Pacific, a railroad between Tonopah and Ely was being contemplated;[2] however, before the railroad companies could find an extended period of prosperity in Nevada for building through Railroad Valley, the highways had begun to replace the railways. In 1911, Tasker Oddie made a successful campaign for governor by automobile all over Nevada. In 1914 construction of the first coast-to-coast motor road in the United States began. But not until federal aid had been extended to the states would a highway between New York and San Francisco be completed in 1927. Because Nevada is over 80 percent federal land, Nevada would become one of the major beneficiaries of the U.S. government's investment in thoroughfares.[3] The Grand Army of the Republic Highway and a golden age of road construction would override the importance of the railway companies in Nevada.

East of Tonopah a series of mountain ranges and valleys ends in low relief to be cut by the northern boundary of Nellis Air Force Range and the Atomic Energy Commission's nuclear test site. Cactus Range, Kawich Range, Spotted Range, Timber Mountain, Shoshone Mountain, Skull Mountain and Pahute Mesa intrude the flats, before the largest of Nevada's military domain ends just north of Las Vegas. "Dry Lakes" to which the mountains shed their rain sit on my map of the range like water-beads left on a pane of glass. My father remembers a house which his younger brother, Robert, bought and hauled from the military land when, after World War II, the destruction practiced here required fewer people. Maybe Robert believed that the prosperity which war brought to the old mining towns of Nevada would carry into peace time, but he was wrong. By the late 1940s Robert, like my father, would leave his house and the state, never to make them his home again. Robert secured a place among Nevada Senator Pat McCarran's law students in Washington, D.C., rather than finish his law studies by mail. Under Pat McCarran's wing, my father would begin his law studies in Washington, too. Nevada has no law school, so Senator McCarran, and Senator Key Pittman before him, would find positions for Nevada students which would allow them to study law in the nation's capital. If the senator was expecting patronage from the Tognoni brothers, he was to be disappointed. Robert chose to practice in Colorado, where he died in a court of law after a career of twenty-seven years. My father elected to pass the bar in Arizona because by 1950, Arizona had become the most active mineral producing state in the West due to its wealth of copper.

At the northeastern corner of the federal government's grand bombing arena in Nevada, we stop. Hot Creek Range stops here too. Its rock cliffs rise behind a combination cafe, bar and gas station where Highway 25 offers a southerly exit. Hot water runs in a tree-lined ditch and through a pipe under the highway's pavement to a house and small trailer park. The water once filled the stone-walled baths of Warm Springs' health resort, which is collapsing beside the plastered, white edifice which we enter. Once a hub of social activity for ranching and mining families, this highway junction has not even been a dependable source of gasoline in the past several years. Inside, my father engages the convivial waitress in conversation. She tells us that she has seen the mobile home park empty out overnight and that most of the men presently living in Warm Springs work at the mines of Tybo and Reveille or on the oil pumps in Railroad Valley.

Tybo, a corrupted Indian name meaning white man's district, is in the Hot Creek Range due north of Warm Springs. Since 1870, when white men followed an Indian to small seams of rich silver ore, Tybo has been producing mineral. The ore includes enough lead to have made Tybo second only to Eureka as the nation's foremost lead producer in the late 1870s. Irishmen, Cornishmen, Central Europeans and Chinese worked in the mines of Tybo and cut timber in the surrounding hills for smelter charcoal. A photograph of three-story dormitories built for the miners during a 1929-1937 revival at Tybo,[4] remind me of a northern Italian mountain town at the foot of Monte Spluga on a postcard signed "Saluti affettuosi, Fratelli" which is among my great-grandfather's papers.

Back on the highway again my father is speaking into his recording machine to make his observations about the long slanting beds of paleozoic limestones tipped up to cap the Hot Creek Range. "Paleozoic" refers to a geologic era once supposed to mark with its fossils the first appearance of life on earth.[5] Horned and raw-boned cattle graze with their calves near the highway, and Rattlesnake Station, which my father remembers, has become Bluejay Station. Between Palisade and Halligan mesas the highway breaks its horizontal, and into the recorder Hale Tognoni hums his geologic descriptions, making tune of the basalt's columnar jointing atop Palisade Mesa. The regularity of the vertically cracked cooling pattern in the basalt indicates that the lava flowed freely. It crept across the flats neither aided nor frustrated by gravity. "We are entering the volcanics," my father announces into his machine, and in the plain before us, cinder cones and lava flows display themselves like museum exhibits. On the cones which rise beside the highway, sagebrush glimmers on the violet-red and black of the smooth curvatures. Where hot rock broke through the placid mounds, the cooled spillways give such clear testimony to geologic event that the red glow, rumble, blast and heat of millions of years ago is alive to the slightest imagination.

North in Hot Creek Valley was once Hick's Station, where "Wild Indian" or "Morey Jack's Boy" and "Rattlesnake Charlie" (Myrtle Tognoni's son by John Williams) exchanged bullets, leaving the Indian and Charlie wounded and Charlie's wife, Mildred, dead. Old Frank Collins, with whom I spoke back in Schurz, was a young man when he helped to track the Indian who killed Mildred. Collins' embellished story of the incident differs factually from the newspaper account in the *Eureka Sentinel*. Around the edge of Charlie's chicken coop door, the Indian's hand appears slowly and transfixes with the best of Shoshone stories. Like rock, poetic imagery is more durable than fact, and geologic events in this high plain millions of years ago hold more factual certainty than human tragedies and affairs that occurred a century ago.

A dirt road to the crater of an inactive volcano intersects the highway, but we are very near Silverton mining camp now, and we are both very anxious. It is fortuitous that we do not accept the volcano's strong invitation today because just over Blackrock Summit, we see a jeep descending Silverton's Treasure Hill on the radar tower road. We hail the driver and on a low crest of the Pancake Range, before the road drops down into Railroad Valley, our car and the stranger's meet and park. His khaki workshirt and pants, his dusty, high-lacing boots, his snug glasses and his lean look are the uniform of the field geologist. Indeed we have chanced to meet the man who is writing the latest geological report of the Silverton mining claims. The lease-holders of our family's claims have asked this man's company to finance further exploratory drilling.

My father tries to convey to this man a sense of our family's history here. In a Napoleonic stance on the black-top where no traffic passes and none, except a distant oil tanker, can be seen in either direction across two valleys, my father cocks his head to listen. The reticent company geologist leans in a disinterested, closed posture against the door of his vehicle. He wants to impress us with his objectivity, and his obedience to scientific measurement. I also take his reserve as an indication that the stakes may be high. Ranchers in this area have jumped the claims, and one major copper company, Phelps Dodge, has recently staked the area with its slick pipe markers. Beginning to stir in me are the emotions of a native whose ancestral burial ground stands to be molested at the hands of large, impersonal economic forces. The company geologist did not notice the Tognoni graves atop the long, black tongue of volcanic rock below Treasure Hill. Painted wooden name-signs stand at the head of three long mounds of sharp rock, but the markers rise so slightly above the sagebrush that they are invisible from most directions. Still, my father returns to our car elated at the luck of having chosen to visit Silverton during the examination by this departing geologist.

When my great-grandfather, J. C. Tognoni, found valuable ore at Silverton in 1912, he may have been attracted initially by similarities to Goldfield mining district where he had already realized success. J. C.'s claims at Goldfield and his claims at Silverton are in ring fractures around intrusive centers or calderas. Volcanics have extruded along the lines of weakness where the mountains broke from the basins on both sides. The most important rock feature of these calderas for mining men has been the rhyolite, akin to glass. Silica is the valuable element of sand from which glass is made, and it is this acidic element which most distinguishes rhyolite from its neighbors. Three types of volcanics, rhyolites, andesites and basalts, arranged on the scale of geologic acidity, put rhyolite and basalt at the extremities. If the hot rock which intruded into and extruded from earth cracks at Silverton had not contained silica, it might have formed basalt. If the acidic hot rock had not cooled quickly where it intruded at Silverton, it would have formed granite, separating slowly into characteristic large crystal grains after which granite is named and from which sand is the eroded product. A "hogsback" branches off from Blackrock Summit where rhyolite which once penetrated the limestone has been exposed and serated by weather. The contact between the rhyolite and the soft limestone at Silverton is J. C.'s ore zone. That was different at Goldfield, but, like Goldfield, the light volcanics beneath the dark basalt are iron stained red, orange and yellow. Iron concentrations are a neon-sign of mineralization.

We pull to the side of the road and trek across a wide, rocky drainage depression and then a short way up the side of the hill to Blackrock Spring. In the altered rhyolite J. C. made this opening for water. It still pools behind a heavy wooden hatch, and on a beam above the dark water, the letters of "J. C. TOGNONI" have been painted bold and large. Smaller desert creatures have burrowed under and behind the timbers to drink from the dark mouth. Cattle and wild animals can drink farther downhill out of two troughs on line with a wood and galvanized tin container which J. C. made watertight with solder. A pipe from the spring feeds a manufactured livestock tank set up by Fellini, who used the spring after my great-grandmother left Silverton. A rubber hose runs from the spring to a halved oil drum of some more recent rancher. When my brothers and their friends helped with the assessment work on the Silverton mining claim, they would climb into the spring and shovel out the accumulated mud. Finally, my brother David poured a concrete roof to frustrate the hill's slow redemption of its secret.

Across the highway from Blackrock Spring rises a tongue of volcanic rock which falls over the summit along the highway into Railroad Valley. Up the side of this fractured black rock climbs J. C.'s road to Silverton mining camp. When my great-grandfather made his discovery at Silverton, he was considered by some who knew him in Duckwater to be a "wealthy old Italian,"[6] and his lawyer, Key Pittman, sat in the U.S. Senate for Nevada. After Senator Pittman's silver purchase act passed Congress in 1918, Harry Stimler, one of the discoverers at Goldfield, incorporated Silverton to raise development money. A newspaper article enthusiastically announced:

> "The Treasure Hill mine (in the camp of Silverton) has been under development by J. C. Tognoni for about seven years, and during that period a great amount of prospecting work has been done. Through the efforts of Mr. Stimler, sufficient money has been raised to explore the ground at depth, and the claims of the Treasure Hill Nevada Mining Company are now assured of development to which the merits of the showings entitle them."

To contribute to development capital, J. C. mortgaged his ranch at Duckwater. When George Wingfield foreclosed that mortgage, he reputedly wanted Silverton for his bank's money rather than the Duckwater ranch. Neither Wingfield's banks, the Monte Carlo Stock Farm or Silverton were destined for good fortune. Not long after Stimler's incorporation of the Treasure Hill mine, silver prices began to fall. When the banks were in trouble, the federal government took the stock farm for an Indian reservation.

While J. C. explored likely ore zones at Silverton with open cuts, tunnels and surface sampling in 1922, the hoisting of ore from the main shaft continued. By 1923, however, J. C. and Myrtle had despaired of Stimler's plan to raise necessary capital, and in that year Stimler forfeited his Treasure Hill claim:[7]

> " . . . I, Myrtle Tognoni, . . . this first day of July, 1923 . . . do locate and claim . . . Silverton No. 1 lode. . . . This claim was formerly incorporated by H. C. Stimler & Co . . . and known as Treasure Hill No. 1. No assessment work was done for the last year . . . therefore I hereby locate and claim the same."

The federal government's silver purchases arranged by Pittman also ended in 1923. Although Pittman continued to work in Washington, D.C., and internationally on behalf of silver mining, not until the Silver Purchase Act of 1934, two years after J. C.'s death, would Pittman's influence in Washington with President Franklin Roosevelt assure copper mines, at least, of a

Silverton mining camp, c. 1930

Myrtle Jacques with her second husband, J. C. Tognoni

market for their silver by-product. In the year of J. C.'s death, 1932, the gross yield from Nevada's mines was only one-seventh of production in 1929, and silver was selling at twenty-five cents an ounce.[8]

On J. C.'s steep road my father and I return to Silverton mining camp. Left behind at the camp after its boom in 1920 were thirteen tents and two wooden structures. Chiatovich and Beko had even started a general merchandise store. When my father first took me to Silverton in the early 1960s, the mine's headframe had been scavenged by local ranchers, and the sun was slowly cremating the one surviving tent house, a veteran of two other mining camps. Its splintered roof beams held skyward the camp's last vestiges of canvas. In the rubble of the camp, my father traces for me the wall lines of the house where his father stayed while working the claims, the outline of the house where his grandparents lived and the site of the tiny cabin which he and his brothers and sister habitated during visits. Beside the rise of earth which marks the doorstep into J. C. and Myrtle's house is a pile of colorful rock—ore samples, each speaking of a hand and a ledge of these mountains. Around the sticks and wire of the old chicken coop, anthropological tidbits grow thick, and still visible between the sagebrush is an unvarnished path to the Beko store where J. C.'s daughter Elva reflected upon her transcient beauty before a full length mirror. Living wreckage at Silverton would be transplanted to government institutions.

Elva had been groomed to be all that her mother, Myrtle, dreamed of being, but she was not prepared for desolation. She learned art, cultured taste, and habits of a lady at the "Sister's School" in Ogden, Utah, and at Saint Mary's College for women in Indiana, from which state came her pioneer grandmother, Mary Cross. At these schools she failed to learn mysticism or discipline's hypnosis—lessons with which Catholicism might have armed her for the pain in her life. She was an orchid among the Nevada road daisies. Senator Tasker Oddie picked her in radiant bloom to be his secretary in Washington, D.C., in the early 1920s. Then in 1931, after two unhappy marriages, she was committed to a mental institution. Perched on Silverton's ridge with the dry wind whipping and rumbling in waves through her thoughts, she was too vulnerable. At Silverton, Elva would leave behind two children and her second husband, Jack Strode, who had hauled ore and had dug into the iron-stained volcanics following his own intuition.

Like her daughter, Myrtle had been beautiful. At the age of sixteen, Myrtle attracted and married one of Duckwater's rich ranchers. A photo, which I believe to be of Myrtle with two of her sisters and her father, has Myrtle posed with an infant on her lap. The twist of her mouth and saucy tilt of her head defy the emotionless expressions expected in formal photographs—a norm to which her sisters and father conform. If this is Myrtle, she obviously doubted that complacency held the self-esteem for which she yearned. In 1887 she divorced her much-absent husband, John Williams, charging successfully that on June 26, 1886, he did "beat, abuse and mal-treat" her in a "cruel and inhuman manner." In the year of her divorce, she traveled to Elko, Nevada, boldly to marry one of her ex-husband's ranch hands—Joe Tognoni (J. C.). Her voice is clear and firm in 1903 testimony in *Nevada vs. Joe Tognoni.* "I should think so," she forcefully replies to Key Pittman's questions, and she speaks of the embattled irrigation water in water-inches, while *men* who took the witness stand declined any knowl-edge of how water is measured. Women would not be allowed to vote in Nevada until 1914, but J. C.'s wife had already grasped a form of personal suffrage for herself. "Aunt Myrt was half-tough," her grandnephew Billy Mendes tells me.

When J. C. died, Myrtle would not allow their son, Joe, my grand-father, to work J. C.'s claims, so he worked his own, calling them the Silver Queen. Mary Celaya, who moved to Silverton mining camp with her hus-band for three months to help mine in the Silver Queen tunnel, answers my inquiry about Silverton with the information that Myrtle was the only woman living there. In those three months, Elva's daughter Joan lived at Silverton for a time too, because Joan remembers Mrs. Celaya. Still, writes Mary Celaya, "things were dead." In the winter of 1934, my grandfather would be interred beside his father in Silverton's black rocks. His fragile health and contemplative nature had been ill-suited to the hard physical labor of his concise life. Near the graves of my great-grandfather and grandfather, Myrtle would endure and persist for another six years. With her faithfulness and fearless companion and helper, Fred Allen (half-Indian), she clung to the mining claims with a tenacity which must put her among the grand old women of the mountains. Not until Fred Allen fell sick and died in Ely did she accept defeat and lose herself to her dreams in the Nye County hospital, there to die in 1954.

In the years that my father watched his grandmother rock herself at Silverton mining camp, she looked out at Railroad Valley expecting the savior in her dreams—the eldest grandson, Nye—to arise from a tiny approaching trail of dust. Two totem-like volcanic stems sit on a grey ridge at the edge of Silverton's mountain range. As Myrtle once did, these monadnocks emerge from their own erosion to peer steadfastly out at the glow of the white alkali flats streaked with unearthly shadows and at the blue mountain range beyond. For me, the "old lady" still prevails here, and despite all the literature to the contrary, the mines of the West have not played out. Human times have deserted them. Decay does not prevail at Silverton. The rat's tail which ends Shoshone stories has not fallen.

Hale Tognoni, sixteen years old, packing ore car up Elephant Mountain to the Silver Queen claims, Silverton, Nevada.

Bronze sculpture by George-Ann Tognoni, inspired by her husband's work as a young man on his family's Silverton mining claims.

9   People's Silver

The quote has been cut from a magazine and pasted over the braille letters of a weighty volume which my grandfather and my father used for a scrapbook. Photographs of public figures and pages from an illustrated pamphlet on Nevada range management make it easy to overlook the preserved lines of philosophy, as easy as it is to pass Silverton mining camp in Nevada without seeing its three graves. How J. C. Tognoni, J. R. Tognoni and Ina B. Tognoni (Conway) came to be buried here is an important episode in the demise of widespread silver mining in the United States. Human accomplishments at Silverton are as fragile as the shadows of braille on the pages of my father's scrapbook and as rich in potential as the rhyolite intrusive at Silverton which lifts and separates Pre-Cambrian sediments into Pancake Mountains. Except for the graves, Silverton mining camp has disappeared. Even in historical catalogs of the many mining camps which have passed like moods across the face of Nevada, there is no Silverton. The silver deposits of the Treasure Hill claims, the Alto claims, the Butte Extension, the Eclipse, the Elephant claims, the General Grants, the King of All, the Manhattans, the Pioneers, the Prince Alberts, the Silver Dollars, the Silver Kings, the Silver Queens, the Woodrats, the Crickets, the Tip Tops and others at Silverton have been stripped of their power to support human life in the twentieth century by the fleeting and erratic value of silver.

Silver once kept the occupation of mining alive in desolate regions like this. Many minerals, found in the company of silver, are not economic to mine without silver's contribution. Today the values in the drill cores,

Puck Magazine, March 2, 1892, portrayal of Nevada Senator
William Morris Stewart, left.
(Courtesy Nevada Historical Society)

which are still being pulled periodically from the earth here, are not dramatic enough to compensate for the low price of silver and the high price of labor; not impressive enough to generate a new Silverton. The history of mining here is as elusive as the braille in my father's scrapbooks. A blind friend tried to read the braille for me, but she could not make much sense from its peculiar combinations of words and numbers. The book was probably discarded by George Halstead, the only blind man of whom I have learned in these parts. At Halstead's birth a midwife administered the customary eye drops, but, according to the story, what looked to be the correct solution was a harmful acid which destroyed the infant's vision. Halstead would never marvel at the world's images, but then he would not struggle with the precepts which might have prevented him from interpreting the world's changing light and movement for himself.

Many times with two good eyes, I have searched the slopes of the only remaining promontory of "Tognoni Limestone"[1] at Silverton. Never, until now, did I perceive the elephant in Elephant Mountain. Finally the surface wrinkles of tilted limestone bend around and down the south face to form the animal's trunk and reveal J. C. Tognoni's vision of the mountain that he named. In the elephant's limestone J. C. found memory of primitive life— worm tracks, trilobites, small brachiopods and etchings of sponges; and in the elephant's path he found the Uncle Sam Fault, a slip in the earth's cracked shell that geologists have traced sixty-five miles north into the silver, lead, antimony and zinc mines of Eureka. From this fault the elephant drank of hot mineralized solutions which have circulated in her between the rhyolite and the limestone. J. C. blanketed the beast with mining claims and shared his vision of the elephant with his son, my grandfather, who would keep faith with the animal's treasure until death. Some may have called my grandfather blind or said that he must have been deceived by the length of the tail or the breadth of the ear when he gave himself to an earthen elephant; but the error which kept J. R. Tognoni from a more glorious destiny and the elephant from being unburdened of her silver ton was as profound in its simplicity as the revocation of George Halstead's eyesight: silver no longer measured value.

The white metal was demonetized, and the United States joined other powerful nationalities in a gold standard. This desertion of bimetallism which had served world trade for thousands of years nudged fine ancient cultures like India's, a silver standard community, or Mexico's, the world's leading silver producer, into poverty from which they have not yet recovered. William Morris Stewart stated the consequences plainly in 1898:[2]

> After the United States and France and the other nations of Europe closed their mints against silver there was no commercial nation where both gold and silver bullion could be converted into coin for the benefit of the owner. The bimetallic tie which made gold and silver one money for commercial purposes was broken and the value of each metal was regulated by the demand for coinage in the countries which accorded it the privilege of mintage. The demand of the United States and Europe for the purpose of coinage fell on gold alone, while the demand for coinage purposes of Asia, Mexico, and South America nearly all fell upon the white metal. There was a greater demand for gold in the gold-standard countries in proportion to the supply of gold than there was for silver in the silver-standard countries in proportion to the supply of silver.

With the untying of the world's bimetallic bonds, the treasure of the elephant at Silverton became a costly burden. In the closing years of the nineteenth century, silver's value as money in the United States only existed upon special act of Congress; and those who proclaimed the virtues of silver were so thoroughly discredited as self-serving that the precepts of bimetallism are lost to our economic thinkers who prowl in dead theory where value has lost the dynamics of duality. Like the mistaken eye drops, the error is most likely unintentional. Even Karl Marx in his volume on the nature of capital equates a group of commodities with gold alone. In so doing, he may be as guilty of inspiring the twentieth century's totalitarianism as the capitalists of the Industrial Revolution who first breached bimetallism's laws. Stewart foretold the outcome:[3]

> The power of the government to create money by the use of paper is undoubted, but the experiment of a proper limitation of the volume of money by human laws, without the automatic rule of regulating that volume by Nature's supply of the two metals, is yet untried. The apprehension that an undertaking by the Government to substitute legislation for the automatic rule ... might result in ruinous inflation or destructive contraction is at present an insurmountable obstacle to dispensing with the use of gold and silver ... If silver is deprived of its money functions, gold must share the same fate, and paper must be substituted for both to rescue civilization from decay.

Why did the price of silver drop at the end of the nineteenth century, never to enjoy exchange values in relation to gold that men had given it for centuries? Silver prices dropped because powerful banking interests and imperialistic governments stopped buying it. Stewart fully develops this answer, but it may be that without having spent time searching for light in the jungle of "economic science" modern readers will have difficulty overlooking unfashionable elements of his style. For instance, Stewart dedicates his book with characteristic bravura to the "young men and women of the United States who are contemplating matrimony." The political economists claimed that the bimetallists, like William Morris Stewart, and those who fought into the 1930s for the remonetization of silver were laboring under the misconception that commodities of gold and silver were universal money "independently of all convention and all law."[4] Clearly the presumption was untrue of Stewart, who wrote:[5]

> The number and variety of commodities that were once used as money ... which now possess no money function ought to suggest to political economists that ... commodities were never money in themselves, but that the money function connected with them ... was created and maintained by force of some law which the people obeyed ... money is the creation of law ... it is stamped or printed on gold, silver or paper, the same as municipal laws are printed on paper and bound in books.

So successfully did Stewart's opponents fortify their thesis that bimetallism had become unworkable in an industrial society that it is now generally unchallenged. Although history had borne out the truth in Stewart's analysis of money, truth remains very unpopular.

> "Very few people will understand this. Those who do will be occupied getting profits. The general public will probably not see it's against their interest." Canto XLVI, Ezra Pound

In 1873, a U.S. Mint Act, designed by admirers of British monetary power and monometallism, failed to include the silver dollar among U.S. coins. At that time the market value of silver in a dollar was about 3 percent greater than the gold dollar,[6] and the gold-dollar had disappeared from circulation by a law of economics as banal as the law of supply and demand. Gresham's Law, well known for centuries before Sir Thomas Gresham's birth, codified the human trait of storing the more valuable of two monies and circulating the other. The increased value of silver would eventually have called the gold back into circulation, but those who held the gold also held power enough to make it the sole standard for national monetary values. The gold rush played a major role in this radical deviation of monetary history.

During twenty-five years immediately after the discovery of gold in California, the value of the world's gold supply doubled.[7] Silver increased in the same period of time by only 30 percent in dollar value, although in the previous 350 years before the gold rush, the world's mines had produced twice as much silver value as gold. When the relative quantities shifted suddenly, gold remained the scarcer metal, but a greater number of nations could use it for a single standard of worth. Since 1546, the world's gold and silver had come primarily from colonies in the New World. After 1546, European miners could not produce the precious metals cheaply enough to compete with foreign sources.[8] In fact, discovery of the Potosi mines in Bolivia by the Spanish might be used as the birthdate of colonialism. European kingdoms began vying for power over the mines of the New World, and the score between them is probably in records, if they exist, of monetary circulation in places like the colonial United States where few mines for precious metals existed. Even after the United States had won its independence, the greater part of the silver coins being used in 1804 were French,[9] and when U.S. law finally forbade the use of foreign coins in the 1850s, an exception for Spanish-American fractional silver pieces had to be made.[10]

According to Stewart, "the right to coin and use the metal which is cheapest, at the option of the debtor, is the cardinal result of bimetallism."[11] So long as the debtor had this vestige of power, national econmies remained fluid; capital could not become thoughtlessly secure; and talent as from the

Latin *talenta*, meaning a unit of weight or money, still had some relevancy to the accumulation of "capital." Monometallism made it possible for those with capital to gain more not through the productivity of their capital but by increasing interest rates. Stewart contends that in 1898 "much of the larger part of the world's indebtedness [was] still unpaid. While some of it may have been liquidated, the aggregate has been largely increased by adding interest to principal."[12] By the end of the nineteenth century, those who labored to produce commodities were fixed as the debtor class, and consequent to the death throes of bimetallism, a long trail of labor strife and violence in the American West began. It started with a bank panic in 1893 after Austria's gross conversion to the gold standard or the export of hundreds of millions in U.S. gold to Austria enabling the Rothchild syndicate to convert two billion four hundred million of Austrian silver bonds.[13]

After silver was demonetized, the most important stimulus to mining would become war, to which the United States turned with greater frequency and on an ever wider scale. Prior to the world wars of this century, Bernard Baruch, one of the most respected economic advisors to the United States government, made a $1 million loan to George Wingfield and George Nixon at Goldfield.[14] Baruch would remain a lifelong friend to Wingfield. Because Baruch spent his literary talents attempting to clarify the differences between war economy and the economic principles of war and of peace, I believe his investment at Goldfield could be interpreted as an attempt to empower peace. When his loan came due, however, Baruch did not exercise his option to purchase stock in Goldfield Consolidated. Maybe he sensed that the economic forces of war were becoming irreversible.

"The depreciation of silver as compared with gold during the twelve years from March, 1875, to March, 1887, was a great calamity to the people of . . . [Nevada]," wrote William Morris Stewart in his autobiography, "and more injurious to the people of the civilized world than famine, pestilence and war combined."[15] Certainly the demonetization of silver dictated the conditions of many lives in Nevada. In this theatre of calamity, my ancestors, who are buried at Silverton, played their parts with honor. J. C. Tognoni and his son, J. R. Tognoni, lost their ranch to the bank in the early 1920s. J. C. moved with Myrtle to his Silverton mining claims while his son, my grandfather, managed the "Bank Ranch." But J. R. soon would abandon the lost home in Duckwater to settle his young family to the north in Eureka, Nevada. In summer months he joined J. C. at Silverton. Ninety miles from their Silverton mining camp, over the Grand Army of the Republic Highway, a man could sell hand-sorted silver ore at McGill for a small return on his labor. Silica in the ore had value for the smelting of copper.

In the silver-rich hills habitated by the dreams of a mine and a mining

town, J. C. herded goats and was content to watch them—his "movies"—
while the course of American mining and politics took a route contrary to his
nature. The stubborn honesty of his goats sustained his spirit in a time when,
like the eagle which I saw near here, J. C. would flee chattering visitors at
Silverton by climbing to his garage roof. There, under the waving Stars and
Stripes, he would perch with his grandson Jackie Strode until customary
privacy was restored. Like a native, he knew where the water and mineral
lay in the land of Nevada and how to use it. He had proven himself at Duckwater, Goldfield, and finally at Silverton; but what he knew had lost its
value as summarily as silver had lost the role of measuring value. Gratitude
for the many blessings of his liberty in the United States braced him in
poverty, but events in 1932 "broke him," in the hard words of Duckwater's
dowager, Beatie Rosevear Halstead.

From the depth of personal tragedy—his daughter Elva's confinement
to the state mental hospital—I believe that J. C. foresaw that the American
government, which he had trusted with patriotic fervor, no longer intended
that each man should have land for his labor. Merciless perception may have
come to him in his suffering: how Goldfield became little more than a ghost
town less than twenty years after mushrooming into Nevada's most populous city; and how the fields which he had carefully worked to bring under
irrigation in Duckwater Valley were being reclaimed by sagebrush. Over
his diggings into what the newspaper called a "100 percent perfect" mining
property at Silverton, the headframe was growing gray and decrepit. Its
sturdy timbers, cut from the pine forest of the Pancake Mountain Range,
had hoisted pay dirt for no more than two years. Likewise, the abilities of
J. C.'s studious and brilliant son, my grandfather, would achieve no greater
prestige than as one of the few, if not the only man in two counties, who
knew how to use a hydrometer. With it he tested the alcoholic content of
brews being distilled during prohibition by local bootleggers like himself.

The newspaper announcement of J. C. Tognoni's death reported an
illness of only six hours. His adoring granddaughter, my Aunt Neva, sus-
pects strychnine poisoning and foul play, but the disinterested tell me that
he killed himself by chasing too many goats in too many rocks. Everyone
remembers that he was laid out by the son of a local rancher who was
studying to be a mortician. Memory seems to revel in this democratic application of science: available even to the non-conformist Italian were the
services of a trained embalmer. As for the story of J. C.'s death by consuming a poison pudding which Myrtle allegedly intended for the visiting
temptress, "Diamond Lil," I cannot lend it credence. Surely the vision of
eternity in the steep blue mountain range beyond Silverton and above the
kaleidoscope of light in Railroad Valley inspired nobility of spirit. Even

Myrtle's daughter Elva did not lose her dignity here on the isolated volcanic ridge of Silverton mining camp. Word came from Tonopah that she had attempted to take her life by hurling herself from one of civilization's upper stories.

If J. C.'s death were a crime, it is a sterile factuality like the earth's appearance of being flat and unmoving. The vigor of something greater passed away when J. C. died. His demise, like the volcanic disruption of the earth's surface at Silverton, marks the end of a long, slow process of shifting weights and pressures. For the economy of the United States this movement had, by 1932, placed responsibility for the world's prosperity and peace firmly on the shoulders of the United States. In the future, world monetary order would depend on the ability of the United States to live within its means. This would become increasingly difficult as men like J. C. were lost, but the unrepaired disruption in our economic fabric which cut the nation loose from important threads of democracy had occurred even before Guiseppi Cristofo di Tognoni (J. C.) took passage on a ship to the North American continent in 1880.

It has been called by some the "Crime of 1873." When the United States broke away from bimetallism to innocently imitate its British progenitors with a gold standard, centralized forces of banking and government began to lift the nation away from its hinges with the land and native resources. Along the fault line an imperial cliff slowly arose to sever America from the fruits of the Spirit. By 1932, the year of J. C.'s death, congressmen who flew bimetallism's last banner from the nation's prominence could not raise the popular cry that had whipped William Morris Stewart, William Jennings Bryan and William Hope Harvey into a frenzy in the closing years of the nineteenth century. William Harvey's book, *Coin's Financial School*, sold over one million copies in two years after the banking panic of 1893; but the half dozen books and voluminous debate which Harvey's book evoked amounted to little more after 1896 than "an almost hopeless mass of facts and theories"[16] and formed but a foothill of erosion beneath the grand escarpment of the United States.

Following Britain and other European nations which demonetized silver, imperialistic foreign policy would thrive in the United States after the desertion of bimetallism. Two years after Bryan's defeat in the 1896 presidential election, the United States entered the Spanish-American War and acquired its first colonies. Even before the gold rush, the British stopped stamping the unit value of their money on silver. British government in the silver standard country of India coincided with this shift in favor of gold. The importance of the American gold rush to Britain is manifest. British investment in mining in California and the American West was heavy. Subsequent mineral development in British colonies such as Australia, South Africa and Canada employed the lessons and technology from American gold fields. The most respected of immigrant miners, called "Cousin Jacks," came from the British Isles, and the United States freighted its ore to Britain for refinement in the absence of adequate local milling facilities. In mid-century the gold rush began to distribute legal tender to the hands of the masses at an astonishing rate—10,000 tons of gold alone in the second half of the nineteenth century.[17] Questions of how to limit the power of those who eventually would accumulate the wealth were set aside. So unimportant had the problem become that the economic system on which world prosperity functioned—bimetallism—was little understood and, in the end, disregarded. As gold too would be replaced by paper.

No chapter on bimetallism is to be found in the *Encyclopedia of American Economic History*, and those who waged the political battles for the remonetization of silver are scorned in the history books as profiteers. The entire "free silver" movement at the end of the nineteenth century is regarded with a lack of intellectual curiosity most peculiar, in light of the undisputed turning point in the U.S. economy at which the demonetization of silver took place: "The succession of depressions from 1873 to the turn of the century produced two responses: internally, a wave of consolidations and the move toward Big Business; externally, the drive to capture export markets, including those of industrialized Europe."[18]

Capital investment in the American West would be abandoned by all but the federal government, which in 1928 approved the construction of the first major dam on the Colorado River. Ghost towns and dying mining camps like Silverton were rapidly fading reminders of natural resources no longer being cultivated by American labor. Productivity has lost its bond with the national monetary supply. The idea that paper money was only a convenient representative of gold and silver and that the government's treasury notes and other credits had to be redeemable in precious metal had been clamorously repudiated. Banks holding war bonds as major assets printed money with ever increasing abandonment of any tie with commodity production. After a long series of banking crises which began in 1873, the U.S. government chartered the Federal Reserve in 1914 "to achieve seasonal adjustment in the amount of currency or to enlarge its supply during panics."[19] In other words, those collecting interest on national debts wanted to be assured that their loans would be honored. Unearned profit or interest rates became the dim light guiding monetary policy. Assets supporting capital were no longer increased by mining gold and silver but by increasing the national debt, and war had no equal in that capability. In the year of the Federal Reserve's creation, the first world war began. Of little consequence anymore were the talents of men like J. C. Tognoni for finding and using local wealth.

The centralization of government and of finance on the British model supplanted less usurious and more democratic economic organization. From 1833 until 1914, the United States had been without a national bank. In 1833, Andrew Jackson had ended the reign of the Second National Bank of the United States by withdrawing all government deposits. Like Thomas Jefferson when the First National Bank was chartered, Jackson distrusted the Treasury Department's goal of basing the government on the political support of the well-to-do. Two years after President Jackson demolished the Second National Bank, he paid off the national debt for the first and only time in the history of the United States. Earlier, in the Battle of New Orleans, which ended British imperialism on American soil, General Andrew Jackson's distrust of the British had served the country well; and it was with equal fury and definite result that he attacked the national bank. It had been modeled after the Bank of England, which monopolized control in world trade as systematically as Britain pilfered man's earthly treasures and hoarded them in the name of history within the marble walls of the British Museum.

When Germany was drawn into industrial competition with the British, it too began to subjugate the producers of raw materials—Mexico, for instance, where German mining companies were prevalent. President Woodrow Wilson would militarily intervene in Germany's economic advances in Mexico, but World War I would draw the United States inextricably into permanent and overwhelming national debt and into European methods of world commerce. Still the United States seems to have retained its innocence or remained ignorant of the forces at work in its economic policies. The amount of money that our foreign investors loaned abroad was never directly related to the possibility of limiting that country's sovereignty. We lent even more money to industrial nations than to "capital-poor countries" where broader political influence might have resulted.[20]

The paradox leads me to believe that we may be close to the truth with inquiries about bimetallism, too close for the comfort of those exploitive forces which are presently liquidating and stagnating the economy of the United States. With the demonetization of silver, an important step was taken by those who profit from war in our "permanent war economy."[21] Power over the money supply or the trading medium between cultures was placed in the hands of a bank with a basic conflict of interests—protecting and increasing the assets of its shareholders as opposed to putting capital in the service of peacefully productive persons. When President Lincoln allowed the greenbacks, despite serious question of constitutionality, to be printed in the interest of this nation's unity, he did so with forebodings, hesitation and the solemn assurance that the greenbacks would be recalled and redeemed with zeal after the war had been won. Instead, that amount of money authorized during the war, but unissued, became a seed of our permanent war economy. The unissued greenbacks would become the first "federal reserve." Few, if any, economists will plainly state this fact, but when President Franklin Roosevelt increased the price of gold from $20.67 to $35.00 an ounce in 1933, there was a flow of gold into the U.S. Treasury which raised the quantity of money and bank reserves without any need for action by the Federal Reserve.

J. C. Tognoni did not live to see the price of gold go up, which might have renewed his hope for silver prices. Upon his death, Myrtle carried on. In Railroad Valley at Chimney Springs, her son had put together a stamp mill and cyanide processor with scavenged parts; but when my grandfather asked Myrtle if he could refine the rich ore in the five gallon tins around J. C.'s diggings, Myrtle said, "No." She unabashedly hoped to lure leasers with the colorful rock in the tins, and I believe that she understood the forgotten positive powers of envy. If self-government is analogous to the government of nations, Thomas Jefferson's words of wisdom may have been in Myrtle's heart: "Confidence is everywhere the parent of despotism —free government is founded in jealousy and not in confidence."[22]

Myrtle forced her son to see Elephant Mountain from a new angle and to make new estimations of its nature. She played upon his pride, and by restraining herself from trusting him with her high-grade ore and with the future of the mine, she coerced my grandfather into developing with his modest means the larger mine. J. C.'s mining claims were her legacy, and she was single-minded in her preservation of them. She had seen headframes erected over too many glory holes. She had observed more than one impressive mill sitting idle. She knew the pattern of American dreams in Nevada whereby the greedy cashed in on the foolish before substantial evidence of a mineral deposit had been collected. Unfortunately, her stubbornness would be translated as selfishness, and when she no longer held sway at Silverton, her grandsons hauled the high-grade into McGill for milling. Although neither my father nor my grandfather had intended to liquidate the family mine, without that ore in the tins, visible proof of the mine's richness disappeared. Some of the hand-sorted ore which was shoveled into the railcar at Ely to provide silica at the McGill copper smelter may have assayed 200 ounces of silver per ton. Geologist Fred E. Young reported in 1920 that such rich samples were frequent at Silverton. But Silverton, like most mines in the United States, was not to follow the model of European and South American mines which produced and employed men over hundreds of years. When money's metal link was unbroken, mines had been like farms and were passed down through generations.

Despite its own and the U.S. government's ignorance of mining, the Tognoni family would manage to hold on to its mine if not produce from it. In 1934, my grandfather followed his father into a grave at Silverton, and the Tognoni children continued a small mining operation on their father's claims. Fred Allen, who cared for Myrtle's needs at Silverton after J. C. was gone; Johnny Mendez, Aunt Neva's husband; my father and his brother Nye would haul a new set of tent houses to the property, congregating them on the opposite side of Elephant Mountain from the Silverton mining camp. They called the new camp "Toonerville" from comic strip geography, which my father explored religiously when he turned his back to the ground to rest.

On Elephant Mountain they drilled with hand steel and hauled the ore off the mountain by horseback. One summer they powered their drill with a homemade compressor which thrived as much on gravity and anticipation as on gasoline. The ore from the tunnels paid more in experience than in silver. The pay dirt they trucked to McGill in the thirties and forties contained an average of only thirty ounces of silver per ton. Underground development at Silverton would cease. In 1920 when geologist Young wrote his report, he included with it a map of J. C. and Myrtle's family holdings which consisted of over a hundred mining claims covering the entire network of silver impregnated fissures in the folded and faulted Tognoni limestone and quartzite. For the future of Silverton, Hale Tognoni looked not only to education at Mackay School of Mines but to the copper industry's methods: open pits and federal support. Hale Tognoni, filled with youthful ideals, would go to Washington, D.C., to add the discipline of law to his geological engineering and not "to get some of that free Democratic money," as his "Uncle" William Mendes disapprovingly quipped.

In the meantime it was my grandmother Ina who kept up the mining claims with her husband, Rex Conway. While J. C. was living, Ina involved herself in his dreams for Silverton, maybe more than Myrtle, who had grown fat and unable to participate in J. C.'s purifying rites of work. It was Ina who shared J. C.'s transcendent vision of America; it was Ina who read the Great Books aloud to her children in their tent at Chimney Springs and ram-rodded her sons into college; and it was Ina whom they buried here at Silverton beside J. R. and J. C. Tognoni. Before she died, my grandmother begged me, a girl of less than ten years, to take her wristwatch from a box under her hospital bed and to keep it. I did not take the watch. Yet I see that I inherited something much more unique to her. She had believed all her life in Silverton, and she gave to me the hope of raising the relationship between peace and enduring mines out of the rubble of history.

10   Blood to a Metal Heart

The seed of our destruction will blossom in the desert,
the alexin of our cure grows by a Georgia slattern,
because a London cut-purse went unhung. Each
moment is the fruit of forty thousand years. The
minute-winning days, like flies, buzz home to death,
and every moment is a window on all time.
Thomas Wolfe

We leave Silverton now. The mine road along which our car creeps is no more than a set of tire tracks which has displaced the desert varnish. Between the parallel depressions, sagebrush grows tall just as it does amid the tiny dark cobbles of black rock which fit so neatly together to varnish the topsoil beyond the road's shoulders. Sagebrush sweeps the automobile's underside and sacrifices a sprig to smoulder and smoke between the hot metal parts which have caught it up. My father is speaking into his recording machine, "The big shaft is straight ahead where we had a map of the Silverton claims posted for years."

He watches the pale white line ahead of us on the steep intersection of Treasure Hill and Elephant Mountain. It is a new road made by leasers to bring in drilling equipment. Ore samples cut by the tri-cone, rotary drill of Howard Hughes' invention, have been blown to the surface where the chips and dust of rock deep in the mountain become the geologist's only proof of the mountain's composure. Despite little real knowledge as to the nature of fluid ore, its source, and the cause of its movement, drill samples are the best clues to where faulting maintained openings through which metal found an upward path. These mountains lie along the jumbled edge of a thrust plate. For a width of ninety miles, a northeastern line roughly bounds the end of one section of the earth's shell where it pinched, slipped, broke and leaked against its neighbor to the east.[1] The resulting geology is complex but profitable. In the permeable sediments left unburied by the thrust plate and its

Joseph Russell Tognoni,
Hale Tognoni's father, in hunting
gear, Duckwater, c. 1920.

volcanics lies the only oil field producing in Nevada. Since 1954, oil companies have been pumping an increasing quantity of very thick petroleum from beneath Railroad Valley.[2]

The valley's narrowed completion, Duckwater Valley, to the north of the oil fields is our destination. Our path into Railroad Valley begins on the volcanic ridge of Silverton which interrupts the gently sloping alluvium at the base of the Pancake Range. East off the edge of the ridge, the road shifts our backs to the old mine shaft and the cool tunnel into Treasure Hill which I remember from my first visit to J. C. Tognoni's mine and mining camp. Our sandy road parts the sagebrush along one side of Silverton's black ridge while the cracked and tar-patched surface of the Grand Army of the Republic hugs the other side like an asphalt reptile. The highway will crest the basalt ridge and intersect our road in the valley. My father points to the remains of his grandfather's corrals at the entrance of "Indian caves" which are under the ridge. If all the stories are true, Indians, desperados and even mustangs have used the dark passages into the basalt. Now the white, pipe claim-markers of Phelps Dodge mining company sparsely surround the caves and the long promontory of volcanics. Between the basalt and the underlying rhyolite, where a reclusive uncle bore his exploratory holes, now Phelps Dodge searches for the silver-molybdenum deposits. Molybdenum or "Molly" is an element for our times because she has the high melting point valuable to speed. Because molybdenum is widely found with copper, it is one of the few metals of which the United States exports more than it imports.

Out to the north of our route into Railroad Valley is Iron King. Its numerous spires of dark rhyolite cut the sky like points of a royal head piece, and at Iron King's foot, antimony has found a home. Unlike the other metals which have crawled toward the surface along this great earth fault, antimony expands when it cools rather than when it is heated, a perversity used diversely by man and so exploited during World War II that eleven antimony mines in Nevada were producing.[3] My father moves his recorder to his mouth again: "The road going north is where the Lockes had their antimony claims. That's the first place where they invaded the Silverton area."

Beyond Iron King in the northerly expanses of the valley, we see Madison Locke's ranch, a cluster of trees and buildings where I remember the dusty windows of a cafe and an old gas pump standing idle by the highway. Four hot water springs and several seeps at Locke's Ranch have built a low hill from carbon and silica solutions.[4] It overlooks one of Nevada's largest lakes of 10,000 years ago, now a tremendous alkali reservoir, a memorial of multitudinous weddings of hydroxides and acids which took place in the waters of Railroad Valley. The sodium-chloride union, commonly called "salt," was so abundant here as to be collected and sold for thirty-five dollars a ton in 1880.[5]

To the east on the other side of the White Plain and Grant mountain ranges in the White River Basin, hydrologists have discovered remarkable discontinuities in the elevation of water springs. From the valley beyond, water flows underground into the White River Basin. West in the broad region of the nuclear test site, the basins have a uniform underground drainage to the southwest; but Railroad Valley seems to be a water system unto itself, closed to subsurface outflow by vast geologic movement. Blind and undesigned forces operate here beneath the surface in the assemblage of permeable contacts with earth's hot core, but boundaries of human time have walled our vision of the water and its potential for perpetuating life. The seemingly bottomless, acidic blue and green pool of hot water in the midst of the reed marsh at Locke's draws one to its edge to stare as if into a key hole.

When a person dreams of life in this valley, he dreams of owning Locke's Ranch. My father is among the dreamers, although he remembers two tall, threatening horsemen—Madison Locke, Jr., and Harvey Titus, husband of Madison Locke's daughter. They rode up to his family's tent at Chimney Hot Springs in the valley. My grandfather warned them to leave or be shot, and he turned his back to their guns. Before he could emerge from his tent with his "coyote gun" the Lockes were riding away, "just two spots of dust in the distance." Madison Locke, Sr., was a Civil War veteran. With script for land which the government gave in payment for military service during the Civil War, he purchased an island of private property in this valley of public land. Adjoining acreage was homesteaded. Descendants of Madison Locke feud with the Tognonis over rights at Silverton even today, but just as Madison Locke's grave marks his land, so the graves of J. C. Tognoni, J. R. Tognoni and Ina Belle Conway brand Silverton mining camp.

With the bones of our forefathers, Earth hides the water and mineral in
Railroad Valley, and like the ancient mines on the island of Cyprus, these
elements precious to man seem to be awaiting a twist of fate. Modern mining on the island of Cyprus evolved from one man's curiosity about the
name "Cyprus." "Copper," said the name of the island. Taking the name
seriously, he dug beneath the surface to find the mines. In Railroad Valley,
the Civil War once brought men to look beneath its surface. In Nye County
along the eastern border line of which Railroad Valley stretches for 200
miles, mine development began in the decade of the Civil War. California
gold-rusher J. T. Williams, a native of Arkansas, helped organize Nye
County in 1863, using Ione, in the far northwestern corner, little more than a
mining camp, as the county seat. Ione gave up its governmental status to
Belmont, where a rush early in 1866 was yielding $200 to $3,000 a ton ore.[6]
During the war, Alexander Beaty, the first settler in Railroad Valley,[7] discovered silver in the Grant Range near what came to be known as Troy.
There the Old English Gold Corporation invested hundreds of thousands of
dollars for mine development.

Later in 1867, silver discoveries were made north of the valley in the
bleak, exposed and wind swept peaks of the White Pine Mountains. During
and after the Civil War, White Pine mining district served as a sort of
refugee camp for men fleeing the desolation in the southern United States.
By 1868, in the White Pine mining district, the towns of Hamilton, Treasure
City, Swansea, Shermantown, Babylon, Eberhardt and Picotillo clung to
the mountains or hid between ridges. The ferment was such that even the
Bank of California and Wells Fargo built branches in Hamilton. Despite the
poor climate and outbreaks of disease, more than ten thousand shivering
miners established themselves in caves, in drafty cotton tents, in huts of hay,
mud and stone, and houses of rough timber, slabs and posts.[8] Southerners
like Ed Halstead, Sr., Captain Clarence Moorman and Madison Locke
owned ranches which became human features as sparse in this countryside
as the springs of water which pock the hostile geology. According to Beatie
Halstead in Duckwater Valley, through it all the men in this emptiness
fought the Civil War over again at every election.

In 1905, William Morris Stewart, father of the American mining laws,
built his last law office in Nye County at the southern border near California's Death Valley. Stewart too had intimate acquaintance with the war's
human suffering. His wife had come from an illustrious southern family,
and U.S. Senator Stewart would aid his father-in-law, H. S. Foote, to escape
the full revenge of Union victors.[9] While Stewart wrote the constitutional
amendment which disallowed "race, color or creed" to bar a man from

voting, he expended his wealth for his wife's self-imposed European exile after the war.[10]

In 1880, when J. C. Tognoni arrived in the United States, every county in Nevada except Nye had been touched by railroads. Although there were more than 250,000 miles of railroad route in the United States by 1914, "more than in all the rest of the world,"[11] railroads would only slice the western edges of Nevada's largest county during the twentieth century. Nye remained uncrossed by steel tracks, and ultimately, the cost of hauling ore would doom the county's mining districts. The expense of teaming ore north to the nearest rail heads in Austin and Eureka continued to be a major consideration to what could become a mine. At the close of the nineteenth century, mining in Nye County virtually ceased and the promise of Railroad Valley was forgotten by most, not my father. He continues to dream of prosperity in the valley.

The oil companies in the Railroad Valley would be served by the combustion engine and the Grand Army of the Republic Highway. Diesel tractors whiz across the valley pulling two tank trailers. Three are legal in Nevada—trains without tracks through Railroad Valley. Early trucking was done by my grandfather and, later, his sons and their friends. They hauled ore, firewood, even houses. Deserted freight wagons sat at Duckwater, and mustangers were trapping horses for horse-meat rather than for horse-power. From the old mine at Troy, Hale and his brother Nye had helped their ailing father truck a three stamp mill into the valley to Chimney Hot Spring. There the stamps were to pound Silverton's ore into powder for J. R.'s humble cyaniding plant, but with silver prices at seventy cents an ounce, my grandfather's operation only weathered one summer.

The popular theory of why so many mines and mining camps in Nye County and elsewhere in the West have been deserted is that discoveries were "supergene enrichments: [In] their prodigal dispersal through the Basin and Range . . . some of the richest silver deposits ever discovered in the world . . . were also the shallowest. There was just so much lying there . . . to print money would take more time than to pick up this silver."[12] Such versions of mining in Nevada leave little room for humanity or truth. Men did not haul ore out of Troy and Blue Eagle, to which my father points below the vaulted precipice banking the far side of Railroad Valley, because it was easy.

The laborious, deep development of most precious metal mines in the West and in the South halted before the Civil War's century was complete. Much of the lead disseminated in our military graveyards of those days came from mines in the Tri-State mining region of Arkansas, Oklahoma and

Missouri. During the war, Union states established foreign imports of these minerals. After the war, the small lead and zinc mines in southern hinterlands stopped producing not because there was no more rich ore, but because politics no longer favored them. The Buffalo River in Arkansas cuts into limestone beds which hold rich zinc-lead deposits, mined on a small scale even in the 1960s, but no more. Currently, the nation finds it much easier to import 76 percent of its yearly consumption of zinc from nations where labor remains cheap. Government experts interpret the lack of mining as lack of ore and have purchased the land for a national river; but, one man whose land the government wished to purchase for this project wanted to be paid for his mineral. Hale Tognoni, with his sons and his associate, Harry E. Nelson of Conroe, Texas, was called in to evaluate the unmined zinc and lead.

Likewise, Hale Tognoni would examine unused mineral lands in Arizona because the government wished to make recompense with the Indians to whom the land had belonged in 1883 when white men took it. In 1978, Hale Tognoni's Mineral Economics Corporation researched the Gila and Salt River mineral province of Arizona for the Indian Claims Commission. It discovered ten small gold and silver mines which could be rich enough to be producing today with proper capital investment. The mines had a minimum value of $100,000 each in a mining market where one particular claim alone sold for $2 million in gold dollars. Mineral Economics also projected ten low grade copper deposits in the province worth a minimum of one-half billion dollars, when developed, or $5 million in 1883 values. In addition, the asphalt and concrete aggregate industry has produced amounts valued at $200 million. The government, accustomed to discounting mineral values on public land, may be rethinking its intention to pay the Indians. The sum has not yet been settled.

Our road slopes gradually into Railroad Valley and jogs my memory of measuring and bagging samples up this slope under a blue sky and relentless sun. This afternoon clouds have begun to gather for tomorrow's rain. My father talks again into his machine: "I made the foolish mistake in 1949 of telling Rex Conway, who was married to my mother, that the oil companies were crazy to drill in Railroad Valley because they were too close to the volcanics. We had just come out of the tremendous volcanic field back by Silverton. Gianella had taught me that there was no oil in pyroclastics (fragmented volcanics), but we had forgotten the sediments."

In 1949, the year his first child (myself) was born in Butte, Montana, Hale Tognoni had just finished his geological engineering degree at the Mackay School of Mines and had been hired by Anaconda Copper Company. He was naturally anxious to display the benefit of his classroom lessons. He was particularly anxious to appear knowledgeable about Silverton. After all, the Tognoni family had made gambling on the geology of the Pancake Range and Railroad Valley a family tradition. One group of oil wells in the valley is called Trap Spring Oil Field. My father remembers visiting a salt water spring with his father to check a trap, the one he believes may have given the spring and the oil field their names.

When Hale Tognoni was last in the vicinity of Chimney Springs in this valley, it had been crusted over by the travertine which spreads from the spring in a tufa mound thirty feet high and one-half mile across. Beneath the white travertine still bubbled the valley's hottest water, 160 degrees Fahrenheit, from which steam rises like chimney smoke to the distant observor. On this trip we find Chimney Hot Springs reopened and fenced by the government "wildlife managers." Around the spring are fragments of my grandfather's cyanide plant, lonely artifacts of history: old pipe used to recycle the cyanide, tank bottoms and the rock with embedded steel rods which held the stamp mill.

My grandfather once began to write the story of this valley and Duckwater, but the yellow pages of his manuscript are only a childhood memory of my father's, like the spots of dust fleeing J. R. Tognoni's rifle at Chimney Hot Springs over fifty years ago. I suspect that J. R. did not pick up his pen lightly. Like his rifle, he lifted it with purpose. Something about this valley stirred him very deeply. Another person's account, entitled "Duckwater Days," was burned, so as not to hurt good people, I am told, and records of the justice of the peace were thrown to the bottom of a well by an outraged woman, they tell me. "Duckwater had a bloody reputation," another informant supplies. The future for life in Railroad Valley seems to have been dammed like Duckwater Creek by the collected and cemented shortcomings of mankind and American aspiration. It is as if the settlers of Duckwater stood on the brink of eternity and turned back in fear; but Railroad Valley still holds the promise of life in every wild flower along the highway. Eternity is too big not to be. No less than in Joseph Conrad's jungle river: in Railroad Valley "the stillness of an implacable force broods over an inscrutable intention."

Children in Duckwater's school with teacher, c. 1903. Frank Collins, bottom left, tells of watching men ride by the school on their way to break J.C. Tognoni's irrigation dam. J.C.'s son, Joe, sulks on the bottom right. J.C.'s daughter, Elva, stands in the middle row, far left.

11 Defiant Dreamers

The marvel of a house . . . is that it leaves its trace on the language. Let it form, deep in the heart, that obscure range from which, as water from a spring, are born our dreams.
Antoine de Saint-Exupery[1]

In Duckwater Valley, the houses of my father's ancestors are relatively young, but their century-old walls appear fit for a millenium. Carved from milky-white travertine, the wall blocks are the remains of hot solution once deep within the earth. Big Warm Spring carried the dilute fluid to the surface, and evaporation from the spring's eighty-two acre lake, now gone, left a silicious mud to bake to hard rock, like a scab over a warm wound. In the lake, reeds grew and died, moulding their own graves in the forming rock. Now hollow, finger-like coffins emerge from walls where they will seem to offer focus to the century of days which hum in my mind, and my hand will reach out to touch them.

We enter Duckwater Valley from the southern end where the water, which has already flowed across Duckwater's ranch land, will sink into Railroad Valley, if unused. In the cemetery at a curve in our road northward are the graves of my great-great-grandparents, Ernest Jesse Jacques and Maria Cross. In this minute yard below the lofty peaks of the White Pine mountain range, the first graves were dug for two Jacques grandchildren in 1880. The McSelf twins, born out of Olivia Jacques, were dead at the age of four months. The children of other Jacques daughters lie here as well: four infants born to Mary Adeline; the adult daughter, Stella, of my own great-grandmother, Myrtle; and two of Myrtle's daughters-in-law. There were seven Jacques sisters altogther. Four or possibly five married men of Duckwater, but only one of the sisters is buried here—the youngest, Mary Adeline, who married William F. Mendes, "Father of Duckwater,"[2] who is also buried in this cemetery.

Alongside of Mendes' grave are the remains of his predecessors in the water war of Duckwater Valley: John W. Simpson and Burton B. Strait, buried here in 1885 and 1896. They were among the first white men to settle in the Valley, and with others they waged the first battle of the war. Mendes, the Portuguese immigrant, would finish that skirmish, and it would arouse in him an appetite for victory satiated on his death bed fifty years later. The names and dates in Mendes' graveyard are clues to a lost story, factors in a conflict which ended without ceremony or examination. Elsewhere in Nevada and the West, the fight for water rights goes on endlessly. On the Carson River, for instance, where the population never dwindled to so few as now inhabit Duckwater, the precious run-off of the Sierra remains wild habitat for fish and rats in the Carson sink. Meanwhile the courts deliberate over questions as old as the Comstock and reclamation of Nevada's vast federal lands stagnates.

On the Carson River, where water conflicts remain in the courts, a daughter of the struggle, Grace Dangberg, has tackled voluminous legal documents to distill the basic problems and issues. She concludes that man is at the mercy of nature; and for the most part, drought, not human vanity, is the instigator of water wars. Certainly, the Comstock mill owners on the Carson River were bound for trouble, especially in drought years, with the farmers and ranchers who had dammed the river upstream; but Grace Dangberg's study, *Conflict on the Carson*, also tends to affirm that resolutions reached between early mill owners and farmers were far less wasteful of our resources than the unresolved court battles taking place at federal expense today. The existence of an Indian reservation in Duckwater Valley leads me to suspect that peace, here too, is being enforced at federal expense.

Unlike Grace Dangberg, I do not have a closely documented conflict to study at Duckwater. I have only my father's stories; the imprint of his enthusiasm for efficient irrigation; a box of unidentified photographs; a few grave markers; the genealogy of the Jacques and Mendes families; the justice of the peace record from 1874 to 1887; incomplete records of court battles; a few property titles belonging to J. C. and Myrtle Tognoni; and the scrambled memories of those who lived or still live in Duckwater Valley.

Among the few pictures which have been absolutely identified is a photo of the Collins family, who now live on the Schurz Indian Reservation far from here. Other than the photograph and old Frank Collins' ballads, the Collinses know only that they lost their land at Duckwater. Indeed, a meadow in the valley is still "Collins Meadow" on the U.S. Geological Survey map. Collins' descendants want to know how the land was lost. William F. Mendes, the titular father of Duckwater, has surviving children;

Water-master Nye Tognoni, left, at work in Duckwater Valley, c. 1939.

Men of Duckwater in the lane along one of the Valley's irrigation ditches, 1903. J. C. Tognoni is second from left.

but his daughter, born in 1900, will identify no pictures, answer no questions. She only asks, "Why would anyone want to dig up the old dirt?" After all, war legend has it that her father, on his death bed in 1931, decreed a settlement by calling together all those with water rights on Duckwater Creek and persuading them each to give a few water inches to what had once been the Tognoni ranch, a ranch which even the "Bank" appears to have sold by 1930.

Duckwater's first major battle over water rights took place between 1877 and 1883 during a time when battles raged all over Nevada between the established and the unestablished. After all, the U.S. government had laid the economic foundation for a consuming struggle to be powerful rather than to be productive and at peace: the United States abandoned bimetallism and the healthy link between labor and money supply. The ultimate rationale for this move was fear that by not adopting a gold standard as the Europeans were doing, the nation would be relegating itself to secondary status in perpetuity. It was popular in those times to call people who stood in one's path to primacy a "crowd" of some sort. On the Comstock, Adolf Sutro would spread the idea of a "Bank Crowd" which was his name for those whom he accused of having selfish interest in denying his tunnel.[3] In Duckwater, the settlers at the lower end of Duckwater Creek became known as the "Lower Crowd" and their motives in preventing the development of irrigation ditches from Big Warm Springs were said to be the desire to monopolize local farm prices by maintaining scarcity.

Only the very hardy found the conflict farcical: Bill Peterson, for instance, who is still mining and prospecting at near ninety years of age. Peterson spent his boyhood on a ranch in the vicinity of Duckwater. But even Peterson warns with the heavy grip of repetition, "You know Duckwater has a very bloody name, you know." He tells a story of Hamilton's boom days in the White Pine Mountains. Wild hay from Duckwater was being sold to freighters at a "tremendous premium." Men died cutting hay on Duckwater Valley's ice. "Some guy would come along and shoot the guy cutting, take his scythe and continue on to harvest the hay." Duckwater's mysteriously plentiful water and its hay were as greedily fought over as any precious metal being dug from the mountains. The earliest water right, Page-Withington, dates to 1866. This certified quantity of water eventually would serve the first homestead, DeFlon Ranch, situated on the confluence of two springs feeding Duckwater Creek. By 1875, John Williams, Myrtle's first husband, would own the ranch. South of Deflon in the 1860s, Isaac Irwin was busy cutting wild hay for freighters to the northwest in Austin. At night, I am told, he slept with a gun in his hand. Irwin would soon establish his own land boundaries in this high desert oasis, as would Strait and Simpson, who lie in the graveyard.

James C. McMinn also homesteaded in lower Duckwater Valley. His glorious parchment deed, dated 1870, is among my great-grandfather's papers. In 1895, J. C. Tognoni received it from the heirs of McMinn. On McMinn's land, J. C. and his wife Myrtle would live and nurture, among others, my grandfather, J. R. Tognoni. The house still stands, and Isaac Irwin's granddaughter, Martha Hawkins, cultivates colorful flags of hollyhock and cool, green vegetation beneath its old trees. She has saved Irwin's lone surviving justice of the peace record, 100 years old.

Deeper into the Valley, beyond the cemetery, is the Jaques house, which, by all appearances, is deserted. Back from the road it sits in the company of a few outbuildings and a handful of trees. The beauty surrounding its travertine walls is wide and stark as if the house were perched alone on a high shore of the ocean. From somewhere near the house, water bleeds from Little Warm Spring at the foot of Duckwater's travertine plateau. A gully has formed along the asphalt where we stand and erodes away the earth beneath our road's smooth surface. Myrtle's son, Charlie Williams, occupied this isolate cottage for years; Indians made it their home; and in 1938, Myrtle gave up the property to save taxes.

Myrtle's first husband and Charlie's father, John Williams, was a tenacious member of the upper settlers in their 1877-1883 battle for water rights. Called *Strait vs. Brown* in the district court for Nye County, the entire list of plaintiffs included Isaac Irwin, McSelf, Simpson and Joseph Mendes, brother of William Mendes. C. A. Brown, John Collins, and John Williams had entered the valley with other defendants as a group in 1872. Led by Brown, who established a road station at Big Warm Spring, the defendants began a ditch from the spring. The Brown Ditch was completed three years later, but in 1877, Brown and his associates also undertook to build a flour mill. This alarmed the lower settlers, who became concerned about their own water rights against growing use by the group at the headwaters of Duckwater Creek. The Lower Crowd began its own ditch, South Ditch, to drain Big Warm Spring, and it instigated several court proceedings. The upper settlers responded by damming the creek. Two homicides are attributed to the ruckus while *Strait vs. Brown* spent seven years in the courts.

The ninety degree Fahrenheit waters of Big Warm Spring had no obvious route to Duckwater Creek. Pouring to the surface at a rate of sixteen cubic feet per second, Big Warm Spring had created a lake. Underground limestone reservoirs of water from the Pancake Range broke the surface to form springs in the northern valley and to become the creek's apparent source; but, after reversal and re-trial, the court in *Strait vs. Brown* ruled that Big Warm Spring was the principal source of Duckwater Creek. This was promptly interpreted as a forced closing of Brown Ditch, although in the years when Brown, Collins, Williams and the others used the water of Big Warm Spring, they did not diminish the supply of water in the creek.[4] Only one defendant, John Williams, Myrtle's husband, had the fortitude to see the court battle through to the final decision in 1883. The others had deserted for a variety of reasons including selling out to the opposition. Williams himself had been compelled to abandon Duckwater for fear of violence.

Religion may have played a role in the early cohesiveness of the upper settlers to which Williams belonged. John Collins may have been the Methodist leader active in Gold Hill on the Comstock whence came many of the gold-rushers who settled in Duckwater. In Nevada, a number of religious groups and utopians, most notably the Mormons, would match faith with the desert. The clammering Protestant sects were eager to test their practical precepts on wilderness. Nevada required cooperation, as the clannish Chinese and Latin miners demonstrated. In Duckwater, the lower settlers were loosely organized around secular law in the figure-head of Isaac Irwin, justice of the peace. Irwin may have been striving to replace lawlessness with a medieval type of communal protection. Duckwater Valley had become the setting for a mystery play in which the daughters of Jacques would be cast in the leading female roles. Not long after John Williams had been financially ruined by *Strait vs. Brown*, Myrtle claimed he had become abusive and divorced him. Her new husband, J. C. Tognoni, eventually would attempt to re-open the Brown Ditch under new state water law and in cooperation with federal reclamation policy. In 1901, U.S. Reclamation Officer L. H. Taylor made measurements of the local waters and issued a report stating that if the waters of Duckwater Valley were concentrated and economically used, they would irrigate more than double the area of land under cultivation. Nevertheless, the Irwin family and William Mendes would not accommodate Tognoni. The old conflict raged through two more major battles and left behind deep scars.

Maria Cross, my great-great grandmother, died in Duckwater after ninety-six years of uproar on the overland trail, in gold-rush California and in Duckwater. Her daughters, Mary Adeline and Myrtle, reputedly were not allowed to attend the burial. My grandfather, young J. R. Tognoni, had been the principal caretaker of old Maria and of her third husband, John Cross. The Mendes family shared the load, but even that matter went to the courts. My father tells his mother's story of Mendes' bringing the old woman and her belongings to the Tognoni doorstep in a winter snow storm. J. R., seeing the Mendes' buggy in retreat, fired a shot to report his displeasure.

Mendes brought Tognoni to court for assault; but in the courtroom, ballistics experts testifying for Tognoni claimed that the hole in the buggy top, which Mendes provided for evidence, could not have been made in the manner claimed. The hole, they averred, had been fired at close range by a gun held over the top while it rested innocently on the ground. Outside the courtroom, I imagine, there were dancing bears and a medicine man; and maybe old Mrs. Cross laughed hardest of all, for she, like Bill Peterson, was a hardy sinner.

My father and I approach Big Warm Spring. A caravan of pick-up trucks and vans is parked on the white mud near the edge of the water hole, and electric music mingles with the hard words of the pool's throbbing, young inhabitants. I have the same uneasy feeling as when I stopped with Dr. Gianella at his childhood home in California's gold-rush country earlier in my pilgrimage. There, too, music and voices sneered at a man come home. Most of the uncertain, adult bodies in the murky pool are dark, and their faces are full and broad inside frames of lank, black hair—surely Indians. One young man on the edge of the gathering in the water volunteers to answer my father's questions. "It's warm!" he tells us by way of introduction. Taking pride in the pool, he informs us that in the mornings before the bathers have disturbed the soft banks, the water is clear, so clear that you can see twenty-five feet to the bottom.

The depth was once reported to be seventy-five feet, so Hale Tognoni cross-examines carefully. His witness responds with silent curiosity. Then, with a backward curl of the head to include all present in the water, the young man tells of their attempts to swim into the wide hole in the pool's side, but even those who reached the hole's edge and gripped rock for leverage could not overcome the current. Together we watch the swelling and swirling near the pool's center where the underground river breaks its concealment by lifting the hole's surface. The young man has been effortlessly treading the water as he speaks. Now, he sends one arm in the air of our shadow to point across the valley in the direction from which the water seems to come. We look into the cliff far behind us, but we find no sign of a river. Out of Big Warm Spring a ditch with an open gate at the pool's edge carries water to the north, Brown's Ditch, the ditch that J. C. re-opened. The lake is gone, and just as Dr. Gianella found when he would try to explain bygone waterways to people in his boyhood home, our listener seems disbelieving and asks no questions. We thank him and walk back around the pick-up truck to our car. There is a warm irony in having the Indians forget us rather than we them.

I have already seen enough to weary my mind with the imponderable for a lifetime when my father makes yet another turn from the now unpaved highway. We are entering a ranch which he describes as his grandfather's, commonly called the Bank Ranch, currently reserved to Duckwater Indians. My father's memories of this place are of shade, running water and the dusk. He points to a travertine building behind a new, more temporary house. The windows of his grandparents' old house hold no glass, the doorways no doors, but the roof and wood floors are surprisingly whole. The trees that cling to the banks of a water ditch behind the house have sheltered the roof and shielded the walls. From the new house, a man approaches our parked car. He will become a valuable guide to the present in Duckwater Valley. He is Allen Lenbeck, one-eighth Shoshone Indian, sometime mine worker, whole-hearted rancher, and Duckwater Valley's official water master. Mr. Lenbeck is not shy, and it is with delight rather than disbelief that he offers up exclamations during my father's stories. Unlike the two geologists, Tognoni and Nusbaum, who met at Silverton earlier today, Lenbeck and Tognoni share a common heritage in this land without which science is impotent here.

Lenbeck rests one hand peacefully on the ledge of his denim pant pocket while he motions from his tightly muscled frame with all of his other arm to illustrate stories of his own. While the two men talk, I finger the travertine wall and enter my great-grandparents' old home. Lenbeck's words must penetrate my historical preoccupations and, so, they reach me like dull thuds of a bell beneath a winter's snow. Nye Tognoni served as water master in this valley in the 1930s after his brother, Hale, carried a petition to the passively hostile ranchers of Duckwater. "I thought we got rid of you Ti-own-ees," one of Isaac Irwin's sons grumbled as he lowered pen to line. Afterwards he offered Hale a drink, but the floating turkey droppings on the open wooden vat of ferment into which Irwin lowered his dipper gave my father no pressing reason to break his youthful abstinence.

Today the nod of Lenbeck's head is heavy with the conflict over water in this valley. Irrigating in Duckwater continues to be a slow process. I suspect no greater acreage is under cultivation now than at the turn of the century, and I doubt whether anyone knows. There is no easy way to dredge the facts from Duckwater, sovereign unto itself and dashing its banks as if they were expectations. In my two visits, I have wondered at the barren, dry countryside in upper Duckwater Valley. Allen Lenbeck would like to see cement pipes in the irrigation ditches to help minimize evaporation. He gives us the figures of yearly loss and points beyond his horse corral to the pile of large pipe by the main road.

Out at the end of Lenbeck's gesture, the road reminds me of that road and ditch along which men walked in a peculiarly solemn row in a 1903 photograph. For a while this photo was my only picture of Duckwater, the

place in so many of my father's stories, but all that could inform me seemed
to be left out of the picture, and I hesitated over it only briefly as I would
over a clumsy snapshot. To where and from where had men made the water
flow? Why does such a large man walk directly in front of my great-grandfather with another following so closely on his heels? What does the man
behind J. C. Tognoni hold? A gun?—the photo appears to have been
scraped here. Now, the figures far behind the two striding men in the
middle ground arouse my curiosity too, and the artfulness of the photo
slowly becomes apparent, as I begin to understand why the picture was
taken.

Someone who knew the shape and cock of each man's hat could probably tell me which of these men is Ralph Irwin, which Paul Irwin; which is
Bill Blair, Henry Lorigan, Charlie Irving. The large man in front is most
probably one of the Irwin brothers, notorious for their size and strength. I
imagine William Mendes was one of what I take to be horsemen, following
in the background. A bullet which entered William Mendes' foot during gun
play in the matter to which the men march, would have made riding a
necessity. But even when the bullets were flying on May 11, 1903, Mendes
never left his horse. He was willing to be shot for what he believed was right,
he told the court in *Nevada vs. Joseph (C.) Tognoni*. Others in the 1903 gun-
fight were less righteous. Either they took cover or reckoned that they were
safe because J. C. rarely missed his aim. If the target was human, Ralph or
Mendes were the likely victims, according to Bill Blair under cross examination at the trial.[7] On the day of the shooting, Ralph was tearing out J. C.'s
irrigation dam. Mendes had done the dirty work two years earlier. The
photograph may be of J. C. Tognoni's arrest or perhaps he is merely being
strong-armed into accompanying other participants to a preliminary examination held two weeks after the incident in the county courthouse at
Tonopah. At that time Mendes claimed that one of J. C.'s bullets caught him
in the foot, and the trial was set for December.

As his lawyer, J. C. hired Key Pittman, not yet U.S. senator from
Nevada. Pittman's successes at Tonopah would start him on a path to fame
as an international proponent of bimetallism and as advisor to President
Franklin Roosevelt. Around my great-grandfather in the early years of
Tonopah, the Key Pittmans and bankers like George Wingfield were gathering power and wealth as William Morris Stewart and W. C. Ralston had
done to the north on the Comstock in the previous century. As on the
Comstock, races of immigrants were marked, not only by skin color, facial
feature and stature, but by their belief in self-worth having no measurement
against another man. These hardy souls willingly labored for low wages. So,
like the Chinese, who in September of 1903, were subjected to violence by

a mob of white workingmen in Tonopah,[5] Italians may have been that group of dark immigrants popularly belittled for a time at Duckwater. The Italians had cut the wood for Eureka's smelters just as the Chinese had laid the railroads; and their position in Nevada social structure may have been just as limited as that of the Chinese. J. C. seemed to have felt at home in Elko to the north, where there was a strong Chinese community. In fact, he and Myrtle were married there, and in Duckwater on the day of the shooting, J. C. was engaged on an acre where he planned to irrigate a potato crop as the Chinese had done around Elko with the waters of the Humboldt River. In any case, while awaiting trial in Tonopah, J. C. would do the prospecting that would make him one of Goldfield, Nevada's founding fathers, and enable him to return to Duckwater a wealthy man.

At the trial in *Nevada vs. Tognoni*, old Maria Cross, mother of both Tognoni's and Mendes' wives, was star witness for the prosecution. She claimed to have heard J. C. exclaim, "I winged their captain," after firing his last shot; but, there is a strong possibility that Mendes shot himself in the foot while drawing his concealed revolver. Then we have my grandmother's version as told to my father: J. C. was aiming at Ralph Irwin's head, and he missed. J. C., himself, testified at the trial that he was aiming at the bridge timber above the dam. Mendes exhibited his boot with a neat hole shot from toe through to heel and a curious tear in the top, which was as poorly explained as why Mendes was wearing his left boot on his right foot.

One thing is certain in the transcript, his fight was only one episode in the war for water rights at Duckwater. Old John Collins, who had lost his battle for water as one of the upper valley defendants, in *Strait vs. Brown*, testified in 1903 on behalf of J. C. Tognoni. So did his son, Truman Collins. John Collins was married to an Indian woman of Duckwater, a fact brought to the attention of the court by the prosecution, to discredit Collins. An Indian employee of Mendes' testified that Mendes was concealing a gun; and behind J. C.'s house on a knoll, a large group of Indian men and women had assembled to spectate on the day of May 11, 1903. The Indians of Duckwater seemed to have a stake in J. C. Tognoni's attempt to use the spring floodwaters that others of the white settlers would prefer to waste rather than to jeopardize their own hoard or their own rights under the law of Isaac Irwin.

Isaac died in 1894, leaving his widow Louisa and their children to carry on at Duckwater. Where the creek enters a corner of the Irwin ranch, U.S. Reclamation Officer L. H. Taylor had built a weir in 1901 to measure the amount of water reaching the creek's lower end. John Collins; John Cross, third husband of my great-great-grandmother; and Serafin Rogantine, Myrtle Tognoni's son-in-law, measured the water running through Taylor's weir after the gunsmoke cleared on May 11. Without J. C.'s irrigation diversion, partially destroyed by Irwin, 400 miner's inches were reaching the Irwin ranch, 100 more than Irwin claimed to be the entirety of the creek.[6] Louisa Irwin had made complaint against J. C. Tognoni not long after Taylor built the weir. Although the suit was withdrawn, her complaint and J. C.'s answer were read into the transcript of *Nevada vs. Tognoni.* J. C.'s answer accused Irwin thusly:

> [of] ... negligently and carelessly permitting the channel of ... Duckwater Creek (below the Tognoni ranch) ... to become so choked with moss, brushes, hay, manure and other debris and obstruction; that said channel could not at such times carry all the waters of said creek ... thereby causing said waters to overflow the banks of said channel and to overflow the adjoining lands and become lost and wasted.

John Collins testified that if the entire creek were allowed to flow, the average volume would be 800 inches per second in an ordinary irrigating season and up to a thousand in June after the spring thaw. Collins and Cross were experienced irrigators and attempted to explain for the court how much water was necessary to irrigate acreage in Duckwater; but as with the miner's inches of water which vary in factors used for measurement according to terrain, climate and custom, so with irrigating: "It takes more on some ground than on other ground; some takes double and another acre takes less." Indeed, because of the complexities of successful irrigation, those writing about Nevada in the 1880s discounted irrigation's future in the state:[7]

> Irrigation is slow and expensive; ditches must be constructed which, unless the land has the proper inclination, must meander according to the surface to give the water the proper motion. If too steep it sweeps away the soil; if too flat the water accumulates and saturates the ground, converting it into mortar that bakes and cracks in the sun. The water must be taken from the ditches in quantities nicely regulated to the nature and requirements of the soil, and constantly watched. Only the sandy soil will stand saturation without damages; even on that a little excess of water will wash the sand away and lay bare the roots of the plants.

Like the dips, spurs, angles and variations of a mineral deposit, the course of water would be difficult to confine, regulate and divide with law. After the gold rush, the rules and customs of miners had governed water rights upon the public domain as well as mineral rights. Out of these rules and customs had grown a doctrine of appropriation "born of the necessities of the country and its people."[8] But the laws were not new. Necessity had dictated law in the past, and Roman law writers had codified the basic principle—the "right of property in water . . . consists not so much of the fluid itself as the advantage of its use."[9] Protection afforded by law to the use of water and to mining defied eastern ideas of territory and private property. The nature of the property right given to water users and to miners could not be framed with lines on a map and still do justice to the movement and change of water and the gamble of mining. So when nature's variety reached the courts of law in the form of human dispute over rights to water or minerals, law could adhere only to a few simple principles and necessarily subjective language like "reasonable use" and "prudent man." Right to water would be protected only insofar as it was being put to reasonable use,[10] and with a mineral discovery, it could be allowed rights of property only insofar as a prudent man would spend time and money developing it into a mine.[11] In both water law and mineral law, the principle of "first come, first serve" lent the only objective justice.

Principles of equity in a land which is rich in minerals but thirsty for regular water supply required continually changing social contracts difficult to tailor out of the fabric of humanity. Loyalties and beliefs necessary to sanity do not change so quickly as the course of water and the width of a mineral vein. In California where transport of water to gold mining sites tapped seasonal sources of water with flumes, aqueducts and ditches of extraordinary ambition, ingenuity and resourcefulness, the laws which grew to govern these enterprises fostered daring. Under them the "father of reclamation" in California, William H. Parks, built the first levee to reclaim Sacramento River swamps.[12] This levee would be destroyed by a mob, which most likely was frightened by the orderliness of Parks' vision and provoked by those who stood to realize immediate profit from Parks' defeat. Parks believed deeply in man's ability to control the river as did other of the glorious men who dealt with the problems of gold mining in northern California. But the confrontation between those who mined and who directed the water and those who grew wealthy from the mines would reach no compromise on the mother lode, where much of the gold remains in the ground. As the land grew populous along California's watercourses, users other than miners began to demand rights which had, under English common law, attached to the ownership of land along a stream—riparian rights or the right to require that the water adjacent to one's land continue flowing for one's own use. The "California doctrine" of western water law attempts to combine both riparian and use rights. Other states, such as Nevada, subscribe to a "Colorado doctrine" which clings steadfastly to western mining law. But even with riparian rights, the problem of apportioning the water of a stream must draw upon principles of appropriation for its solution. With riparian rights, "the amount allocated by decree . . . is never permanent, but is subject to modification as the needs of the several riparians or the available supply of water changes."[13]

The first federal laws recognizing the miner's customs in the distribution of water were part of the 1866 and 1870 federal mining legislation. The 1866 law was entitled, "An Act granting the right of way to ditch and canal owners over the public lands, and for other purposes." In 1877, the Desert Land Act further clarified the federal government's policy for use of water on public lands:[14]

> "... the right to the use of waters ... shall depend upon bona fide prior appropriation not to exceed the amount of waters ... used for the purpose of irrigation and reclamation ... All surplus water over and above such actual appropriation and use, together with the water of all lakes, rivers, and other sources of water supply upon the public lands and not navigable, shall remain and be held free for the appropriation and use of the public for irrigation, mining and manufacturing purposes subject to existing rights."

After the passage of the Desert Land Act, patents issued for lands in a desert stage or territory carried with them no right to the water flowing through or bordering on them. This 1877 codification of irrigation law coincided with the first court battle in Duckwater, and in retrospect, the decision in that case would seem to be a court protest of deviation from riparian common law. Those who had begun to put the water in Duckwater Valley to greater use, even a flour mill, were defeated by those who wished to maintain the stream flowing past their land. Other courts, however, would help define the principles of western water law in their variance from riparian rights:[15]

> The rights of a riparian owner in and to the use of the water flowing by his land are not the same in the arid and mountainous states of the West that they are in the states of the East. These rights have been altered by many of the Western states by their constitutions and laws, because of the totally different circumstances in which their inhabitants are placed, from those that exist in the states of the East, and such alterations have been made for the very purpose of thereby contributing to the growth and prosperity of those states, arising from mining and the cultivation of an otherwise valueless soil, by means of irrigation.

Not until 1901 did Nevada seize the right to make state water law. In that year the Engineers Act affirmed state government's commitment to irrigation: "An act to provide for the measurement of streams, the survey of reservoir sites, the determination of the irrigation possibilities and of the best methods of controlling and utilizing the water resources of the state."[16]

As with the Desert Land Act of 1877, so with the Engineers Act, a battle of the water war at Duckwater ensued. In 1901, J. C. Tognoni took the law to heart and tested his rights under it against the established landholders on the creek. He had come to Duckwater as an immigrant ranch hand around 1880. He worked on the Mendes spread, on Strait's homestead and for Williams. J. C. also found work in Elko on the Humboldt River where the Central Pacific Railroad unloaded freight destined for the White Pine Mining District just east of Duckwater Valley. In Elko the state university may have had something to do with the quality of the English that my great-grandfather learned and the value he placed on books. In 1887, a divorced Myrtle Williams joined J. C. in Elko to be married. Together they returned to Duckwater in 1892. For a time J. C. worked cattle with his brother Louie to the north of the valley at Head Spring, also known as Big Louie Spring; and in 1895, Myrtle and J. C. purchased the homestead of J. F. Earl, a rancher in the lower valley who had run afoul of Isaac Irwin's widow. Earl lost a good portion of his ranch's water rights to her in a court battle, so that when J. C. purchased his first land at Duckwater, although the creek ran through it, he had rights to but fifty inches to irrigate his 160 acres. (A miner's inch of water to an acre is a general rule of irrigation sufficiency.) In the year that J. C. bought his land, "unknown persons" were stopped by Myrtle from tearing out J. C.'s first irrigation structure on the creek, according to testimony in *Nevada vs. Tognoni.*

After the introductory hostility, my great-grandparents would seem to have been ignored for five or six years; and in this peace they prospered. A drought in 1889-90 in the West had driven homesteaders out, leaving private property to be gotten for paying the taxes. This J. C. and Myrtle began to do in Duckwater, buying up deserted tracts in the upper valley. Then *Nevada vs. Tognoni* took my great-grandfather out of the valley to seek his fortune in Goldfield until 1905, when the state finally passed water law designed to loosen the power of riparian clenches on the waters of the state. Under the influence of the U.S. Reclamation Service, Nevada's first law for the appropriation of water provided: "Whatever may be the quantity claimed, the amount beneficially used, within the limit of a particular appropriation, is the amount which the law recognizes and all that a prior appropriator can hold."[17] The Act of 1905 provided for the appointment of water commissioners or water masters, and once again trouble flared at Duckwater.

When J. C. returned in 1905 to pursue dreams of irrigating, he met with obstinate and determined opposition. I showed J. C.'s photograph and biography from a Goldfield publication to Beatie Halstead, still living in Duckwater. She did not recognize "Ti-own-ee" as a successful mining man of Goldfield. She had her own version of how he came into the fortune with which he returned. Big Louie, a legendary figure in the history of white settlement at Duckwater, died in 1905. Big and blond, Louie did not have the dark features and slighter stature which many of his Italian compatriots enjoyed. His unfenced land holdings had been acquired under the old "three mile law" whereby a man could stake a spring of water as his own and lay claim for grazing purposes to three miles in every direction. The breadth of Louie's holdings and the grandeur of his personal presence lent themselves to general belief that he was a wealthy man. Mystery surrounding his death provided grist for fable, and Duckwater's crusading water warriors suspected J. C.'s wealth had been ill-gotten.

By 1906, J. C. and Myrtle had accumulated 960 acres of land north of Big Warm Spring, and J. C. submitted his application to the water commissioner to develop irrigation works from the spring. But the commissioner, receiving a protest from Louisa Irwin and being warned of past hostility in Duckwater, delayed processing either the application or the protest until he was removed from office. His successor quickly approved J. C.'s plan in September of 1908; but J. C. was compelled to settle in the courts. In a separate suit, Louisa Irwin took her neighbors and even her sons into legal proceedings to get a decree from the court regarding each appropriator's share of the water in Duckwater Creek. The court gave her every jot of guarantee that written language could provide.[18]

> ... adjudged and decreed to be quieted and confirmed in said plaintiff forever;—and ... defendants ... co-defendants ... each, every and all of them, ... are hereby strictly and absolutely restrained and enjoined perpetually from diverting, conducting, carrying away, or in any wise or manner interfering with or obstructing the waters or flow of Duckwater Creek ...

The word "use" continued to flaw Louisa Irwin's security. She had the right to *use* 7.15 cubic feet per second of time of the flow of Duckwater Creek until on June 13, 1910, the court of law serving Duckwater once again gave over to eastern common law which the western states were attempting to modify. Judge Averill found in *Tognoni vs. Louisa Irwin, et al.*, contrary to the state engineer's judgment, that Big Warm Spring was the primary source of Duckwater Creek, and he ordered:

> [T]hough there is unappropriated water in the supply upon Big Warm Spring Plateau, the appropriation thereof is hereby declared to be detrimental to the public welfare and to invade or impair the rights of other appropriators, unless works of control are constructed as hereinafter set forth ... plaintiff shall bear the expense of putting in all works of control necessary to secure to the users of water below him their appropriations as fixed by decrees of the court ... and to ascertain and ... to determine unappropriated water.

Thereafter, Judge Averill proceeded to specify, in effect, that J. C. should not only open the old Brown ditch but also the South ditch dug by the lower valley settlers in 1877 and later abandoned as soon as the upper valley settlers were defeated. What my great-grandfather did, I'm not certain. The waters on the plateau of Big Warm Springs are gone and the Brown Ditch is open today, but on July 6, 1914, Ralph Irwin "on behalf of Louisa Irwin" filed an affidavit that J. C. had diverted water upstream resulting in only five and one-half second feet flowing to the Irwin ranch. . . . J. C. was found in contempt of the 1910 court order and fined $250 or one day in jail for each two dollars of the fine. About this time, he began his prospecting at Silverton.

Uncle Sam had come and tried to distribute the water amongst the people of Duckwater, as my great-grandfather would have said it; but Uncle Sam needed men of courage like himself and courts with the vision to respond with necessary vigor to the challenge of irrigating Nevada. The heartbeat of humanity went unheeded at Duckwater and leaders tuned themselves to the "pulsations of pocket books" as William Jennings Bryan warned when the United States demonetized silver. Nevada, the "silver state," and men who worked on her land never recovered. Allen Lenbeck, however, still has his dreams for Duckwater Valley. He and two other men have formed a corporation to try transferring water for irrigation with vacuum trucks like the ones they have used when employed by the oil companies in Railroad Valley. Lenbeck's expression of discouragement in this endeavor due to lack of capital brings my father rising. In him, the spirit of his grandfather is strong. In Duckwater, he is like a ghost returned to shake up the dead. The very old think that he is Nye Tognoni just as two generations ago they made legend out of J. C. Tognoni's older brother, Louie. The old-timers puzzle over this new man who does not answer to the name "Ti-own-ee" but calls himself a son and talks of all that men can do to reclaim the land rather than sit liquidating the progress of their fathers while the wilderness once again overtakes them.

12   Red Rock Pass

These proceedings may at first seem strange and difficult,
but like all other steps which we have already passed over,
will in a little time become familiar and agreeable: and until
an independence is declared, the continent will feel itself
like a man who continues putting off some unpleasant
business from day to day, yet knows it must be done, hates
to set about it, wishes it over, and is continually haunted
with the thoughts of its necessity.
Common Sense, Thomas Paine, 1776

As we drive the short dirt lane from the Bank Ranch out to the main road through Duckwater Valley, I chide my father, telling him that he most likely has given Allen Lenbeck a false impression of wealth. But I talk as a cautious stranger in Duckwater Valley, and maybe underestimate the respect between the two Nevadans. Optimism like my father's may not be just the privilege of wealth in Nevada, but the spirit necessary to happiness where the earth is hard, dry, hostile and expectant of sacrifice. We argue only briefly as my father turns an eye inward to his memories of driving this road many times before. In this chapter, we will not go far. Behind us lines of force radiate widely, and ahead of us they converge at Red Rock Pass, where the calm, like the mid-space between poles of a magnet, produces the tense clarity of suspended animation. It is late afternoon and shadows are calling to the landscape as my father reminds me that this road cuts, not only through the mountains, but through himself. "There is a path which no fowl knoweth, and which the vulture's eye hath not seen."[1]

My father speaks to me of a twenty-mile walk which he took in the rain when his truck broke down and slid into the deep mud of the road's desolate shoulder. Another time, eight inches of snow and a load of wood did not stop him from commandeering his vehicle over Red Rock Pass to sail across Little Smoky Valley and beyond where the Fish Creek Range and Diamond Mountains harbored his home—Eureka. Wonder seems to move my father's

J. C. Tognoni on his Silverton claims, c. 1915. His success in Goldfield, Nevada, had made him a wealthy man. Site of his own grave and that of his son and his son's wife.

voice more than ever at the pass: "I remember my brother Nye driving our father's coffin up over this pitch in the rain and mud." From behind in a car with the rest of his family, my father watched his brother and the vicissitudes of the wooden casket. Silverton, where J. R. Tognoni would be buried after the humble, yet relentless, funeral procession, is 100 miles to the south at the other end of the Pancake Range of mountains. Normally, traveling dead moved in the opposite direction toward Eureka, where civilization's graveyards might preserve a person's memory; but my grandfather wished to be buried in the scene of his dreams, not his compromise. So his young family hazarded the grip of Red Rock Pass; and after the ease of the flats through Duckwater and Railroad Valley, the caravan climbed back into the mountains at Black Rock Summit and Silverton.

For Hale Tognoni, roads into the mountains along our path have meaning as neighborhood alleys might have in other boyhoods. While he steers the steady climb of our gravel road, he crooks his neck repeatedly at significant junctures. Below our road to the east, he tells of a shaft where those who saw a meteor come to Earth dug, but he does not speak of his desire to see this terrain of his father's words. According to J. R. Tognoni, the face of Moody Mountain was all torn up at the end of an arch of light which once mysteriously torched the night sky, another meteor. Etched into meteorites which have been recovered on this planet are celestial cuneiforms similar to those on Babylonian clay tablets. The scientists have given them a name and for the encyclopedias, they theorize that the markings are vestiges of a crystal organization in the iron-heavy rock. But, it is apparent that the Babylonians have been more positively translated than the stars, and like my father's first geological fossil, which came from these same hills, the meteorites are reminders of how little we understand.

My father is putting ethereal concerns aside when he continues, "This area has oil potential," and points out a drill road up over a hill to the east. Still the facts of commercial potential do not rob his voice of its gentleness and do not inspire it with dogmatic tones of practicality to which I am accustomed. I look to my map of the Pancake Range where "Coal Mine" and "Oil" confirm the organic layers of these mountains. As a geological engineer in Washington, D.C., Hale Tognini spent the summer of 1950 drilling into the sediments of this continent for Carnegie Institute's Department of Terrestrial Magnetism. His measurements aided in the study of changes in the direction and intensity of magnetic polarization in crustal materials of the Earth. Carnegie Institute maintains magnetometer stations all over the world and has sent a metal-free ship around the globe to take readings. The data has probably found use in isogonic maps for navigators to correct "true north." Ordinarily, Hale Tognoni might assure me that in some sanctified catacomb of abstracted science, the terrestrial magnestism measurements waste in their application to mining; but at Red Rock Pass on this afternoon, human persuasion seems to have found a silent niche.

After my father's summer of traveling for the Carnegie Institute, and after the nation's entry into the Korean War, he was back at work for the Corps of Engineers as a civilian. During World War II, as a member of the Corps, he supplied camps with water, power and sewage plants, and otherwise participated in employment of science in the Philippine Islands. With the Corps in 1950, he tested materials and equipment for roads and airfields; but he was soon to leave Washington, D.C., and a subsequent job searching land titles in Rockville, Maryland. Acceptance into law school in Idaho brought him home to the West where he would finish law studies begun at American University in the nation's capital.

Southwest of our progress is Big Louie Spring, the water supply around which the first Tognoni in Nevada, Antonio Luigi di Tognoni, according to legend, built his ranch. On a second journey through the Pancake Range, we will find Big Louie Spring. The cold wind on that expedition allowed no lingering to trace fully the clues to bygone human activity. So I tromped the dust and weeds to finger only briefly the metal and glass debris of the most recent stockmen. On that spring journey to Big Louie Spring, we traveled south along the edge of Big Sand Springs Valley, at the northern end of which are "Ruins" according to the U.S. Geological Survey map. From our path along the foothills, lines of human entry and retreat took off, straight and white, across the valley's grassy expanse. At Portuguese Spring, I walked into the Pancake Range toward Railroad Valley with my father. We were there to determine the boundaries which J. C. Tognoni, J. R. Tognoni and the Collinses intended for their Black Oil association mining claims of 1919 and to examine the discovery. At Portuguese Spring, black liquid seeped from the side of the hills, and two white, equine skulls, splashed and stained with dark mud, stared from the spring's black sumps.

Overlooking the scene was the red face of a hill which Frank Collins had told me was near the "rocks which would burn." My father and I oriented ourselves to the red prominence until, as we passed over the pinon mane of the ridge, the red mountain sunk into Big Sand Springs Valley behind. Following the mustang tracks, we descended on the soft, black soil into a sanctuary for Indian tea and cactus. A black, shale reef distinguished our lower path and probably attracted recent prospectors who staked this cul-de-sac with four-by-four posts and rock piles into which they slipped mining claim location notices as required by law. We read the names, but we saw no one.

In 1920, one year after J. C. Tognoni and his associates located the Black Oil claims, oil was removed by Congress from the workings of the mining laws. Government agencies would lease the right to remove the oil but would keep the land, contrary to earlier mining law which disposed of the land as incentive to beneficial mineral development. That was before government grew possessive of the land and resources in Nevada and the western states; before human population commensurately dwindled; and before accusations became thick as the weeds over old homesteads: "They cut down all the pine-nut trees. They fraudulently represented the mineral potential. They overgrazed the wild grasses." Ironically, it was not the divisiveness of these complaints which left the people fractured and powerless against federal custody and economic policies. It was the westerners' failure to face controversial issues for fear of splitting the supporting groups in projects for which they wooed federal funding. A period of drift began which is well characterized by the conceits of the reclamation law of 1902. That law provided for the advancement of loans at no interest for the construction of irrigation facilities, but it made vague provisions for the prevention of the inevitable land speculation accompanying federally financed water and power projects. The law required that land benefitting from the water projects be in parcels no greater in area than 160 acres, the acreage allotment under the general homesteading laws.

Two-thirds of the land which reclamation projects would eventually provide with water were private lands, but one of the first questions before the Reclamation Service was whether private lands should be allowed the benefits of the reclamation act. On that point, the homesteading acreage limitation caused confusion. Not until 1926 would another act attempt to practicate prevention of speculative profit. The Omnibus Adjustment Act furnished the secretary of the interior with the power to fix the sale price of private land in excess of 160 acres without consideration for proposed water works.[2]

Still the existence of private lands and private utility companies remained incompatible with public water works until President Franklin Roosevelt pushed the projects through to provide employment. In the Central Valley of California, for instance, a Granger association resisted a Corps of Engineers dam because it feared the Corps would turn the dam over to the Kings River Water Users Association rather than retain government administration. According to the Grangers, the users association would sell the power to Pacific Gas and Electric Company, and an indirect government subsidy allowing the Grangers to pump water from the lower watershed would be lost.

Pacific Gas and Electric had been born of the gold rush. Mining gave self-sufficient economic function to a wide range of aqueducts, ditches and dams which served the ore bodies. Agricultural uses for the land increased to serve the mining, but the sense of the whole, the need of the second for the first, is not a part of our recent intelligence. Soil can be enriched for agriculture, but our ore bodies are our inheritance from the earth. Without the mines, the state and the farmers could not afford to pay even the interest rates of the Reconstruction Finance Corporation for loans to build water projects.[3] Yet, the farmers fought with the miners, even destroying the private attempts to direct the water beneficially for all concerned.

Like the southern United States, the western states had problems peculiar to their region and land. To live on that land, social systems grew up out of necessities, not dogma. People, not laws, made homes and marshalled the water. The laws which they used were never better than the people who used them, and where they conflicted with natural law and God's law, they were, in time, altered. But history has been written by the reformers whose interpretation of man's disinheritance of the earth would have us believe that the men who depended on the land for their sustenance, like my father and his father before him in Nevada, and like Irwin and Mendes and Locke for that matter, were slow to appreciate nature and quick to ravage her. These same historians ignore national enchantment with the economic relaxation provided by the nation's first military thrusts abroad at the turn of the century. While our nation transferred its capital investments from the western states to foreign locations of cheap labor, it divested the law of any motivation to make our land productive and robbed the courts of the duty to equitably and efficiently settle disputes between men. The simpler path of allowing man's strife to be dissipated by federal patronage found every rationalization, and war distorted economic realities with its inherent disregard for cost. Desertion of the American landscape became a form of genocide in our permanent war economy. Men who would live from the land have died off, and we romanticize the shrill threat of the coyote and the outlaw who have preyed on domestication in the valleys and mountains of the West for centuries.

Chief among the people who have been weakened by federal patronage have been those of Indian descent. In 1887, the federal government reversed the Indian Non-intercourse Act of 1790. The 1887 legislation attempted to allow Indian persons freedoms which would open the way to their entry into the American economy. It began the distribution of communal tribal property to individual tribal members and allowed that individual Indians could participate in commerce.[4] In Duckwater and at Goldfield and Silverton, J. C. Tognoni and his son J. R. had a good number of Indian partners and friends under this new scheme. Harry Stimler out of the mountains near Goldfield was the son of an Indian woman and was J. C.'s partner at Silverton. The Collinses, also of an Indian mother, participated with the Tognonis in both ranching and prospecting. But, in 1934, when the ranchers and silver miners of Nevada and the west were losing their shirts collectively, Congress passed the Indian Reorganization Act, granting to the American Indian special privileges if he would again don the garb of his tribal forefathers.

In Duckwater, a 3,785 acre Indian reservation would be created, but those of Indian descent like the Collinses, who had land of their own, would be swept away along with the white ranchers. I suspect that the Collins ranch was lost to the bank, which in turn lost the land to the federal government, as happened to the Tognoni ranch. Those who passed the Reorganization Act naively thought of themselves as preservers of cultural heritage, but their cause, like most successful causes, served larger economic convenience. During the Great Depression, the Nevada banks of George Wingfield were thrown into receivership. Wingfield's assets were tied up in sheep and probably silver and gold properties.[5] Drought was killing sheep, and the U.S. Treasury was killing gold and silver. The drought ended and the Reconstruction Finance Corporation did not lose a dime on its loans to the sheep ranchers.[6] Wingfield, however, lost his banks. The head of the Reconstruction Finance Corporation, which administered the liquidation of the Nevada banks, admitted that one man's guess was as good as another's in assessing the probable worth of many a bank's investments. He freely admitted that a great many unsound banks were allowed to resume business.[7] Wingfield's politics must have been weak. His Bank Ranch became part of the Duckwater Indian Reservation.

Resentment, distrust, guilt and inertia accompanied the increasing number of reservations in the western states. By asserting unique Indian rights against non-Indian interests or the rest of the society into which people like the Collinses had integrated, the Indian agencies were synchronized with reclamation patronage and federal administration of public land in general. Maybe we can find an element of humor in this grand orchestration when we see that it all came together despite the good intentions of congressmen. The Indian Reorganization Act, according to Senator Wheeler of Montana, would inhibit bureaucratic controls in Indian government.[8] The Taylor Grazing Act of the same year, 1934, was to provide for the "highest use of the public land pending . . . final disposal."[9] The powers of the Bureau of Indian Affairs have not waned under the Indian Reorganization Act, and features of the Taylor Grazing Act have helped halt final disposal of public lands due to the growth of land agency prerogatives.

The loss of liberty which accompanied the loss of land in the western states was not academic. In Nevada it struck at the heart of the people. I am reminded of a story which Beatie Halstead told me of a man who spent his life in Duckwater. She pondered the picture in her mind silently, promising lucidity. According to Beatie, the man had been content with the small salary, room and board which the Halstead ranch afforded him. On the day when Beatie announced having applied for a social security number for him, he made only a perfunctory protest before walking to the barn where he was later found hanging beneath the coils of a noose.

The climb to Red Rock Pass is sadly familiar in the long shadows of afternoon: "Forgive us our trespasses as we forgive those who trespass against us." Hale Tognoni pulls my thoughts back from the deceptively warm color of the hills which close in on our path. "My father had a wood camp set up right back over the hill from here. He was chopping firewood and hauling it into Eureka. These old scrub cedars make good wood . . . We had a Dutch oven full of beans and salt pork that we kept warm or cooking all the time . . . Sometimes we had beef that we would get from ranchers . . . My father would hang the quarters on a tree. It would freeze and we would shave off the pieces of meat to eat."

The debt and sacrifice for federal supervision has become clear in recent times, and slowly the government is beginning to give back to the people the responsibility for their own productivity. Unfortunately it gives back the means—the land and its resources—even more slowly. In Duckwater Valley behind us, J. C. Tognoni fought corruption, and waste in the distribution of water. His faith in the ideals of democracy never slacked and he left behind a legacy for his grandson, Hale Tognoni. Through his own son, J. R., J. C. passed a belief in the benevolence of nature toward those who keep faith with the law of the land. As my father speaks, I feel the road becoming more familiar and agreeable, straight as an arrow across Little Smoky Valley into Eureka County. "Frank McBride built this road without the use of surveyors or engineers," my father tells me. I see this road when I dream of the way through the valley to a path beyond the broken promises of our past.

Eureka, Nevada (looking west)

13   Mountain Link to the Past

*"Eureka is not a ghost town . . . No attempt has been made
to change Eureka. Eureka is absolutely authentic as it
stands. To change this town would be to destroy a very
rare and wonderful piece of Nevada's heritage. We
would like to keep Eureka just as is is . . ."*
Historical Society, Eureka County, Nevada

Pavement meets gravel like past confronting present in Little Smoky
Valley, which we traverse on our way to Eureka. At Red Rock Pass, we
crossed out of Nye County into a western corner of White Pine and now,
where the asphalt cuts a dusty seam across our path, we enter Eureka
County. Presently, Eureka's ties are to the north and to the gold mining near
Carlin which has recreated a well funded county seat in the town of Eureka.
Remote human settlements in these basins and ranges of central Nevada,
like Duckwater, once relied upon Eureka as the closest rail connection.
Now, Ely near the major copper mine in White Pine County serves Duckwater's ranchers. As for Eureka's future, it awaits the completion of a prolonged penance in a twilight zone unresponsive to human generation. The
night and dawning for Eureka seem to be captives of geologic time.

In Little Smoky Valley and its northeastern extension, Newark Valley,
ranches show themselves as green interruptions widely spaced along the
meeting place of valley and mountain. Electrical power has made the
pumping of water possible for ranching nearer to the byways and liberated
the sparse population from the natural springs in the mountains; but, the irrigation systems envisioned in 1909 are still a dream: "The valleys are mostly
arid, but where irrigation is applied the soil will produce an average of forty
bushels of wheat to the acre, and sixty bushels to the acre have been har-
vested in the richer soil."[1] In 1880, the Eureka-Palisade Railroad deposited
Guiseppi Cristofo di Tognoni in this country. He and others under the

sponsorship of Italian padrones came from the foothills of one of the world's great mountain ranges—the Alps. They came with the hope of owning a piece of this new, uncultivated land, and they brought with them not only experience valuable to the mines but a land ethic which had transformed dry and deforested foothills of Lombardy into gardens with a "system of irrigation that has been nowhere excelled and rarely approached in the degree of perfection":[2]

> ...men have drawn the subsoil waters to the surface and taken the streams that flow down from the Alps, especially the waters that come from the reservoir lakes of Lombardy, and the diverting them into an amazing network of canals adjusted finely to slopes and grade, have spread their blessing over the land. The Cistercian monks it was, of the Chiaravalle abbey, that seven centuries ago began this work, which succeeding generations have developed. Diversity and abundance of crops are a consequence; hay yields several cuttings a year, and dairying thrives—'Whoever has meadowland has everything,' says the proverb.

Another proverb from the same land warns, "Chi ha terra ha guerra"—who owns land must fight.[3] Behind us in Duckwater Valley, Guiseppi, to become Joe or J. C., would learn the truth of the old proverbs in the new land.

Once across Little Smoky Valley, we skirt the Fish Creek Range and the lips of Secret Canyon to Chalk Pitch at the top of which Highway 50 crosses Nevada's mid-section and will take us north to Pinto Summit. "Used to be we would have to grind up on our lower gears. To get over the top of Pinto Summit was a real sweat." At a curve in the summit road, a set of trees glimmer in silhouette against the dusk and mark the site of a ranch house where a woman whom my father remembers, Mrs. Schaefer, worked the land with her two sons. No more. At the ranches behind us, Hale Tognoni once knew people. Now he knows electrical power and corporations. His father, with a hydrometer and knowledge of specific gravities, was one of the forerunners of advanced technology among the people in this country-side. He tested the whiskey of bootleggers. He, J. R., would haul discarded corn mash back to his family's pigs. The porkers would fatten in a bacchanal rite of stagger while beneath their unsteady feet one of the great mining districts of the American West languished.

Between the ancient lake beds of Lahontan on the west and Bonneville Basin on the east, rises a "rough mountain block standing out prominently by itself ... almost as completely isolated from its neighbors as the longer parallel ranges," wrote geologist Arnold Hague in a monograph about Eureka mining district for the United States Geological Survey in 1892.[4] My father's copy was a gift from Sam and Harry Morris, two miners in Secret Canyon who applauded his decision to return to Mackay School of Mines after World War II. In the days when theories of mineral deposition were young and controversial, Hague and a number of his illustrious colleagues explored the shafts and tunnels of the Eureka mines like vivisectionists of the earth's body. Frequently these geological studies were sponsored by legal disputes as to the ownership of a lode deposit once it led the miners underground beyond the surface boundaries of the mining claims. In the famous court battle between Eureka Consolidated Mining Company and Richmond Mining Company in 1877, the geologists even created glass models of the ore deposits for the court's edification. Circuit Court Judge Stephen Field, to become the first Supreme Court justice from the far western states, wrote of being charmed by the decorum of the dispute between the scientists. His decision is still cited for its strong differentiation between the language of science and of law:[5]

> [The mining laws] were not drawn by geologists or for geologists; they were not framed in the interests of science, and consequently with scientific accuracy in the use of terms. They were framed for the protection of miners in the claims which they had located and developed, and should receive such construction as will carry out this purpose.

Ultimately the dispute was settled by a compromise which overcame the limitations of both science and law.

Around the great ore body of Eureka District an industrial society was growing. Sixteen smelters and a railroad connection with the Central Pacific gained for the mining camp the title "Pittsburg of the West." Its 6,000 inhabitants in 1882 and over 2,000 in the community of Ruby Hill, only two miles distant, composed a social structure as highly differentiated and resilient in character as the displaced blocks from neighboring ranges which formed the Eureka Mountains. Approximately 75 percent of all adults in Eureka in 1880 were foreign immigrants. There were the German metallurgists and miners, the Welsh smelter and furnace builders, the Slavic miners, the French service personnel, and the Italian charcoal burners.[6] In the people and in the geology, time had concentrated nature's elements in disturbances and weaknesses of the substance. All around Eureka, volcanics intrude, fall and flow over paleozoic sediments. The granite which forms the deepest foundation of this earthern surge has been exposed only on the north end of Prospect Mountain, the highest peak. Approximately ten thousand feet high, Prospect Mountain is visible to us on the west side of our road northward. Alternating beds of shale and limestone warped within the mountain to grind and crush its elements. Those rocks which stood the pressure and retained original character, although displaced and flattened, were flexible like the shale. Others, more crystalline in structure, have metamorphosed into geologic specimens peculiar to Eureka, as in the Phoenix Mine where a mysterious black rock contains large quantities of magnetite and fool's gold.

When the pressure which built and altered the rock within these mountains broke a path to the surface, it could do so with such force as to blow the magma violently into the air where it burned to ash and settled on these mountains to flow like mud, lubricated not by water but by hot air. Beneath the volcanics and in immediate proximity to where ore would be deposited, trapped magma cooled in more recent centuries to a rhyolite record of fissures and faults. Intrusions at Ruby Hill and Prospect Mountain frequently followed the course of least resistance or the contact between types of rock. Sometimes left behind in the rock is a flow chart. Fluctuation in pressure moved rock particles back and forth within intruding liquid rock. The moving particles broke more pieces of wall rock into the magma and oriented the long fragments in the direction of the flow.

Consequent to rhyolite intrusions, the ore body came into being, largely through solfataric action. For the U.S. Geological Survey at Steamboat Springs in 1948, my father studied and measured this process of circulating Earth's nutrients to its skin. Changes of sulphides to oxides from the decomposition within rhyolite contributed necessary elements and functions to the earth blood. A secondary type of deposition is in the limestone. Solvent action of downward trending water carried the carbonic acid of decomposed limestone through fissures enlarging them to crevasses and caverns. Where a casing of clay confined the metal-bearing solutions to crushed and shattered limestone, mineral was left behind in depressions like those at the Ruby Hill.[7]

The crags and cliffs on the surface of this great organism of geology into which my father and I drive first attracted prospectors in 1864. They discovered an outcrop of mineral ore and, to test it, threw pieces into their campfire where a flow of metal surprised them. "They could not believe it was silver, and it was too hard for lead. However, it was metal, and they exclaimed, 'Eureka,' locating their claims and organizing a district under that name."[8] The ore, however, was not to be separated into its lead, gold and silver components without careful study. The hasty furnaces of New York capitalists were, therefore, abandoned until 1869 when, in the aftermath of the Nevada gold rush to White Pine County, prospectors retreated to the bountiful ores of Eureka and to methods of smelting in the Old Testament. The Egyptians of the New Kingdom had learned to separate gold from silver by melting their compound, electrum, in a crucible at high heat with salt and lead. The salt reacted with the silver and lead to form chlorides which could be skimmed off and re-smelted for their metallic content.[9] In the beginning, most of Eureka's ore went to England for smelting, and much of the district's mining development was financed with English capital.[10] Smelting with new draft furnaces was soon so successful that the only limitation seemed to be the size of the operation. By the end of 1882, half the dollar value of the ore which has been removed from the Eureka Mountains was achieved. One-third of it was gold and 225,000 tons was lead.[11] Even so, in 1884, Joseph Story Curtis reported for the geological survey that, with the exception of some few mines, "the properties of Prospect Mountain have been slightly developed . . . and in the upper levels of the Richmond mine important ore bodies may be discovered by careful prospecting."[12] The *Eureka County Resuscitant* later claimed that progress in methods of reducing ores would work effectively in Eureka District if the "normal values" of metal were restored, but that shafts could be sunk no deeper until settlement of the question of bimetallism.

The British interests in Eureka were most likely coining the silver for trade with the silver-standard colony of India. In the United States, silver coins were being hoarded or melted down for export. They were not in circulation. The California mother lode and her children throughout the American West and Australia had increased gold by a quantity equal to all of that which had been mined previously by man. Phenomenal quantities of gold flooded the mints and the markets. Gold was the metal in circulation. By Gresham's Law, "bad money" had driven out the "good," or that money of greater scarcity and rising price left circulation. In reality there was, of course, much more involved than a dictum of economic science. During the American Civil War, which came on the heels of the gold rush, specie payment was suspended to allow floating of the greenbacks which financed the war. Simultaneously, discoveries of silver on the Comstock were augmenting the silver supply. Still, this new silver was not enough to drive the metal back into circulation. Even war's inflation had not affected the price of silver. Here it may be of importance that the British favored the Confederacy. When specie payment resumed in the United States in 1879, silver was still being mined in abundance. It was bringing $1.152 per ounce in 1878.

The United States' use abroad of a heavy "trade dollar" for a few years; the issuance of silver certificates; the expanding need for small change or fractional coinage kept silver's price high enough, but by 1890 prices had reached a peak. During the natural fall in silver price, acts by the government and by banking concerns brought about the decline of silver value and retarded a respondent price climb by gold. Both silver and gold would eventually be replaced by an ever-growing quantity of debt notes or paper money, and Eureka's brilliant future flickered out.

"If things be let alone till silver money be a little scarcer, the gold will fall of itself," wrote Sir Isaac Newton in 1717. As Master of the Mint in

England, Newton was responding to the edict which forbade persons to give or receive gold "guinea" coins at a higher price than twenty-one silver shillings. Contrary to the thinking of Newton, the king had issued an edict attempting to defeat Gresham's Law by keeping the guinea in circulation instead of allowing the change in tide to silver in England. Trading by the English East India Company had caused an outpouring of silver to India and an influx of gold into England. Over four million pounds of gold was minted between 1713 and 1717.[13] If silver were allowed to buy off this abundant gold, the British would have lost their trade advantage in dealings with India and elsewhere in the East. The silver could have favorably represented the labor of the Indian people in world market value.

So Britain began to control rather than adjust to the waves of commerce. Previously the government had conformed the weight of coins to market value with periodic flexibility. In recorded English history the biggest single change in coin weights came under Edward IV in 1464. English gold was flowing to foreign mints where higher prices prevailed, so Edward IV increased by 25 percent the quantity of coin created from a pound weight of metal. He would be criticized for the large amount of metal which he kept as his cost. In 1560, Elizabeth I conducted the "Great Recoinage" made possible by an influx of silver from the Americas. She stabilized silver prices for 135 years and began a "new era of accountability in English monetary affairs." Crown and private holdings in the American treasury were 98 percent silver after 1560. The industrial revolution to follow would bring fatal threats to man's ability to adjust his legal tender to changing realities.

By the 1690s, philosopher John Locke had sanctified the British Treasury's mint weights rendering the government powerless to adjust them. Man began to manage monetary supply with diminishing regard to cost or the time intervals of functioning bimetallism. The banker's tinkering with interest rates would replace the metal link between money supply and the labor required to claim natural resources. By 1816, devaluation of British currency after the Napoleonic Wars took the form of a gold standard act. In other words, the British government would no longer freely coin gold and silver. It would attempt to set the price of gold by taking all gold and only some silver. The nations of the European continent eventually followed suit, and the treasuries began to dump their silver on the market in the 1870s. Consequently, gold became the scarcer good money of Gresham's Law, and the U.S. government stopped freely buying the "bad," silver.

When the United States deserted bimetallism, it abandoned the nation's investment in the rich mining country of the West. A brief revival of mining in Eureka followed the First World War during a time when investors were happy to surrender rights of ownership and all voice in the nation's enterprises so long as dividends came regularly.[14] By 1931, silver, Shakespeare's "pale and common drudge 'tween man and man," was at the lowest price since the second half of the thirteenth century. President Franklin Roosevelt made an ill-advised attempt to raise the price of silver, but in the 1930s, neither gold nor silver controlled money supply in the United States. China, the one remaining silver standard country, would make the leap to paper without even toying with a gold standard.

The desertion of metal standards unleashed national governments to borrow and lend with little or no regard to the productivity or natural resources of separate peoples and lands. Gone was the discipline of indestructible legal tender which metal had come to represent for the people of the trading world for centuries—electrum, gold, silver, copper, bronze and brass. Left behind in the U.S. Constitution are bimetallism's vestiges: "No State shall . . . make anything but gold and silver coin a tender in payment of debts; . . . Congress shall have power . . . to coin money, regulate the value thereof and of foreign coin, and fix the standard of weights and measures."[15] Eureka's real history abides in tideous volumes of economics where it becomes apparent that Eureka has changed despite the assurances of the historical society. The black and white over Pinto Summit trade dominance without warning. Eureka is vitality surrounded by a ghost town. Blink and Eureka is a live town with a ghost's heart. "Welcome! Rock and Bottle Hunters Paradise, Eureka, Nevada" reads the sign beside our road.

With their dogs, Hale Tognoni and brothers pulled garbage collecting wagon in Eureka, Nevada, c. 1929.

Much of the wood cut and hauled in wagons like these was burned in large stone kilns to make charcoal for smelters like those in Eureka, Nevada.

14   Miner's Destiny

*They speak of events of a year ago as of events that
scarcely anyone can remember as if a current of
oblivion had swept over them. Finally, they speak
of things that occurred five, six, ten years previously
as of things so remote that memory no longer
suffices to keep their record, as if not one but
ten generations had supervened upon them.*
Robert F. Foerster

In Eureka we find a motel where we have reservations. It is not the
place my father had intended for us to stay, but I willfully convince him not
to take the time to make new arrangements. We change for dinner and, in
the dusk, drive up past my father's boyhood home to the cemetery of the
Benevolent and Protective Order of the Elks. In modern mining towns, the
Elks are common, but they were not among the early groups here. In the
hills above Eureka, to the west, the Catholics, Masons, Odd Fellows and
Pythians, Chinese, a mortician named Schwamb, and the City of Eureka
fenced their separate territories for the dead. The Jews removed their own
to an isolated position south of Eureka.

Eurekans looked after their dead, their knowledge, their property and
their prejudices with a variety of secret societies and chivalric brotherhoods
phenomenal to the size of the community and inspired by dark memories of
the Civil War, which many of Eureka's early prospectors had survived.
Beneath Eureka in the white, volcanic froth called "tufa," they dug passage-
ways in which they secreted themselves like veins of mineral ore. The
Masons built their meeting place underground, and masonic officer Reinhold Sadler, who became Nevada's governor in 1898, connected his home in
Eureka to his place of business by tunnel. The Silver Party, sister to the
Populist party in national politics at the turn of the century, would begin in
Eureka in the mold of a fraternal order—the Silver Club.[1]

We enter a grove of marble headstones and cedar trees, and in the twilight my father pauses before the graves of the departed whom he knew as a boy. Tomorrow morning on the unshaded hill of the Catholic cemetery, we will find the grave of Big Louie Tognoni. He is surrounded by at least a dozen compatriots from the town of Tognoni and by the members of their families. Italians are as thick as the dust here, but J. R. Tognoni's family is not among them, with the exception of Johnny Mendez, his daughter Neva's husband of Spanish descent. J. R. drifted from the Catholic Church to which his unhappy sister Elva clung. His children would become hard-driven people who adopted work as a sacrament at a time when Christians were as intersected as the crossroads to Eureka's cemeteries where the self-guiding tour warns: "Rattlesnakes have been seen in these areas so caution is advised."

Tomorrow I will take my father's photograph beside the marble monument into which Big Louie's name and origin were carved in 1905. "Weep not. He is at rest." My father heard stories as a boy about how Louie had helped many of the Italian immigrants in Eureka. In fact, Louie may have been responsible for a large number of the people planted here with him. The world reputation of Eureka's mines and their promise of afford-able land lured Louie to this countryside. The Italians were part of a great immigration to America which was accompanied by flourishing times for mining in the United States, just as centuries ago in Germany, mining pros-pered in a period of major movements of people.[2] Even so, in the Western United States Italian immigrants would be comparatively few. Most Italians from Italy's northern mining provinces went to South America where mining had a history commensurate with the mining skills and traditions which Italians had developed in the Alpine foothills of their mother country.

Louie was from a northern region near Lake Como, Italy, where communes had trades and whoever took up that trade with an intention to emigrate had the support of those who had preceded him and become es-tablished abroad.[3] The traditional padrone would guide the newcomer in his first ventures; but this system was to be corrupted to allow a few to grow excessively wealthy at the expense of their countrymen. Because Louie left public life in Eureka to live in seclusion on his ranch in the hills north of Duckwater, he may have rejected the profiteering which contributed to the Italian War of 1897 in Eureka. By the late 1870s the production of charcoal, originally a task which the Chinese laborers accepted, had been seized by organizations of Italians. In 1876, the *Eureka Daily Sentinel* claimed that Italians constituted 75 percent of the migrants coming into Eureka; but their usual ten dollars per week income was less than one-half that paid to common mine workers.[4] Nonetheless, the tenacious Italians prospered, unlike the Chinese who had been among the earliest miners in Eureka County and who had once been present as the majority of the 500-man labor force which completed the Eureka-Palisade railroad in 1895.[5]

Like those Chinese railroad crews who struck for higher wages until thirst broke their resolve in Diamond Valley, the Italian laborers too would forego the comforts of contentment to organize for their rightful share of profits. By so doing they were demanding a realistic assessment of the whole cost of sustaining the phenomenal production of mineral from Eureka. By 1878, the furnaces of Eureka were consuming in excess of 16,000 bushels of charcoal per day, and for thirty-five to fifty miles around Eureka the pinon, dwarf cedar and mountain mahogany had been cut to leave bare hills. The venerable logs in the cabin of G. T. Tannehill, prospector and first mining claim recorder of Eureka Mining District, may be of a bygone size but the forest around Eureka has returned. On this summer evening in 1981, sheep and deer are grazing amongst the trees near the highway.

In 1879, the major smelters which were consuming the forest reduced the price of charcoal from thirty to twenty-seven cents per bushel.[6] Charcoal contractors attempted to pass this cut in price down to the already underpaid woodcutters and burners. Finally, the complacent Italian laborer laid down his tools. No longer would he respond to his meagre portion of the wealth with "we are ignorant and do not know English. Our boss brought us here, knows where to find work, makes contracts with the companies. What should we do without him?"[7] In Europe in the preceding century, the charcoal burners' guild had developed into a secret revolutionary society which caught the imagination of the Italian people who associated ideas of independence, unity and liberty with Carbonarism. It is likely that the charcoal burners of Eureka District felt themselves to be in the old Carbonari tradition.[8]

The Eureka Charcoal Burners Protective Association would find their strongest opposition not in the large smelting companies nor in the government but in the charcoal contractors and wagon drivers. Violence ensued in August of 1879:[9]

> A posse of nine men, headed by Deputy Sheriff J. B. Simpson, attacked a coal ranch at Fish Creek, about thirty miles from Eureka and opened fire on about a hundred coal burners. Five of the latter were killed, six were badly wounded, and several were made prisoners. None of the Sheriff's posse were injured, although it is claimed that the coal burners were well armed, and fired the first shot.

The Italian minister in Washington asked for an investigation, and the Italian consul and vice consul from San Francisco inspected the final scene of the

Italian war. The matter died, and never again would the burners overtly challenge Eureka's economic forces. The demise of silver mining had already begun, leaving unanswered many of the questions of cost which the burners were raising.

Physical calamity in the long, narrow canyon of Eureka matched the cultural strife between the human settlers. The course of events took on literal aspects of a melting pot. Hot streams of molten ore were constantly running from Eureka's fiery furnaces and a heavy black cloud of smoke hung over the town or the "Big Ditch," as locals pronounced it. Eureka's chief fame at the nation's centennial celebration in 1876 was its advancements and experiments with furnaces. In fact, Eureka existed because a persevering group of mining men successfully reduced argentiferous lead ores for the first time in American history. This achievement, however, unleashed some of the major problems of industrialization in this little pocket of humanity in the great American Desert.

Mining men assaulted the industrial problems in Eureka much as they had done with the stubborn lead ore. They laid pipe up the side of the hills to deliver the smoke high in the air where it would be blown away from town. The problem of fire among Eureka's wood buildings was solved after three disastrous conflagrations by quarrying the volcanic tufa on which the town rested and constructing stone buildings. Heavy iron doors hang on the windows of the historic edifices. They were used to contain fire, protect interiors and fend off other damage to valuable window glass. Eureka fought fire with fire. Volcanic fire had toughened the "fire-proof" building blocks. Fire forged the iron window shutters and melted the bronze for casting the bells which sounded Eureka's fire alarms. When increased quantities of silver went into the alloy of a bell, as at the Presbyterian Church, the bell would sweetly beckon as opposed to the shrill outcry of the feathered Phoenix which preyed upon Eureka.

The slag dumps and sites of old mills with their glazed brick and shaped scoria—remnants of the Eureka melting pot—were my father's playground. He has not learned to see them with foreign conception so that they remain beautiful in his sight. Other of his schoolmates in Eureka have not been so fortunate. One very successful Eurekan recently spoke to my father with contempt for the slag dumps of their home town. In the same worldly breath, he slandered a Nevada oasis as careless mine waste and destruction. Despite this man's haughty position, he no longer possesses the God-given power to wonder like a child at the irregular swellings across otherwise slick, slag rock nor at the long, low mesas of tailings so uniformly eroded in mining towns.

Hale Tognoni has worked all his life surrounded by volcanic terrain, nature's self-desolution. The very uplift of the Great Basin, no feat of man, left behind barren alkali flats. But when, in the nineteenth century, man briefly knew this land with the power of God and western science, he made the lonely desert his garden. The salt of the valleys was collected, purified and sold.[10] Williams Salt Marsh northwest of Eureka wastes today, but elsewhere there are signs that man will again reap the bounty of the Earth. Coal strip miners on the Navajo Indian Reservation at Black Mesa are shaping acres of mine spoil into a catchment basin that channels meagre rainfall into a series of ponds where solar-power pumps the water to orchards and gardens;[11] and in Pennsylvania, man-made mountains of black residue from the processing of anthracite are being burned to produce heat and energy. The remaining ash may become road metal and building blocks similar to the volcanic cinders of the western United States.[12]

In Eureka, much of what man learned about the land is beneath the surface. Tunnels fed men into the earth and ore out. In 1883, Eureka tunnel measured 2,008 feet in length, and through Prospect Mountain a tunnel cut for a distance of 2,350 feet.[13] In these subterranean pathways and in the adits of the mines, all of man's art and science was holding against the elements in constant change within the earth. In Eureka a geologic fault divides the countryside, displacing the sediments like Leonardo Da Vinci or Einstein intruding upon the static and dogmatic to express the effects of change, movement and time. Eureka's major fault raised the southwestern section of the terrain 500 feet and in some places 2,000. It extends from Ruby Hill through a southern line of mines, and very early it became the focus of geological maps.

In one Eureka mine an iron door would be set into soft Dunderberg shale near the intersection of the Locan shaft with Eureka's great fault. The door was intended to hold back the water which would rise along the fault to flood the mine. A crew of miners was ordered to mine beyond the door into the fault. When their drill hit the water, the pressure shot the drill back into its operator and sent him and the rest of the men running. They slammed the door behind them, but the water only hesitated before flattening the heavy obstruction beneath its flood. As the men were elevated out of the mine, rising water licked their boots. The Locan shaft would be abandoned to water at the 2,000 foot level although the Cornish pumps which served the shaft had allowed miners to go down 470 fathoms or 2,820 feet in Cornwall.[14] Today the world's deepest mine in South Africa reaches into the earth 12,200 feet or more than two miles.

At the 800 foot level of the Locan shaft in the 1940s, Hale Tognoni would participate in building the pump station for the Fad shaft, which would go down 2,200 feet. Hale worked behind a three-man crew of miners whom he would observe in off-hours at a saloon in Eureka. During day shifts, Asher, Dasher and Baby Face would break drill and blast the new ground. A mucking crew would follow to haul away the ore, and at midnight, Hale would come in with the timber crew to set steel supports for the back or roof. Frequently, the lead miner, Asher, would burn up ground at a rate that won bonuses for every member of the operation. So my father's curiosity was laced with gratitude at the saloon where he watched Asher, his partners and their women engaging in their domestic affairs. Asher was the personification of mining gospel—"Put the rock in the box." With the entirety of his demeanor, he cut short any philosophic speculation in favor of physical reprisal in which he and his partners habitually engaged. The women, Butte Babe and her brick-like, Paiute Indian girlfriend, participated equally with the men in the scuffles and bestowed their favors in counterstroke. What might have been labeled promiscuity in the light of day had a kind of honor in the dark habitats where they met in a proud disclaimer of superficiality. The Babe had earned her name underground in Butte, Montana. In the 1940s women were forbidden underground, so the Babe entered the mine disguised as a man.

However much my father might have admired Asher, the lead miner's destiny was apart, and my father's vision was not to be confined to dark tunnels. His mother, although she could be as hard with her words as the Babe, had labored to make of her children educated people of recognized accomplishment. As such my father is uneasy as we walk into the bar of the Eureka restaurant on main street where we will eat dinner. He knows no one among the young ranching families who are seated at the dining tables and who have been participating in Sunday horse activities. Near a second entrance, two young men rest their limbs heavily at a table and take turns disappearing to the washroom. One speaks not at all while the other loudly flirts with the energetic waitress. The diners learn that he has been working on a drill rig this day, which we might have guessed from the blackened condition of his attire. My father battles with the disrespect he reads in their conduct. When in the field he insists that his men clean up for dinner. It is a noble rite which mining engineer Clarence King in his role as head of the geological survey used to carry to full fantasy. Camped on a terrace overlooking Salt Lake Valley, he explained to a dinner guest his immaculate linen, silk stockings, low shoes and clothing without wrinkle:[15]

> "It is all very well for you, who lead a civilized life nine or ten months in a year, and only get into the field for a few weeks at a time, to let yourself down to a pioneer-level, and disregard the small elegancies of dress and manners which you can afterwards easily resume, because you have not laid them aside long enough to forget them. But I, who have been for

years constantly in the field, would have lost my good habits altogether if I had not taken every possible opportunity to practice them. We don't dine this way every day, but we do so whenever we can."

In addition to cleaning up for dinner, my father's habit is to philosophize at the dinner hour; but homecoming has unsettled him, and he does not elaborate on his beliefs in man's behavior being as critical to environment as water, land and plant, nor does he pontificate on his statement for the Arizona's Governor's Committee on Arid Lands, "we must respect the orderly process by which social and resource policies are implemented." In the street behind the restaurant, pipe is being laid for a sewage disposal system which Hale Tognoni proposed twenty-five years ago when he returned from World War II and his duty with the Corps of Engineers. He wanted to donate his services, but his uniform generated jealousy rather than trust. He and I are tired. Only this morning we were in Tonopah, eight chapters behind us.

Sleep and the morning bring renewal, and we gas up the car at the garage of a high school classmate of my father's with whom he talks at length. We buy a shovel in a hardware store where again Hale Tognoni gains recognition and information. After breakfast at the cafe-saloon of an oriental couple, we stroll the main street. The cold air still awaits the sun's rising above the eastern wall of this bucolic gulch. Suddenly, my father is stepping more quickly, and we cross the street. We are following from afar a tall, thin man who moves slowly through the shadows along a street which ends sharply at a row of houses set like caves against the cliff. On the cross street I remember my father coming together for the last time in Eureka with his brother Nye at my grandmother's funeral. Finally, Hale calls out, "Tony," and the man turns. Tony DePaoli probably had little reason to expect this reunion with a man who as a boy called him "Tony Pie" and his brother "Johnny Cake," but he does not seem surprised. Mr. DePaoli is not feeling well, and although he remembers my father and his family with fondness, he seems anxious to return to his easy chair and the care of his wife. When my father asks him if he knows where in town that there might be a library of old mining books, he walks us gently back to the main street and to the open door of a store front over which the letters GMDC have been routed in new wood.

The sun has begun to warm the air as Ms. Clemens, descendant of Orion Clemens, the first secretary of the Territory of Nevada, welcomes our visit. Remembering the first line of Mark Twain's *Roughing It*: "My brother had just been appointed Secretary of Nevada Territory . . . ," I inquire. Ms. Clemens speaks with disparagement of her famous literary uncle, but in good humor she ushers us to the inner office. With an account of the dog team with which my father and his brothers collected Eureka's garbage in the late 1920s and 1930s, she graciously introduces us to three young men of General Mineral Development Corporation.

My father takes from his wallet his own calling card—"Mineral Economics Corporation"—but I am sure he would much rather respond to inquiries about the dog team before discussing business. In Eureka while J. R. Tognoni was still alive, he built his sons a wagon with a set of shaves and a breaching for dogs. With this outfit and improved versions to follow in time, mongrel dogs of Eureka, led by an unusual coon hound named Kayo, could move as much as 400 pounds of garbage in both forward and reverse. The garbage, or that part of it not required by the dogs for their services, was fed to pigs, and the pigs were eaten at home or raffled on the roulette wheel in a local bar. My father frequently tells the story of that trash collection system in the context of his mining philosophy. For him it serves as an allegory for the total use of the products of a mine.

Also to become of allegorical importance, although Ms. Clemens is not familiar with the exploit, would be the trucking business of the Tognoni Brothers. Over the high roads of Eureka, east to Ely, Nye and Hale drove six-ton loads of rock. They dug the rock from mine dumps and transported it to where cooperation between wealthy railroad men and investors like the Guggenheims of New York had succeeded in building twentieth century mining towns at Ely and McGill. The copper smelter at McGill would smelt ore from small silver and gold mines in its vicinity because it needed the sand or silica in the process of burning off non-metallic impurities from its Ruth copper mine. Nye would sample mine dumps when other trucking business was slow. He leased the good ones. He also leased the Buckhorn mine dump in the mountains northwest of Eureka after he and Hale had hauled away its eight miles of pipeline and its camp houses during the mine's liquidation. The gold ledges of Buckhorn had been discovered in the twentieth century, and financier George Wingfield erected a power plant in Beowave to run a 300 ton cyanide plant built in 1914. But the Buckhorn vein pinched out in 1916, and the new mill was dismantled. A revival at the Buckhorn mine twenty years later left a dump for Tognoni trucking after 1937. Nye's one canvas bag of rock from the Buckhorn dump showed eight dollars per ton in gold, higher than any dump he had previously sampled. Half so much would have been enough to begin shoveling, and he and Hale fell prey to a type of fever common and economically fatal in American mining country, although excusable perhaps in the temperament of young men. Nye and Hale feverishly began hauling enough of the Buckhorn dump to fill the required railcar side-tracked for the convenience of such operations at Nevada Consolidated's station in Ely.

Unfortunately, the new deposit of earth which the Tognoni brothrs were making in the railcar was of greater permanence than either of them knew. Rather than silica, the Buckhorn dump was fine clay, and it was wet, 20 percent water due to weather conditions. The railcar became a mold and the ore a huge wet brick clinging to the rough metal surfaces of its new home. In the end, the ore gave four dollars per ton in gold, but the deduction of McGill's labor expenses for having the ore mucked out of the railcar and the absence of any redeeming silica left the brothers with a deficit. At that point, they had no alternative but to return their trucks to the finance company and paste unpaid gasoline bills in their scrapbook of youthful momentos. As a consulting engineer, Hale Tognoni recounts the Buckhorn flash in the pan virtually every day to illustrate the importance of having trained and experienced men sample and outline mineral deposits. More than the expense of such expertise, too often the time for thoughtful evaluation of a mining property is out of step with established rhythms of mining in the American West. The pattern is to mine immediately the high-grade from each new discovery in order to defray costs of initial development rather than to purposely study the ore body to attract the kind of capital investment which will allow the profitable marketing of the larger quantities of lower grade ore.

In 1881, there were fifty producing mines in Eureka mining district and "thrice that number that could be made productive at a very small outlay."[16] In the early twentieth century there were 400 mines held under valid titles, 250 of which were on the county assessor's books as producers.[17] Where mines received adequate capital investment, they paid off. The Diamond Mine, for instance, had only $10,000 in production before being bonded to capitalists in Salt Lake City to gain development money. After the necessary equipment was purchased for $60,000, the miners were able to extract enough ore to raise the mine's net value to $1 million.[18]

GMDC's geologist and my father talk about the success of current mining operations around Eureka. They talk in that small circle of men who do not have to be convinced that the riches within the earth will give plenitude and contentment to man sooner or later. Yet the young geologist's kneeless blue jeans, leg-cocked manner of sitting, and his unruly hanks of blond hair speak more of youth than authority. Maybe among the things he defies with his appearance is the bigoted generalization that the mines are played out.

Current operations rely on the gold content of the ore, just as Clarence King had pronounced over one hundred years ago. Inasmuch as he placed the profits that had arisen from the mines to the production of that metal, he regarded Eureka as a gold-bearing camp. The Diamond Mine and Windfall

Mine directly west of Eureka are currently leaching gold with returns of .035 ounces per ton, profitable at $110 per ounce. The early miners never saw this micron gold which is detectable with an atomic absorption spectrograph. It is widely disseminated and microscopic. Recent mining around Eureka is primarily in the shallow zones where it exists. Recovery of deeper deposits awaits adequate capital investment.

Before returning to our motel and resuming our journey beyond Eureka, we walk back into the neighborhood where we met Tony DePaoli earlier; and we find Stella Genzoli's house. She allows us to interrupt her compulsory breakfast of bran nuts, but she has to see us out quickly because of her job—picking up the morning bank mail from a small air strip outside of town. As we leave, she hails a man across the street who is working in the yard beside his freshly painted white house. Standing in the healing warmth of the morning sun, Jim Morrison is glad to talk with a contemporary. Like Tony DePaoli, he has not been well, and he gives the conversation a slowly measured quality in high contrast to the crocheted vigor of Mrs. Genzoli and her sitting room. He speaks about the mining operations in the area with concern for employment opportunity as does my father: mining on Alligator Ridge above Newark Valley; work by Phillips Petroleum near Hamilton; new mining at Tybo near Silverton where a power line has reduced costs. They talk while the puppy at Morrison's feet on the other side of the fence wildly spends itself. Such unbounded animal energy has been of little avail to Eureka for many years.

15 Beneath the Wounds of Greed

*. . . The inevitabilities which historians are
fond of asserting at best only raise questions.*
Rodman Paul[1]

As we drive out of Eureka to Duckwater, my father is making the drive
in his memory when he trucked a house, one half at a time, down main street
with a friend perched atop to lift the overhanging power lines. It is a warm
day and Little Smoky Valley is bright and without shadow in our direct
course back to Duckwater. I will interview Beatie Halstead and others for
most of the day while my father travels mountain roads to Silverton with
Allen Lenbeck as chauffeur. At Silverton I am to meet them. There, I am
savoring the sweet expectation of walking alone to the family graves when I
see Lenbeck's red pick-up approaching on the sandy road beside the
volcanic platform of Silverton's townsite.

Before sunset and before Lenbeck's return home, the three of us will
make an excursion out into Railroad Valley to Chimney Hot Springs. My
father is interested in what the hot water has deposited on the colorful banks
of a narrow stream which trickles across the travertine from the spring's
fenced pool. Allen and I help him to dig and sack his samples, and we
occupy ourselves with talk of Indian rice grass and the medicinal value of
tea from the yerba munson's white flower, while Hale Tognoni, deep in
thought and memory, examines the spring. What my father and his family
had here at Chimney Hot Springs is gone. It was gone except for vanishing
subtleties virtually as soon as human occupation and use ended.

Myrtle Tognoni was once the grand old lady of this landscape, but she
died impoverished, fattened and corrupted with the easy and sinless white
sugar which she once scraped from the wedding cake of a grandchild when
her senility was left unattended. Like the mines of the American West, her

children would not fulfill their promise; her daughter Elva, the most beautiful woman in Nevada, according to some, spent her mature life in an institution for the mentally deranged, there to be rescued by her own daughter, Joan, a little over ten years later. Now, while Elva's son Jack prospects Nevada in his father's footsteps, Elva lies waiting in Lovelock for death, much like her own mother. Elva's brother, the grand old lady's son by J. C. Tognoni, was my grandfather. At the age of forty-three, leaving behind four children, his body was lowered into a grave at Silverton. The children are scattered: my father in Arizona, his sister in California. The youngest son is dead and buried in Colorado. The oldest, known as "Tag" in mining towns of the Southwest, runs a tri-state tax service and is the modern idea of what an old-timer should be—grizzled and searching, surrounded by discard below a vast horizon. He is in the Nevada history books:[2]

> Natural wealth and scanty population in a sovereign state are a combination that makes opportunity now as earlier, especially for young men . . . [In 1940] . . . Nye Tognoni, twenty-two years old and a sophomore at the University of Nevada, ran for the legislature of Eureka County, canvassed personally from house to house, and won by a huge majority. Healthy, liberal, intelligent, he could anticipate a career . . .

Nightfall is a matter of illusive degree as Lenbeck leans out the window of his truck to get a closer look at the animal tracks in the soft dirt of our road back to the highway and to Silverton. In the day's afterglow, my father and I depart. It is dark when we reach the Warm Springs roadhouse. Inside, there is no dinner, so we drive on to Tonopah and the Mizpah Hotel, where we eat at the last occupied table. The enduring presence which will link this day to the final day of our trip is my great-grandfather, J. C. Tognoni. In the morning, we will visit the natural monuments to him outside Goldfield, surely the only town in the United States with a sign on its main street reading "Gold Mines for Sale."

> Splendid, magnificent, Queen of the Camps,
> Mistress of countless Aladdin's lamps,
> Deity worshipped by kings and tramps.
> The lure she is of the West.[3]

After the gold rush to California and to the rest of the far western United States and Alaska, there was one final blast of glorious gold mining in southwestern Nevada. "Goldfield," they called it, and it lured the nation's prodigal sons. In the infant years of the twentieth century, several thousand of them descended like a cloudburst into the sagebrushed flood plain at the mouth of Death Valley. In the sprinkle of men that preceded the flood had

Goldfield, Nevada, 1981

Outlying mining district of Goldfield, c. 1905. J. C. Tognoni, left, on horse.

been Joe Tognoni, Italian immigrant and Duckwater rancher. He would sell or gamble away and make gifts of his mining claims in gestures of generosity befitting the flamboyance which would govern Goldfield. As the easily hired language of the day would have it, Joe was the "Father of Vindicator Mountain" from which came a portion of $15 million in gold during 1906 and 1907. It is no promotional exaggeration to say that Goldfield was one of the greatest gold mining camps the world has ever known. Goldfield averaged $100 to $500 per ton of ore when ore out of Tonopah, twenty-five miles to the north, was averaging $40 per ton; and the longest continually operating gold mine in the United States, at Lead, South Dakota, was getting $5 per ton. Even California gold had generally run only $5 to $20 per ton of ore.[4]

Despite the phenomenal wealth, most of the early miners of Goldfield did not seek to invest even a small portion of their energy in permanence. The nation's great capitalists were skeptical of mining investments. In a political climate turned against silver, they had lost millions in grand schemes to go deeper into the crevices of mines like the Comstock. Without mining capitalists, a leasing system which had flourished in Tonopah spread to Goldfield. It lasted three years until Goldfield Consolidated Mining Company brought a degree of efficiency and systematic mining to the rutted landscape; but the new order had no deep root. Where wild greed had sizzled brashly on the surface only the day before, Goldfield Consolidated spread its clawing tunnels in a broad and hasty circle just beneath the dust. Rather than use the profits near the surface to develop the deeper deposit, the Consolidated operation would pay its stockholders $30 million in dividends, three times that paid by any other gold mining company in a period of one year.[5]

Of the six ore reduction mills and sampling plants erected in 1905, only two of them were in use three years later. Five plants were built after 1905, but by 1915, only the Goldfield Consolidated was producing. Goldfield Consolidated would close down in 1918, but during the next twenty-two years almost three and a half million dollars in gold would be recovered from its tailings, indicating either that the milling was being done with equipment which was quickly outdated, or it was being conducted at a pace inconsistent with efficiency. One of Goldfield's first mills lasted less than two months. Within three years after ore was shipped by wagon from the desert reaches of Goldfield, three railroads had arrived in the camp: one, like the darting tongue of a snake out of Death Valley, would retrieve Goldfield's wealth for the Santa Fe line; one linked Goldfield to the Southern Pacific and to Tonopah; and the third from Las Vegas to the smelters of Utah was destined to be replaced by a highway. After only fourteen years of use, the Las Vegas to Goldfield rails would be torn from the Nevada desert and sent to Russia.[6]

All indications were that the mineral values at Goldfield would increase at depth. Mines below the oxidized zone showed continuous values and to the north at Tonopah, valuable veins had been found at 900 feet without diminishing mineralization.[7] Tonopah was to have a more permanent existence than its neighbor to the south, outdistancing Goldfield in production although Goldfield's ores were richer.[8] The northernmost stone monuments to mining claims in Goldfield would become like the "witness heap" which Jacob and Laban of the Bible set up between them in the desert out of Mesopotamia, "hillocks of testimony" to diverging paths. "And God keep watch between thee and me."[9] Goldfield would go beyond the veil of mining morality. "Promoters with rascally motives flourished."[10]

George Graham Rice epitomized the men who prevailed. He would write his Goldfield exploits in a book entitled *My Adventures with Your Money*. Gathered in Goldfield were men of action like the state had not seen since the Comstock, but the law bound them, and they would break it. Diamondfield Jack Davis, namesake of the townsite near a group of J. C.'s claims, had been sentenced to hang in Idaho; my great-grandfather himself had been on trial for assault in Tonopah just previous to the rush to Goldfield; and George Graham Rice, alias Jacob S. Herzig, had spent time in New York State Reform School and the state prison before coming to Nevada. His big promotions, all of them for the customary million dollars, dominated the Goldfield Mining Exchange. He encouraged the public to spend $200 million on stocks in 1905 and 1906, and in 1907, he would help to start a miniature Goldfield without the gold at Rawhide, Nevada. The law called him a crook, but others might well have called him a gambler, of which Nevada mining was in perpetual need.

After the gold rush to California and before the boom of Goldfield, many had "learned to their financial advantage that a gold rush was an eminently exploitable phenomenon, an entrepreneur's delight, a way for a man to make a small fortune in everything from canned goods to bartered flesh."[11] Phrased less passionately, the most pressing problem during the first fifty years of the twentieth century was the division of the profits from production between labor, management, government and finance, each progressively demanding a larger percentage of the take. Only a few seemed to go about their business quietly. In 1882, before the rush to Alaska in the 1890s, John Treadwell, a mining engineer, purchased a lode mining property on Douglas Island near Juneau. The ore from this mine was reportedly poor, but Treadwell calculated that with up-to-date methods and machinery, the lode could be worked at a profit. He acquired $400,000 in initial capital investment and was still producing at the turn of the century. In 1923, I find evidence in an Alaska Bureau of Mines bulletin, Treadwell Mining Company was still operating at least one neatly planned underground Alaska mine and paying its labor a healthy six dollars a day.

Judging from this meagre set of facts, Treadwell was that rare type of man capable of bringing to American mining slow and purposeful projects, bereft of greed. Hale Tognoni and the company of mining engineers and geologists who have associated themselves with him are of that same type. To survive in domestic mining of this century and to follow the practical dictates of their sciences, they have brought together a group of mineral properties under the manifold protection of Mineral Economics Corporation (MEC). Like Treadwell's mine, the most remote of MEC's mineral development is in Alaska. Ten miles inland from Platinum, Alaska, where the Bering Sea meets the southwestern corner of the state at Goodnews Bay, is a tight little mining camp in search of a new generation. The camp's dredge on the Salmon River (the minnow of a wholesale dozen Salmon Rivers in Alaska) was paid for with a loan from the federal Reconstruction Finance Corporation. From 1938 to 1975, the Goodnews Bay Mining Company, formed by Charles Johnson and brothers Andrew and Ed Olson, mined 641,000 ounces of coarse platinum from the deposit, but MEC engineers estimate that less than 50 percent of the mineral has been recovered. If this platinum deposit were mined at the rate of 10,000 ounces per year according to a disciplined program of development, it could provide 1 percent of current platinum consumption in the United States for forty years.

Although the Reconstruction Finance Corporation was not originally designed to make investments or to speculate in the nation's mining industry, it became involved in loans to mineral developers during the depression years and for strategic minerals during the War years. In the aftermath of the industry's own excesses and reaction in the form of the Securities Exchange Commission, trust lay amputated from the slowly disintegrating corpse of domestic mining in this country. Trust, which may never have been a strong member of commerce between men, was particularly weak during "antitrust" years which wet-nursed the Great Depression. Mining, like Christianity, requires sustained faith and sobriety of thought. Inquiries by those wishing to secure a profit in mining without a degree of trust have common sense answers; but on this crucial issue Hale Tognoni stoically quotes Winston Churchill: "The trouble with common sense is that it is not common."

According to Tognoni, clays like those in the upper bench of the Platinum property have been redredged with improved equipment throughout the world from three to seven times, and each time an amount equal to that from the initial operation was recovered. MEC recommended newly developed clay dispersing methods and the fabrication of processing and mining equipment which would go deeper into the Alaska deposit. It would also drill on the probable source of the platinum above the placer streams in the mountains; and it would pay for planning, so that instead of careless mounds of dredge debris, Platinum Park might be created. But Tognoni has failed to convince current purchasers and operators of the old dredge that boom and bust habits do not transplant with permanence to the extremely exacting climate of Alaska.

In Nevada, MEC has accumulated data on mining districts and mines such as the J. C. Tognoni properties: an exploratory producer at Silverton; patented claims on the outskirts of Goldfield which were bought for taxes by their current owner; and the unpatented association Black Oil claims where there are classic indications of an economic deposit. Like the Combination claims at Goldfield which became one of the most successful producers in the district, the Black Oils were located not because an economic mineral deposit was measurable on the surface, but like the outcrop of quartz on the Combination, oil seepage on the Black Oils becomes significant in light of producing oil wells within a ten mile radius. In 1903, the Combinations were the closest valuable ground to already discovered rich ore.[12]

In Arizona, MEC's engineers participate in the search for the southern portion of the huge disseminated copper deposit which has been mined at Ajo, Arizona. Geological structure in and around the Ajo open pit copper mine indicates that Ajo's deposit may be only the upper portion of a deposit sliced from its source to the south and thrust along a plate of the earth's surface to the present location of the Ajo pit. MEC's wollastonite-copper prospect is to the south of Ajo and is largely covered by sharp ridges of a metamorphosed limestone called wollastonite. Here stressful activity in the earth's crust has transformed limestone into a tough, crystalline, white rock that has become increasingly valuable. U.S. manufacturers are using 55 to 70 percent wollastonite in low-cost wall tiles, according to the geological engineer on this project, Harry E. Nelson. In addition to the wollastonite which breaks the desert on these claims to form one of the largest known deposits of the mineral in the west coast region, there exists a possible disseminated gold deposit and a probable massive sulphide deposit enriched with precious metals. Like geologists examining a single rock, geophysicists have flown over the earth here to calculate its hidden components of this portion of earth with unseen waves of magnetism, gravity, electricity and sound. Induced polarization indicated a mineral anomaly of the magnitude existing over proven copper deposits in the Southwest. Geochemical samples have confirmed that a peculiar concentration of precious and base metals exists on the claims. "Pathfinder elements" such as mercury, bismuth, cadmium and tungsten leave a telltale trail to deposits of these metals. Such signposts are what geologists today depend upon to induce finance to help develop tomorrow's mines.

Further north and east in Arizona's San Pedro Valley, geophysical photographic equipment reacted with infra-red while flying over the site of a number of old gold and silver diggings along a contact between intrusive structures and ancient sediment in Paige Canyon near Cascabel, Arizona. The anomaly found by Mobil Oil is in the vicinity of folded sediments steeply dipping to dramatic termination against granite. On the surface is a ubiquitous mantle of geologically juvenile Gila conglomerate "resting unconformably on older rocks."[13] The infra-red of geophysical equipment and Red Hill beside Paige Canyon give witness to mineralization impregnating the rocks and filling the cavities beneath recent sediment in the region; yet Mobil Oil's exploration department drilled only two shallow holes before abandoning the project. MEC maintains these capped drill holes, hoping one day to take them to 3,000 feet.

Frequently the oil companies lack the experience, incentive and forbearance which are vital to hard rock mining. The oil companies, which have taken over many American mining corporations, do not understand the need for sustained development nor the long lead time necessary before production. Lost to the oil company's mode of operation and the current system of federal taxation which guides profitability is the rule of thumb by which mining men trained in the old schools engineered mines: you must outline one ton of ore in the earth for every ton mined. The oil companies understand a big outlay of capital for a drilling platform, which they can immediately write off as a tax loss; and if they strike oil, necessary funds for production are easily secured. Little subsequent expenditure is required to recover the initial investment. In addition, big mining companies, in general, lack genuine incentive to mine the entirety of a deposit, the parameters of which are determined by economics and efficiency. If a company increased the known supply of its mineral, it lowers the demand and the selling price and often increases taxable assets.

To the west of Cascabel beyond Tucson, Arizona, on the Papago Indian Reservation in the Cababi (hidden springs) mining district, MEC engineers have studied several groups of patented mining claims. Since the late 1700s and as late as the 1960s, the silver mines on these properties have been sporadically worked. Estimated production is at least five hundred tons of ore containing silver, gold, lead, copper and zinc worth almost three million dollars in today's market. The owners are hopeful that a healthier U.S. metals market will allow mining companies to follow the ancient "leads" and structural clues to the deeper ore deposits. Unfortunately, in most old mines like these in the Cababi District, records which might save expensive drill holes now were not kept, and records kept by the Bureau of Mines and the U.S. Geological Survey, although valuable, are limited.

Another old mine on the Papago Indian Reservation which deserves attention is in the Gunsight Hills where MEC helps to maintain fourteen patented lode mining claims and a patented five-acre millsite. Gunsight Consolidated Silver Mining Company incorporated in 1881. Old maps indicate that the vein was developed to a depth of 400 feet and samples taken from ore left behind by the early miners would be worth $56.55 per ton at today's prices and 80 percent milling recovery. MEC estimates that if ore being mined in the 1880s was produced today, it would be worth $200 per ton. Harry E. Nelson conservatively estimates probable tonnage in the Gunsight vein at almost two and a half million. If the development program set out by MEC yields favorable results, the underground workings could be reopened and a mill facility built to take the Gunsight Mine back into production.

The O'Flaherty mining claims, one mile north of Magma Copper Company's mine at Superior, Arizona, and one-half mile south of the old Silver King Mine, run along a fault parallel to the veins of the mines on either side. Hale Tognoni demonstrates a vein deposit by tearing through a sheet of paper in a zig zag and by moving the two halves along the tear. Knowledge of how earth faults slip to make room for mineralization can guide miners when overlap, of the two paper halves, or tight areas in the ground leave only a thin "lead" to the next opening filled with broken rock and valuable mineral. Like the Silver King, Newmont Corporation's Magma Copper Mine to the south of the O'Flaherty is closed now; even though it has one of the most competent of mineral veins at depth. For many years Magma Copper Company followed it from rich pocket to rich pocket of sulphide copper ore. Underground vein mining to the depths reached in a country like South Africa is non-existent in the United States. Mining companies in the United States have gone to less labor intensive disseminated deposits which are extracted by open pit operations or, as with the world's largest underground copper mine at San Manuel, Arizona, by a system of block caving. Advanced engineering allows miners to take the ore out from under a section of earth and lower the overburden in a manner that wedges and packs it into a new home above the cavernous mine.

On claims such as the O'Flaherty's, MEC recommends consolidated ownership with the Silver King mine to the north in order to finance the kind of high technology now available to geologists and mining engineers, such as satellite photographs for the mapping of geological structures which will be used to project locations for exploratory deep drill holes. If the ore found is amenable to cyanide reduction, then MEC would recommend the reactivation of a cyanide leaching operation on the Silver King. The drilling is expensive and does not provide public investors with the kind of visible results for their money that premature construction of a mill would give. Too many of the mining companies which have gone after public investment resort to such a mill before the quantity and quality of the ore to be milled has been adequately determined.

In California MEC has evaluated the dump from an old mill, the Daggett Reduction Works in San Bernardino County. The mill reduced ore over seventy years ago, leaving in its waste an estimated 2.6 ounces of silver per ton. The Corporation believes that modern cyanide leaching techniques, which allow the agglomeration of crushed ore into charcoal-like briquets, will release as much as 65 percent of the remaining silver into cyanide solution when the briquets are heaped and sprayed with the toxin. If silver prices should reach fifteen dollars an ounce, as they most probably will, a $400,000 investment on the Calico claims would yield a $2 million profit, if all 170,000 tons of the dump give up 65 percent of their precious metal content.

Elsewhere a sample processing unit for microscopic gold particles awaits funds. In the wide, level section of a desert river in Arizona which seasonally drains the mineral-rich Arrastra, Bradshaw, Weaver and Santa Maria mountains, a natural catch basin has been formed for heavy minerals. Gold, silver, platinum, magnetic iron, tungsten, tin and zirconium, as well as others, have been found in samples from River Gold. According to famed geologist Waldemar Lindgren, at least five thousand feet of erosion has occurred in the Bradshaw Mountains alone. From the mountains the water channel on the claims forms a loose, water-saturated bed which has acted as a filter, precipitator and collector suitable for a large scale dredging operation such as has been successfully employed in several other placer basins of the world. A German exploration group projected the presence of a clay collector bed in the mid 1970s. In the early 1980s, Canadians promised to finance the first phase of a development program, but defaulted just as MEC was ready to build a sample processing unit capable of determining the quantity of micron gold in the samples. In the accomplished portion of the program, ten drill holes were put down to a maximum depth of 100 feet. With the reneging of finance, the ten tons of samples from these drill holes were put in storage to await processing, and while the dike built east of the narrows at River Gold to divert flood waters from drilling operations has disappeared.

In the Silver Mountain mining district on the west slope of the Bradshaw Mountains, MEC is developing another set of unpatented mining claims in an amphitheatre-shaped canyon four miles square. The high molybdenum content of the copper ore on the seventy-three claims called Copper Basin has been subjected to drilling programs by Coleman Morton, Exxon Mineral Company and Utah Construction and Mining Company. Silver increases toward the periphery while molybdenum appears to increase in depth. With possible silver, molybdenum and other copper by-products, Copper Basin should become more valuable than other more developed copper mines.

Ultimately, California mining historian Rodman Paul asked the only really pertinent question at this juncture in American mining history:[14]

> Did many good claims that need only labor and funds to become paying mines go begging because of the madly speculative frame of mind that dominated so many Californians during the hectic period that was ushered in by the discovery of the Comstock Lode or did economic politics outside of the mining country and a revolution in investment law deprive labor and funds from good prospects?

In Goldfield, where the "madly speculative mine" met with a natural treasure trove during the early years of the twentieth century, the reasons deep development did not proceed may be as simple as the obscurity of J. C. Tognoni, his springs and his mountain in Goldfield mining district.

George Wingfield (Courtesy Nevada Historical Society)

16 Water from the Rock

... mining is the Cinderella of our political economy ...
C. C. Williams, Jr.[1]

The past may have been cumbrous to our journey, but our last day seems shackled to the present. Neither of us remembers to fill up the gas tank of our Futura, rented in Sacramento. Coming out of Goldfield, near Beatty, Nevada, we lose power and roll to a stop. The ranch house behind about one-half mile is reassuring, but two men in a pick-up truck charitably rescue us. They themselves are passing through from Arizona on business. Later, our car will begin belching smoke out from behind its front wheels during each stop at traffic lights in the bright and broad tunnel of casino-hotels at America's neon crossroad—Las Vegas. It is Cinderella's ball with the romantic boredom as exposed and colorful as the geology of the mountains beyond the city's asphalt gathering of lost sheep.

The morning of our day we spend finding Tognoni Springs and Tognoni Mountain. On geological survey maps and in a bulletin of the Bureau of Mines,[2] these reminders of Joe Tognoni's career in Goldfield mining district are several miles northeast of the town of Goldfield. They are just over the Esmeralda County line in Nye County. When mining claims here were first recorded, the district was called "Grandpa," and it was mistakenly declared to be in Nye County; however, the major portion of the dead volcanic center and its eruption into the biggest U.S. mining boom town of the twentieth century, was soon properly identified as an Esmeralda County occurrence. A prospector in an earlier mining district of this region of Nevada prophetically christened his district and the county from a French novel in which the gypsy Esmeralda entertained the city of Paris with a "wild dance of death or disappointment to thousands."[3] Esmeralda County had its boundaries changed by acts of 1869, 1875, 1883, 1911 and 1913. In addition, parts of the county were once claimed by California. Aurora, the first county seat of Esmeralda, simultaneously served as the seat of government for Mono County, California, until a joint boundary survey put the early mining boom town in Nevada. Understandably, boundaries of Esmeralda had been incorrectly drawn on some early maps. There was little of permanence besides the geology of this countryside to suggest territorial demarcations.

In the mineral deposits and mines the residents of Esmeralda developed a faith resilient enough to become tradition in a sparse population. The land had a strong spirit. When the State of Nevada was first organizing, Esmeralda County would not ratify the first draft of the state constitution because of the clause allowing taxation of the mines as property. Esmeralda's people understood better than most that to tax mines rather than production was to waste capital investment and to strike at the roots of any hope of growth. Surrounded by the clean vistas of God's creation, they knew future economic health for Nevada without mining would be as vapid and empty as Christianity without Christ. William Morris Stewart, first senator from Nevada and "Father of the American Mining Laws," set up his last law practice near Esmeralda. He was cut off from her by an extension of the same county line which separated Tognoni Springs from the bulk of Goldfield district. In his autobiography, Stewart would apologize for the inevitable injustices of the county lines which he helped to create in 1861, but on the issue of taxing the mines, Esmeralda and Stewart were of one heart and mind.

Senator Stewart was possessed by his vision for Nevada's function in the body of the nation, and he railed with vigor so awesome as to become impossible for the master of sacrilege, Mark Twain, to ignore. In the *Territorial Enterprise* for which Twain served as a journalist in Virginia City, Twain wrote a parody of the state's constitutional convention.[4] In this literary burlesque Twain appointed himself chairman of the convention, superintendent of buffoonery. To Stewart he responded:

> "I have been reporting and reporting [your] internal speech for the last thirty days . . . When I want it, I will repeat it myself—I know it by heart . . . if you can't . . . say it backwards, or sing it to a new tune, you have simply got to simmer down for awhile."

Stewart's speech in the Twain caricature:

> "Mr. President: I insist upon it . . . when you tax the poor miner's shafts and drifts, and bed-rock tunnels, you are not taxing his property: you are *not* taxing his substance;—no, but you are taxing the shadow from which the substance may eventually issue or may not; . . . in a word, sir, you are

taxing his hopes, taxing the aspirations of his soul; taxing the yearnings of his heart of hearts."

In 1908, when William Jennings Bryan ran for the third time as the democratic nominee for president of the United States, Bryan pledged to send a Missouri mule to the precinct which gave him the largest percentage of votes; the mule went to Goldfield, new county seat of Esmeralda.[5] Goldfield became the capital of southern Nevada in the years of Theodore Roosevelt and William Taft's presidencies, and in 1907 when three companies of federal soldiers were sent into Goldfield by request of Nevada Governor Sparks, the population was almost twenty thousand. Three years previous, Goldfield had been but a loose huddle of prospectors. Three years afterward, it had begun to return to its humble beginnings. The U.S. Census counted only 4,838 residents in 1910, and by 1920, only 1,500 dwelt in Goldfield. In 1923, a fire devastated Nevada's last mining metropolis, and large portions of what had grown from the "loosest moneyed, highest-spading camp of all"[6] went un-rebuilt.

From 1904 to 1918, Goldfield yielded over eighty-three and a half million dollars in mineral, an average yearly production of more than five and a half million, most of it gold.[7] In Goldfield's prime, a man could lease a claim and dig it out while reveling in every debauchery devised by man to insulate him from the Great American Desert. The "cribs" of the whores or "sporting girls," as Nevadans have called them, were, like horse stalls, in rows with each girl's name emblazoned on her door. Outside in the night, the crackling of the roulette wheels and the "dull thump of distant dynamite"[8] were as persistent as the wind whistling down from the barren hillsides above the town and across the gleaming, salt-encrusted plains. Where lizards had dared only to dart from brush to brush, 60,000 people gathered on Labor Day in 1907 to watch "Battling Nelson," the "durable Dane," fight the "black boxing wizard," Joe Gans, for a record purse of $30,000. Man eroded man atop a dome of earth into which stresses of unknown origin found relief in a very complicated system of fissures, like a map of hell, unaccompanied by any considerable displacement of the rock. The battle ended during the forty-second round, with Gans being declared the winner on a foul. According to George Graham Rice's account of the fight, Gans stated after the twentieth round that he couldn't win but he wouldn't lose.[9]

Writing for *Mining and Scientific Press* in 1908, historian T. A. Rickard would document the immorality at Goldfield.[10] Like the geology of the district, changes were evident in Goldfield although causes still dwelt in regions where facts and hypothesis, inference and speculation are indistinguishable without difficulty and consequently political dogmatism finds congenial soil.[11] Just so, the process by which the ores of Goldfield were deposited remains unknown, a subject of controversy, disguising the gold's genesis, the host rock changed texturally as well as chemically in the temescent mineral deposit. Yet, as rare as the richness of the ore at Goldfield is the stage of erosion which reveals rather than obliterates the geological transitions—ancient granite and metamorphics covered by sediment and then by volcanics.[12] Outcrops of the older rock are surrounded by wide concentric zones of successively younger formations which map change without revealing process like the passage at Goldfield into a new century for mining. The demise of domestic mining in the United States would be so like Goldfield sediment eroded to reveal lively metamorphics that T. A. Rickard would pen "Rich Ore and its Moral Effects" for a journal devoted to objectively measured events.

Stealing, called high-grading, reached new heights of imagination and rationalization. The owners of mining claims at Goldfield (1,115 claims surveyed for patent, 838 patented[13]) had no idea of the richness, extent and ease of working of the ore bodies; so they leased claims on a 25 percent royalty for one year. If the tenant struck pay ore, the mine soon would revert to the owners, with development work accomplished. The tenant's primary concern became to raise as much rich ore as possible in a given time. In order to keep peace with his labor force he ignored the gold which left his mine by surreptitious means. Scores of so-called assay offices sprang up to traffic in dishonestly acquired high-grade ore.

Even after leasing ended in Goldfield and George Wingfield and George Nixon succeeded in consolidating a number of rich producers, the high-grading continued. A comparison of mine production with mint figures for 1907 indicates that total stealings from Goldfield Consolidated Mines Company was fully one million dollars.[14] In the next year, despite labor union problems, the high-grading was ended, but the transgressions at Goldfield recurred wherever failure to attract capital investment for development of a mine led to a lease on unexpectedly rich ore. In National, Nevada, for instance, the original locators anticipated that they would lease in order to develop the ground. They filed location notices on thirty-four claims in 1907 knowing that they could not begin to do the necessary work on all of them without leasers.[15] In changing the mode of mineral exploration in the twentieth century away from the lone grubstake of the previous century, Goldfield's leasing was a step toward the corporate position that mining has increasingly and necessarily become. In Europe coal and metal mining were the earliest stimuli to the development of true joint enterprise along the lines of the modern corporation. The mining companies exhibited those qualities which are the earmarks of true corporate organization, including a "side-issue" relationship to the furnishers of capital.[16] Only in Goldfield could George Graham Rice have become audacious enough to write a book entitled *My Adventures with Your Money.*

But if something were being gained in the progress of American mining, something was also being lost. In the 1907 session of the Nevada State Legislature, the political laboratories of sentence and phrase overturned the traditional ninety days allowed for doing location work around a discovery monument. The new state law gave only twenty days for a claimant to put his corner and sideline monuments on the ground. "With ninety days," cried the reformers, "the prospector has the opportunity of swinging the claim to take advantage of a neighbor's strike." Yet only after location work did the prospector know enough to lay out corners and sidelines in good faith. The longer period, therefore, encouraged more accurate claims and discouraged claims where the discovery could not be substantially supported by subsequent work. In Goldfield, substance, honesty and faith were being juggled in a game with no winners unless distrust and envy could be said to enjoy victory over the spirit of the law.

Goldfield was the culmination of America's gold rushes, as was the rush to Alaska which preceded it by only a few years. At Dawson, Alaska, the saloons, cat houses and lawyers had already set up business by the time the miners arrived. At Nome, miners rushed to make claims in the names of relatives and friends until forty people had effective control of 7,000 acres of potentially rich mineral ground on gulches and creeks of the Snake River.[17] This went against California gold rush tradition and the vigor of American mining law, but discoveries on the beaches at Nome made the rush into a poor man's proposition once again, and Nome would become the last major, free-placer region in the history of the mining frontier. The beaches would be panned out in a year, and as in California, hydraulic mining and dredging, requiring joint enterprise, would begin. The value of the mineral removed during Alaska's first ninety years under the flag of the United States, two-thirds of it gold, repaid Alaska's purchase price more than 150 times.[18]

Southerner Key Pittman had joined the rush to the Klondike. He became the lawyer for Australians who attacked corrupt government in Dawson, and the first prosecuting attorney in Nome during the "lawless winter of 1899."[19] In 1903, Pittman would be my great-grandfather's attorney in Tonopah where he was tried concerning the foot wound of William Mendes and the battle for water rights at Duckwater. Beyond the American gold rushes, Pittman would use his powers of diplomacy against the entrenched capitalists who had become as kings in the countries from which Americans had immigrated. But by the 1930s, in a time period paralleling fading monetary value for silver and gold, the Old Dominion Mine in Globe, Arizona, would seek out the influence of Joe Kennedy, first director of the Securities Exchange Commission in much the same way that early American land companies had applied for grants to the Lords of Trade in England.[20]

During the last gold rushes to Alaska and Nevada and alongside the demise of legal tender secured by mineral production, every major theory which would drive the Securities Exchange Commission and the evolution of anti-trust doctrine would be born in the United States. The commission, ostensibly created to meet disparities in state laws, would not, however, alter the fact that the money raised on stock exchanges does not go to mineral development, after the original purchase, but to speculators. Today if a company asks for one million dollars, for example, in a stock issuance and succeeds in showing a profit, the stock will probably rise in value, but none of the increased value necessarily becomes capital investment in the mine. A new issue of stock, with every assurance to protect the speculator, must be drawn up for new capital. In Nevada, "Irish dividends" continued to rake off the cream since so many Nevada corporations were created before the existence of the S.E.C., especially in Goldfield. With an Irish dividend the corporation pays dividends on excess assets as well as, or instead of, paying on production earnings. On the basis of such supposed distribution of profit, the company's stock may increase in the exchange houses where corporate directors could then unload their shares in a canny liquidation of the company's assets.

Goldfield Consolidated incorporated under the laws of Wyoming[21] and the guidance of Charles S. Thomas, former governor of Colorado. In Colorado "apex" language in revised federal mining laws met its match in non-apexing geology similar to Goldfield's. The problem was partially alleviated by leasing practices which allowed a discoverer to locate many claims as a blanket on a probable mineral deposit, and the location of the highest point of a vein or the apex became unimportant. In Goldfield the law of the apex would not be invoked with the same bitterness and ingenuity as in Butte, Montana, and in Colorado. In Goldfield compromise and consolidation reigned in a 1908 agreement between the Jumbo Extension Company and Goldfield Consolidated. Frederick L. Ransome applauds the agreement in his report of the Goldfield district. He congratulates the engineers who established the facts, the lawyers who interpreted the legal bearing of these and the companies who accepted them.[22] In Ransome's estimation, the compromise deserved to rank as one of the important events in the history of the district.

Positive inducement to mineral exploration and development came in the 1930s when President Franklin Roosevelt raised the price of gold from $20.67 per ounce to $35.00; but, the heavy hand of the Securities Exchange Commission would send men who had once productively gambled in the mines of Nevada into less closely regulated and newly legalized Nevada casinos. The Reconstruction Finance Corporation, created to guide national recovery from the great economic depression of the late 1920s and the 1930s, had to amend its enactment articles to allow for speculative loans in mining during World War II. Prior to the amendments, the law required that the Finance Corporation opine formally that the mining operations made possible by R.F.C. loans would result in profits. Furthermore, the loans could be made only to those already engaged in development of mineral deposits excluding those with undeveloped discoveries.[23]

From 1940 until 1945, Metal Reserves Company under the R.F.C. handled the major portion of mineral investments. In 1941, director of the R.F.C. Jesse H. Jones reported that $72,500 had been loaned for mining since 1934. With the war, concern over domestic production of minerals escalated. The large strategic mineral companies, like Aluminum Company of America in Pittsburgh, Anaconda Copper Mining Company in Butte, and Basic Magnesium Incorporated of Cleveland, would get millions of dollars in 1941 loans. Still the developers of new mining properties for graphite, tungsten and mercury would be given only $20,000 each as a general rule.[24] In the case of some minerals such as zinc, which is an ingredient of cartridge brass, the R.F.C. loans or "premium payments" were made necessary by ceiling prices held by another arm of the federal government.[25]

The Reconstruction Finance Corporation was not dissolved until the early 1950s. After the war, it continued in part as an institution for the encouragement of small business. According to Director Jones, testifying before the Senate Banking Committee in 1949, the R.F.C.'s intention was to help those who saved in the form of fixed assets when they could not get their financing elsewhere. Frequently, after the R.F.C. had approved a loan, private financing institutions would buy the debt notes.[26] To the miners, there are no assets so fixed as mineral deposits, so the post-war function of the R.F.C. would seem especially suited to curing the domestic mining slump, but a world-wide war economy had locked into gear, leaving the problems of peaceable material development at home unresolved.

In addition to the drought in mining capital which has existed since World War II, popular views on land use began to legislate against mining. In California, where mining was the economic base for the greatest agricultural state in the nation, the disassociation with mining came early in the history of the state. Powerful men of California were insistent that mining and farming were incompatible on the great western watershed of the

Sierra, although flooding, of which the farmers complained, continues to the present day, long after the hydraulic miners ceased their work. As early as 1880, the hydraulickers were having to defend themselves before a public land commission; but they failed to convince the state that every industry of the people contributes to the immense deposits of eroded sediment seasonally carried out of the mountains and into the valleys and bays along the Pacific Ocean.[27]

> Agriculture contributes very largely to it; grazing contributes to it through the animals running over and dragging up the mats of roots and loosening the soil, and subsequent rains washing it away. The lumbermen contribute to it very much; every log he drags over the roads loosens the earth, and eventually it is washed into the rivers. Every wagon-rut, railroad, and county road contributes to the sediment that flows into the canyons . . . I have known the cutting of a wagon-road along the mountain-side to so take away the props to the soil on that side that heavy winter rain carried the whole mountain-side down, acres upon acres, with the forest trees upon it, until it obliterated the marks of the road.

The difficulties between farmer and miner were not new. Copper miners in colonial Connecticut were unable to resolve their conflicting claims with land owners,[28] and in England special courts were created to handle the grievances between landlords and free miners. When the courts were operating, the miner was being encouraged with every sort of privilege, including non-military service. At one point convocations of miners could even veto legislation from Parliament.[29] In those days the government depended on its mineral wealth for a large share of its power, and the term "coinage" represented metals stamped and taxed before any sale was permitted.

In England, just as in the United States, domestic mining would go into periods of decline. During one such period, the Society of Mines Royal supplanted free mining to grant licenses or leases to capitalists and corporations. The society's influence and methods of operation became pernicious, tending to check private mining companies and leading landowners to conceal traces of ore upon their grounds rather than to exploit the property.[30] A group of London merchants secured from a Massachusetts court in 1645 a twenty-one year monopoly of iron making and of the management of all iron mines then known or thereafter to be discovered. Free men were allowed to purchase shares in units of not less than fifty pounds in the Lynn Iron Works which came of this monopoly, and shareholders or members were to be free from militia duty and enjoy no export tax;[31] but, not until the discovery of gold in the American West would mining become invigorated in the United States. In England the Society of Mines Royal died in 1852.

In our century of declining domestic mining, the federal land agencies have inherited the role of the Society of Mines Royal. The files of countless mining claims where the governor has intervened in Arizona show the government frankly admitting that it intends to make the profits on developed mineral deposits while in the same breath deny that any mineral exists that would support the mining claimant's property rights. Many mineral deposits are in remote areas, and communities like Colorado City, Arizona, have survived only because they used not only the agricultural potential of the land but its mineral wealth as well. Yet, to keep their mining claims in recent years, Colorado City has had to fight countless legal battles not with claim jumpers but with federal officials wishing to collect fees for leasing.

Today the public land agencies which interpret and administer the laws of mining would have difficulty understanding a statement by the father of those laws, William Morris Stewart: "I have prevented the auctioning of mines." Stewart was relentless in his understanding that mining in the American West meant opportunity for each man despite his monetary fortune; that liberty and its protection resulted in the discovery and development of minerals which countless minions of foreign kings and slaves of pagan fear had only trampled under foot. Liberty was at J. C. Tognoni's core. Those who tell stories of J. C.'s success at Goldfield, like Oscar Streeter who held a seat on the Goldfield-Tonopah Stock Exchange, gave the impression that J. C. was a learned mining man rather than an Italian immigrant with little formal education. In Goldfield he was free to use his God-given intelligence toward the achievement of his ends, which would seem to have been charitable by the nature of the memorials to him on the outer limits of Goldfield mining district—fountains of water where volcanics once quietly flowed onto the surface.

When Frederick Ransome wrote his professional paper for the U.S. Geological Survey on the Goldfield mining district in 1908, Tognoni Springs were frequently correlated: "One of the best places in the district to observe the effusive character of the andesite and to distinguish the superposition of flows is in the steep slope just east of the northernmost of the three Tognoni Springs."[32] The slope to which Ransome refers may very well be Tognoni Mountain, from which the water seeps. J. C. had an affinity for volcanics, the rocks here near Goldfield are very similar to the rocks at his Blackrock Spring near Silverton. The volcanic activity at Goldfield has completely died out. Mines and springs where volcanism has not been so deeply mortified give forth hot water and gases. Tognoni Springs, according to Ransome, are cool.

The springs mark the separation between past and future at Goldfield with the geological transition from intrusive dacite on the west and extrusive dacite on the east. The dacite was the principal country rock of the larger mines, but ore bodies in the district's andesite, particularly in the Daisy mine near Diamondfield and Tognoni Springs, promise deeper deposits.[33] Diamondfield, one of the five townsites organized in the district, is four miles northeast of Goldfield townsite and almost a mile west of Tognoni Springs. Ransome would divide the mines of the district into two groups, which he designated as Goldfield and Diamondfield. Only 5 percent of the mineral from the entirety of Goldfield mining district came from the Diamondfield group of mines.[34] This lesser division of Ransome's may have been a focus of early prospecting where the geology was more familiar than in the extraordinarily rich and shallow deposits neighboring on the southwest.

All over Goldfield district, shafts from 200 to 400 feet in depth were put down and abandoned, often within a few months. The shafts quickly became unaccessible and unsafe, and those who could give witness to the geological secrets within disappeared. The heaps of earth which they left behind will perplex geologists for centuries to come. Just so, my father, the geologist, reluctantly indulges my fascination for things left behind in a junk store on the highway through Goldfield. To him the artifacts are like mineral samples on a dump, divorced from their stories, their settings, their meanings; so I browse only briefly and buy an old bank note which once sufficed as currency in this region where legal tender could not be gotten fast enough.

Our road out to Tognoni Springs is like a tunnel through a theatre of gold mines. On both sides of the road, sun-bleached piles of earth rise in cones around shafts; the grey timbers show like hats on ghostly thespians. Occasionally a skeletal headframe rises to silhouette itself against the clouds of this bright and haunted stage. Out beyond the silent throng as we approach Tognoni Springs, a shack hides a watering trough from our view. The wild burros who drink there scatter up a slope of Tognoni Mountain, where they wait just far enough away to be easily mistaken as Joshua trees, instead of the rootless variety of life that the water here supports. From a source higher in the rocks of the mountain's craggy southern face, the water only trickles into the empty trough.

In the shack with its garden of rubbish, old and new, there is evidence that a young mother may have joined the burros here recently. Alongside the telling clues of her presence are the first pages of *Acts of Love* by Elia Kazan: "This is the way people really talk, argue, make up, lash out." Near the pages is a tiny medallion on which has been pasted the photographed face—rosy, open and smiling—of an Indian woman. My great-grandfather suffered the absence of his wife and family to prospect here at Goldfield.

He would sell his mining claims to an eastern investor, and he would give others away to those who showed him kindness. Like his wit and humor, his acts of generosity were characteristic of the true gambler. Then he took his wealth back to Duckwater, to his family and his beloved irrigation projects. He gambled and won in a district where the unusual richness of the ore was matched only by the remarkable irregularity of the mineral deposits.

The facts about J. C. Tognoni and his mining claims in Goldfield have been difficult to gather because those who have preceded us in examining records and documents of this mining district have not been interested in material germane to our purpose. Significant conclusions about Goldfield are daring, but the only evidence which we have found for the common presumption that Goldfield was mined out is an extensive exploratory drilling program by Newmont Mining Corporation. Even so, the Diamondfield area may not have interested Newmont. What does seem evident is that something important to the spirit of mining in the United States sleeps in Goldfield. So I try to answer the shuttle bus driver from Hertz Rent-a-Car to the airport terminal in Las Vegas, when he inquires about the shovel we carry aboard his transport.

Too tired to speak as we fly into the sunset, we listen to the excited talk behind our seats from some very large men who have just been in attendance at a boxing match in Las Vegas. It is welcome chatter suited to our unflagging optimism that the earth provides equality of opportunity, but that men differ in responding to it. Political changes effect the geography of world mineral production far more than geologic fact, making it unsafe to draw conclusions as to whose foot will fit the glass slipper of mining.[35] I wonder if these young men behind me know that Gans and Nelson had to go forty-two rounds in Goldfield.

J. C. Tognoni with claim monument.   *J. C. Tognoni, c. 1915.*

Endnotes

Introduction

1. Agricola, *De Re Metallica*.
2. *Ibid.*, introduction by Herbert Hoover.
3. Lyons, Eugene, *Herbert Hoover*, p. 68.
4. Bennett, Russell H., *Quest for Ore*, pp. 22-23.
5. Twain, Mark, *Roughing It*, p. 168.
6. Young, Otis, *Western Mining*, p. vii.
7. Agricola, *op. cit.*, p. xxvi.
8. *Ibid.*, pp. 11-12.
9. Dunning, Charles H., *Gold from Caveman to Cosmonaut*.
10. Joraleman, Ira B., *Copper*, p. 22.
11. Lavendar, David, introduction to *Gold and Silver in the West* by T. H. Watkins, p. 11.
12. DeKalb, Courtnay, "William Morris Stewart," *Mining & Scientific Press*.
13. Stewart, William Morris, *Congressional Globe*.
14. Sparks, Jared, ed., *The Works of Benjamin Franklin*, Vol. II, p. 347.
15. *U.S. vs. Desert Gold Mining Co.*, pp. 442-43.
16. *Ibid.*, p. 477.
17. Van Dyke, John C., *The Desert*, p. v.
18. Smith, Lee, "Armand Hammer and the Phosphate Puzzle," *Fortune*.
19. Van Slambrouck, Paul, "First oil, now minerals," *Christian Science Monitor*.
20. Agricola, *op. cit.*, p. 16.

Chapter One—Whispers of the Gold Rush

1. Bidwell, John, et al., *New Helvetia*.
2. Lienhard, Heinrich, *A Pioneer at Sutter's Fort*.
3. *Woodruff vs. North Bloomfield Gravel Mining Company*, "The Debris Case," 16 Fed.Rep.25.
4. "An Act to create the California Debris Commission and regulate hydraulic mining in the State of California," March 1, 1893.
5. Borthwick, J. D., *Three Years in California*.
6. Greenbie, Sydney and Marjorie, *Gold of Ophir*.
7. House Executive Document, 1880, testimony of Aaron Sargent.
8. Clark, William B., *Gold Districts of California*.
9. Kelley, Robert L., *Gold vs. Grain*.

Chapter Two—Abandonment

1. Angel, Myron, ed., *History of Nevada,* facing p. 56.
2. Clark, *Gold Districts of California.*
3. Kelley, *Gold vs. Grain.*
4. Powell, J. W., *Annual Report* of the U.S.G.S., "Geology of Leadville."

Chapter Three—Echoes from Walls of Time

1. House Executive Document, 1880, Report of the Public Lands Commission, testimony of G. F. Allardt and D. A. Ostrom.
2. *Ibid.,* L. L. Robinson, p. 188.
3. Rickard, T. A., *A History of American Mining,* pp. 19, 37.
4. Paul, Rodman, *California Gold,* p. 243.
5. *Ibid.,* pp. 122-23.
6. Littlepage, John D. and Demoree Bess, *In Search of Soviet Gold.*
7. Temple, John, *Mining, An International History.*
8. *Ibid.,* p. 115.
9. *Multiple Use, Inc. vs. Rogers C. B. Morton, Secretary of the Interior,* Ninth Circuit Opinion, Oct. 2, 1974.
10. Shutes, Milton H., "Abraham Lincoln and the New Almaden Mine," *California Historical Quarterly.*
11. House Executive Document, *op. cit.,* testimony of F. J. Wrinkle, p. 439.
12. Pound, Roscoe, "The Law of the Land," *Dakota Law Review.*
13. Young, *Western Mining,* p. 58.
14. Kelley, *Gold vs. Grain,* p. 64.
15. House Executive Document, *op. cit.,* testimony by H. S. Bradley, John S. McBride, John McClay, James McGillivray, B. B. Redding, L. L. Robinson and A. W. Von Schmidt.
16. Dunning, *Gold from Caveman to Cosmonaut,* p. 82.
17. "Banks and Banking in California in the Fifties; Early Legislative Prohibitions," *Mercantile Trust Review of the Pacific.*
18. California State Constitution, Article IV, Sec. 34.
19. Paher, Stanley, *Nevada Ghost Towns and Mining Camps,* p. 130.

Chapter Four—Up Against the Sierra

1. Shinn, Charles Howard, *The Story of the Mine,* pp. 1-2.
2. Stewart, William Morris, *Reminiscences.*
3. Elliott, Russell R., *History of Nevada,* p. 1.
4. *Ibid.,* quoting C. F. Dutton, geographer.
5. Royce, Sarah, *A Frontier Lady,* pp. 27-28.
6. Miller, Max, *Reno.*
7. Angel, ed., *History of Nevada,* pp. 149-65.
8. Royce, *op. cit.,* p. 107.
9. Laughlin, J. Laurence, *The History of Bimetallism in the United States.*
10. Stewart, William Morris, ed., *Silver Knight-Watchman,* August 15, 1895, p. 1.
11. "Gold-to-Silver Ratio Strategy," *Research Study,* North American Coin & Currency, Ltd.
12. Hardy, Charles O., *Is There Enough Gold?*

13. Lehrman, Lewis E., "The Case for the Gold Standard," Morgan Stanley Investment Research.
14. Powell, *Annual Report of the U.S. Geological Survey*, 1880-81.
15. Rocha, Guy Louis, "Nevada Mining Law, Eminent Domain, and Historic Preservation," unpublished paper.
16. Winter, Wayne, ed., *Western Prospector and Miner*, March, 1982, p. 8.
17. Symmes, William, "Decline and Revival of Comstock Mining-II," *Mining and Scientific Press.*

Chapter Five—Chant of the Survivors

1. Paher, *Nevada Ghost Towns and Mining Camps*, p. 79.
2. *Ibid.*, p. 63.
3. Lanner, Ronald M., *The Pinon Pine*, p. 122.
4. Public Law 46, February 25, 1920.
5. Hansen, Clinton J., "Why a Location System for Hard Minerals," *Rocky Mountain Mineral Law Institute.*
6. 29 Stat 526 (1897).
7. Williams, C. C., Jr., "Conservation of Mineral Resources: A Brief Survey,"*West Virginia Law Quarterly and The Bar.*
8. *People vs. Association Oil Co.*, 1930, Santa Fe Springs oil field in California.
9. Williams, *op. cit.*, p. 259.
10. Peck, Raymond A., Jr., "And Then There Were None," *Rocky Mountain Mineral Law Institute*, pp. 26-27.
11. *U.S. vs. Midwest Oil Co.*, 1915.
12. Peffer, E. Louise, *The Closing of the Public Domain*, pp. 131, 316.
13. Taylor, Paul S., "Excess Land Law," Report by Special Advisor on Reclamation, Senate Document, 1924, p. 111, quoting *California Law Review*, Vol. 52, 978.
14. Lanner, *op. cit.*, pp. 132-33.
15. Reich, Charles A., "Bureaucracy and the Forests," Center for the Study of Democratic Institutions, p. 4.
16. Clawson, Marion, *The Federal Lands Since 1956*, p. 27.
17. *Western Rebel*, Nevada periodical, 1980, p. 1.
18. "Hualapais Hire Mexican Oil Hunters," *Arizona Daily Star*, 1982, p. 2.

Chapter Six—Legend of the Family Mine

1. *U.S. vs. Haskins*, Secretary of the Interior's decision, April 22, 1935.
2. *U.S. vs. Haskins*, A-3037, Dec. 19, 1966, Stipulation 23130, Ninth Circuit Court of Appeals app. Oct. 3, 1969.
3. *U.S. vs. Haskins*, 505 F 2nd, 246 (1974).

Chapter Seven—Moon on the Sagebrush

1. Television program on the Great Depression, Public Broadcasting Station, Phoenix, Arizona, 1981.
2. Robinson, Florence B., "Tonopah Nevada, Mizpah, 1907," public relations pamphlet.
3. Shamberger, *Goldfield.*
4. "Guidebook to the Geology of Four Tertiary Volcanic Centers in Central

Nevada," Nevada Bureau of Mines and Geology Report 19, 1974, p. 49.

5. Paher, *Nevada Ghost Towns and Mining Camps*, index under "Wingfield."
6. "Joe Tognoni," anthology of famous characters of Nevada mining districts, p. 77.
7. Unknown volume, "Joe Tognoni," p. 51. The page has been ripped from its source and pasted in a scrapbook kept by Hale Tognoni and his father.
8. Raymond, R. W., "Biographical Notes of Clarence King," *Transactions*, p. 631.
9. Lord, Elliott, *Comstock Mining and Miners*, pp. 61-63.
10. Stewart, *Reminiscences*, p. 130.
11. Zanjani, Sally Springmeyer, *The Unspliced Rail*, pp. 14-15.

Chapter Eight—Journey into Silence

1. Unknown volume, "Joe Tognoni." *See* endnote 7, Chapter 7.
2. Elliott, *History of Nevada*, p. 117.
3. *Ibid.*, p. 264.
4. Paher, *Nevada Ghost Towns and Mining Camps*, p. 353.
5. Fay, Albert H., *A Glossary of Mining and Minerals*, p. 486.
6. Stephen, Charles, "Trying for a Change: Sixteen Years in the White River Valley, Nevada," *Nevada Historical Society Quarterly*, p. 145.
7. Location notice, Nye County Recorder's Office, Tonopah Courthouse.
8. Elliott, *op. cit.*, p. 291.

14. Lanner, *op. cit.*, pp. 132-33.
5. *See* Royce, Sarah, *A Frontier Lady*, pp. 27-28.

Chapter Nine—People's Silver

1. Young, Fred E., "Geological Report on Silverton Mining Property," 1920.
2. Stewart, William Morris, "Analysis of the Functions of Money," Senate document, p. 19.
3. *Ibid.*, p. 10.
4. Laughlin, *The History of Bimetallism*, p. 5
5. Stewart, *op. cit.*, pp. 3, 4, 24.
6. Hepburn, A. Barton, *A History of Currency in the United States*, p. 230.
7. Laughlin, *op. cit.*, p. 116.
8. Temple, *Mining, An International History*, p. 33.
9. Hepburn, *op. cit.*, p. 51.
10. *Ibid.*, pp. 66-67.
11. Stewart, *op. cit.*, p. 7.
12. *Ibid.*, p. 14.
13. *Ibid.*, p. 18.
14. Shamburger, *Goldfield*, p. 195.
15. Stewart, *Reminiscences*, p. 358.
16. White, Trumbull, ed., *Silver and Gold or Both Sides of the Shield*, Introduction of W. H. Harvey by H. M. Thomas at Illinois Club debate between Harvey and Prof. J. L. Laughlin of the University of Chicago, p. 25.
17. Temple, *Mining, An International History*, p. 76.
18. Magdoff, Harry, *The Age of Imperialism*, pp. 35-36.

19. Trescott, Paul, "Central Banking," *Encyclopedia of American Economic History*, p. 744.
20. Becker, William H., "Imperialism," *Ibid.*, p. 884.
21. Melman, Seymour, *The Permanent War Economy.*
22. Bryan, William Jennings, *The First Battle.*

Chapter Ten—Blood to a Metal Heart

1. Jerome, S. E. and D. R. Cook, "Relation of Some Metal Mining Districts in the Western United States to Regional Tectonic Environment and Igneous Activity," Nevada Bureau of Mines Bulletin 69, p. 2.
2. Scheid, Vernon E., dir., "Mineral and Water Resources of Nevada," Nevada Bureau of Mines Bulletin 65, pp. 54-56.
3. *Ibid.*, p. 59.
4. Garside, Larry J. and John H. Schilling, "Thermal Waters of Nevada," Nevada Bureau of Mines Bulletin 91.
5. Angel, ed., *History of Nevada.*
6. Paher, *Nevada Ghost Towns and Mining Camps*, p. 355.
7. Angel, *op. cit.*, p. 516.
8. Paher, *op. cit.*, p. 247.
9. Letter to Andrew Jackson, May 2, 1865, *The War of the Rebellion*, public document, II, 8.
10. Hermann, Ruth, *Gold and Silver Colossus.*
11. Martin, Albro, "Economy from Reconstruction to 1914," *Encyclopedia of American Economic History*, p. 97.
12. McPhee, John, *Basin and Range*, p. 154.

Chapter Eleven—Defiant Dreamers

1. Saint-Exupery, Antoine de, *Wind, Sand and Stars.*
2. "W. F. Mendes," anthology of *Nevadians*, 1910.
3. Stewart, Robert E., Jr., and Mary Frances Stewart, *Adolph Sutro*, pp. 77-80.
4. *Tognoni vs. Irwin*, "Opening Brief for Plaintiff," p. 27.
5. Chan, Loren B., "The Chinese in Nevada," *Nevada Historical Society Quarterly*, p. 266.
6. *Irwin vs. Tognoni*, "Complaint," 1901.
7. Angel, ed., *History of Nevada*, p. 135.
8. *Lux vs. Haggin*, 69, California, 450.
9. Martz, Clyde O., *Cases and Materials on the Law of Natural Resources*, p. 28, quoting from *Water Rights in the Western States*, by Wiel, 3rd ed., Sec. 18.
10. *Ibid.*, p. 126.
11. *Castle vs. Womble*, 19 L.D.455, 1894.
12. Kelley, *Gold vs. Grain*, pp. 71-72.
13. Martz, *op. cit.*, p. 124, note 6.
14. *Ibid.*, p. 41, Act of March 3, 1877, c. 107, Sections 1, 19, Stat. 377 (43 USCA, Sections 321.)
15. *Clark vs. Nash. See* Martz, *op. cit.*, p. 43, note 6.
16. *Tognoni vs. Louisa Irwin, et al.*, "Reply Brief," p. 38.
17. *Ibid.*, p. 31.

18. *Irwin vs. Tognoni, et al. and Risch, et al.*, "Decree," 1909.

Chapter Twelve—Red Rock Pass

1. Job 28:7.
2. Roos, Robert de, *The Thirsty Land*, pp. 77, 91.
3. *Ibid.*, p. 36.
4. Israel, Daniel H., "The Emergence of Tribal Nationalism and Its Impact on Reservation Resource Development," *Colorado Law Review*, p. 620.
5. Shamberger, *Goldfield*, p. 230.
6. Jones, Jesse H., *Fifty Billion Dollars, My Thirteen Years with the RFC*, pp. 42-43.
7. *Ibid.*, p. 441.
8. Israel, *op. cit.*, p. 668.
9. Taylor Grazing Act, June 28, 1934.

Chapter Thirteen—Mountain Link to the Past

1. "Eureka County Resuscitant," presented to American Mining Congress, 1909, p. 9.
2. Foerster, Robert F., *The Italian Emigration of Our Times*, pp. 108-9.
3. *Ibid.*, p. 115.
4. Hague, Arnold, *Geology of the Eureka District*, p. 3.
5. *Eureka Consolidated Mining Co. v. Richmond Mining Co.*, 1877. See Martz, *Cases and Materials on the Law of Natural Resources*, p. 481.
6. Shepperson, *Restless Stranger*, p. 121.
7. Curtis, Joseph Story, *Silver-Lead Deposits of Eureka, Nevada*, p. 78.
8. Angel, *History of Nevada*, pp. 425-26.
9. Young, *Western Mining*, p. 280.
10. Angel, *op. cit.*, p. 430.
11. Paroni, Genevieve M., "A Brief History of Eureka, Nevada."
12. Curtis, *op. cit.*, p. 4.
13. Jastram, Roy W., *Silver, The Restless Metal*, pp. 19-21.
14. Josephson, Matthew, *The Money Lords*, p. 53.
15. *U.S. Constitution*, Clause 1, Section 10, Article I; Clause 5, Section 8, Article I. See A. L. Fitzgerald, *The Thirty Years War on Silver*, p. 174.

Chapter Fourteen—Miner's Destiny

1. Elliott, *History of Nevada*, p. 184.
2. Lewis, George Randall, *The Stannaries*, p. 73.
3. Foerster, *The Italian Emigration of Our Times*, p. 125.
4. Shepperson, *Restless Strangers*, pp. 121-22.
5. Chan, "The Chinese in Nevada," *Nevada Historical Society Quarterly*, pp. 283-84.
6. Shepperson, *op. cit.*
7. Foerster, *op. cit.*, p. 326.
8. Earl, Philip J., "Nevada's Italian War," *Nevada Historical Society Quarterly*, pp. 53-54.
9. Angel, *History of Nevada*, p. 438.
10. *Ibid.*, p. 436.

11. Salisbury, David F., "How a former Arizona strip mine was turned into valuable farm land," *Christian Science Monitor*.
12. Dvorchak, Bob, "Coal town's longtime eyesore may become magnet for jobs," *Arizona Daily Star*.
13. Curtis, *Silver-Lead Deposits of Eureka, Nevada*.
14. Lewis, *op. cit.*, p. 13.
15. Raymond, R. W., "Biographical Notes of Clarence King," p. 635.
16. Angel, *op. cit.*, pp. 431-32.
17. "Eureka County Resuscitant," p. 21.
18. *Ibid.*, p. 19.

Chapter Fifteen—Beneath the Wounds of Greed

1. Paul, Rodman, "The Beginnings of Agriculture in California," *Essays and Assays: California History Reappraised*, p. 37.
2. Lillard, Richard G., *Desert Challenge*, p. 13.
3. Stout, Wesley, "High, Wide and Handsome," *Saturday Evening Post*.
4. Lillard, *op. cit.*, p. 254.
5. Stout, *op. cit.*
6. Stout, *op. cit.*, p. 19.
7. Forward Mining Development Company, "Facts about Goldfield, Nevada," p. 6.
8. Stout, *op. cit.*, p. 18.
9. Genesis 31: 45-52.
10. Lillard, *op. cit.*, p. 262.
11. Watkins, *Gold and Silver in the West*, p. 142.
12. Shamberger, *Goldfield*, p. 175.
13. Shannon, Charles W., "Geological report on Cascabel property, Arizona," April 1972.
14. Paul, Rodman, *California Gold*, p. 263.

Chapter Sixteen—Water from the Rock

1. Williams, C. C., Jr., "Conservation of Mineral Resources," *West Virginia Law Quarterly and Bar*, pp. 247-75.
2. "Guidebook to the Geology of Four Tertiary Volcanic Centers in Central Nevada," Nevada Bureau of Mines and Geology Report 19, p. 49.
3. Carlson, Helen S., *Nevada Place Names*, p. 109.
4. Angel, *History of Nevada*, p. 82.
5. Shamberger, *Goldfield*, pp. 165-66.
6. Stout, "High, Wide and Handsome," *Saturday Evening Post*.
7. Shamberger, *op. cit.*, p. 173.
8. Lillard, *Desert Challenge*, p. 252.
9. Shamberger, *op. cit.*, p. 92.
10. Rickard, T. A., "Rich Ore and Its Moral Effects," *Mining & Scientific Press*, pp. 774-75.
11. Ransome, F. L., *The Geology and Ore Deposits of Goldfield, Nevada*, p. 197.
12. *Ibid.*, p. 60.
13. Shamberger, *op. cit.*, p. 173.

14. Ransome, *op. cit.*, p. 18.
15. Schreier, Nancy B., *Highgrade*, p. 20.
16. Livermore, Shaw, "Early American Land Companies," p. 41.
17. Watkins, *Gold and Silver in the West*, p. 142.
18. Johnson, Hugh A. and Harold T. Jorgenson, *The Land Resources of Alaska*, pp. 284-85.
19. Lillard, *op. cit.*, p. 78.
20. Livermore, *op. cit.*, p. 78.
21. Ransome, *op. cit.*, p. 20.
22. Ransome, *op. cit.*, p. 23.
23. Senate Reports Nos. 1649, 1650, Oct. 20, 1942.
24. House Report 5667, Sept. 16, 1941.
25. Jones, *Fifty Billion Dollars*, pp. 445-46.
26. Hearings, Senate Committee for Banks and Currency, Subcommittee on RFC, June 22, 23 and 30, 1949, p. 35.
27. House Executive Document 1880, Report of the Public Lands Commission, testimony of John McDonald.
28. Livermore, *op. cit.*, p. 51.
29. Lewis, *The Stannaries*, pp. 67-68.
30. *Ibid.*, pp. 41-42.
31. Livermore, *op. cit.*
32. Ransome, *op. cit.*, p. 54.
33. *Ibid.*, p. 22.
34. Shamberger, *op. cit.*, p. 30.
35. Leith, C. M., Cleana Lewis and J. W. Furness, *World Minerals and World Peace*, pp. 100-101.

Bibliography

Books

Agricola, Georgius. *De Re Metallica*, 1556. Translated by President and Mrs. Herbert Hoover. New York: Dover, c. 1950.

Angel, Myron, ed. *History of Nevada*. Thompson and West, 1881. Reprint. Berkeley, Calif.: Howell-North, c. 1958.

Bennett, Russell H. *Quest for Ore*. Minneapolis: T. S. Denison & Co., c. 1963.

Bidwell, John, William L. Loher, Captain Sutter, William F. Swasey. *New Helvetia*. San Francisco: Grabhorn Press, c. 1939.

Borthwick, J. D. *3 Years in California*. First printed in Edinburgh, Scotland, 1857. Reprint. Oakland, Calif.: Biobooks, c. 1948.

Brennan, John A. *Silver and the First New Deal*. Reno: University of Nevada, c. 1969.

Bryan, William Jennings. *The First Battle*. Chicago: W. B. Cankey Co., c. 1896.

Carlson, Helen S. *Nevada Place Names*. Reno: University of Nevada Press, c. 1974.

Clark, William B. *Gold District of California*. San Francisco: California Division of Mines and Geology, Bulletin 193, c. 1970.

Clawson, Marian. *The Federal Lands Since 1956*. Washington, D.C.: Resources for the Future, Inc., c. 1967.

_____ *Man and Land in the United States*. Lincoln, Nebr.: University of Nebraska, c. 1964.

Curtis, Joseph Story. *Silver-Lead Deposits of Eureka, Nevada*. Monographs of the U.S. Geological Survey, Vol. VII. Washington, D.C.: Government Printing Office, c. 1884.

Dangberg, Grace. *Conflict in the Carson*. Minden, Nev.: Carson Valley Historical Society, c. 1975.

Dunning, Charles H., with Ralph Sadler. *Gold from Caveman to Cosmonaut*. New York: Vantage Press, c. 1970.

Elliott, Russell R. *History of Nevada*. Lincoln, Nebr.: University of Nebraska, c. 1973.

_____ *Nevada's Twentieth Century Mining Boom*. Reno: University of Nevada, c. 1966.

Fay, Albert H. *A Glossary of Mining and Minerals*. Washington, D.C.: U.S. Department of the Interior, Bulletin 95, c. 1948.

Fitzgerald, A. L. *The Thirty Years War on Silver*. New York: Greenwood Press, c. 1903.

Foerster, Robert F. *The Italian Emigration of Our Times*. Cambridge, Mass.: Harvard University, c. 1919.

Gilbert, Milton. *Quest for World Monetary Order: The Gold Dollars System and Its Aftermath*. New York: John Wiley & Sons, c. 1980.

Greenbie, Sydney, and Marjorie Greenbie. *Gold of Ophir: The China Trade in the Making of America*. New York: Wilson-Erickson, c. 1937.

Hague, Arnold. *Geology of Eureka District*. Monographs of the U.S. Geological Survey, Vol. XX. Washington, D.C.: Government Printing Office, c. 1892.

Hardy, Charles O. *Is There Enough Gold?* Washington, D.C.: Brookings Institute, c. 1936.

Hawtrey, R. G. *The Gold Standard in Theory and Practice*. New York: Longmaus, Green & Company, c. 1947.

Hermann, Ruth. *Gold and Silver Colossus*. Sparks, Nev.: Dave's Printing, c. 1975.

Jastram, Ray W. *Silver, The Restless Metal*. New York: John Wiley & Sons, c. 1981.

Johnson, Hugh A., and Harold T. Jorgenson. *The Land Resources of Alaska*. New York: Arno Press, c. 1963.

Jones, Jesse H., with Edward Angly. *Fifty Billion Dollars, My Thirteen Years (1932-1945) with the RFC*. New York: MacMillan Company, c. 1951.

Joraleman, Ira B. *Copper*. Berkeley, Calif.: Howell-North, c. 1973.

Josephson, Matthew. *The Money Lords: The Great Finance Capitalists, 1925-1950*. New York: Waybright and Talley, Inc., c. 1972.

Kelley, Robert L. *Gold vs. Grain*. Glendale, Calif.: A. H. Clark, c. 1959.

Lanner, Ronald M. *The Pinon Pine: A Natural and Cultural History*. Reno: University of Nevada, c. 1982.

Laughlin, J. Laurence. *The History of Bimetallism in the United States*. New York: D. Appleton & Company, c. 1896.

Leith, C. L., Cleana Lewis, J. W. Furness. *World Minerals and World Peace*. Washington, D.C.: Brookings Institute, c. 1943.

Lewis, George Randall. *The Stannaries: A Study of the English Tin Miner*. Cambridge, Mass.: Harvard University, c. 1907.

Lienhard, Heinrich, trans. by Marguerite Eyer Wilbur. *A Pioneer at Sutter's Fort, 1846-1850*. Sacramento: California State Library. No. 3 of the Calafia Series, c. 1941.

Lillard, Richard G. *Desert Challenge*. New York: Alfred A. Knopf, c. 1949.

Lindgren, Waldemar. *Ore Deposits of the Western United States*. New York: Rocky Mountain Fund, c. 1933. American Institute of Mining and Metallurgical Engineers publication.

Lindley, Curtis H. *American Law Relating to Mines and Minerals Lands*. San Francisco: Bancroft-Whitney Company, c. 1897. 3 volumes.

Littlepage, John D., and Demoree Bess. *In Search of Soviet Gold*. New York: Harcourt, Brace and Company, c. 1937.

Livermore, Shaw. *Early American Land Companies: Their Influence on Corporate Development*. New York: Commonwealth Fund, c. 1939.

Lord, Elliott. *Comstock Mining and Miners, 1883*. San Diego: Howell-North, c. 1951.

Lovering, T. S. *Minerals in World Affairs*. New York: Prentice Hall, c. 1943.

Lyons, Eugene. *Herbert Hoover*. Garden City, N.Y.: Doubleday, c. 1964.

Magdoff, Harry. *The Age of Imperialism*. New York: Monthly Review Press, c. 1969.

Marcosson, Isaac F. *Anaconda*. New York: Dodd, Mead and Co., c. 1957.

Martz, Clyde O. *Cases and Materials on the Law of Natural Resources*. St. Paul, Minn.: West Publishing, c. 1951.

McPhee, John. *Basin and Range*. New York: Farrar, Straus, Giroux, c. 1981.

Melman, Seymour. *The Permanent War Economy*. New York: Simon and Schuster, c. 1974.

Miller, Max. *Reno*. New York: Dodd, Mead and Company, c. 1941.

Paher, Stanley W. *Nevada Ghost Towns and Mining Camps*. Berkeley, Calif.: Howell-North, c. 1970.

Paul, Rodman W. *California Gold, The Beginning of Mining in the Far West*. Lincoln, Nebr.: University of Nebraska, c. 1947.

Peffer, E. Louise. *The Closing of the Public Domain*. Stanford, Calif.: Stanford University, c. 1951.

Ransome, F. L. *The Geology and Ore Deposits of Goldfield, Nevada*. Washington, D.C.: Government Printing Office, c. 1909. Professional Paper 66, U.S. Geological Survey.

Ravage, M. E. *The Story of Teapot Dome*. New York: Burt Franklin Reprints, c. 1924.

Reich, Charles A. *Bureaucracy and the Forest*. Santa Barbara, Calif.: Center for the Study of Democratic Institutions, c. 1972.

Rickard, T. A. *A History of American Mining*. New York: McGraw-Hill, c. 1932.

_____ *Man and Metals*. New York: McGraw-Hill, c. 1932. 2 volumes.

Robbins, Roy M. *Our Landed Heritage*. Lincoln, Nebr.: University of Nebraska, c. 1942.

Roos, Robert de. *The Thirsty Land*. Stanford, Calif.: Stanford University, c. 1948.

Royce, Sarah. *A Frontier Lady*. Lincoln, Nebr.: University of Nebraska, c. 1932.

Saint-Exupery, Antoine de. *Wind, Sand and Stars*. Translated by Lewis Galanteire. Cornwell Press, c. 1939.

Schreier, Nancy B. *Highgrade: The Mining Story of National Nevada.* Glendale, Calif.: Arthur H. Clark Co., c. 1981.

Shamberger, Hugh A. *Goldfield.* Carson City, Nev.: Nevada Historical Press, c. 1982.

Shepperson, Wilbur Stanley. *Restless Strangers: Nevada's Immigrants and Their Interpreters.* Reno: University of Nevada, c. 1970.

Shinn, Charles Howard: *The Story of the Mine.* New York: D. Appleton and Co., c. 1896.

Stegner, Wallace. *Angle of Repose.* New York: Fawcett-Crest, c. 1971.

Stewart, Robert E., Jr., and Mary Frances Stewart. *Adolph Sutro.* Berkeley, Calif.: Howell-North, c. 1962.

Stewart, William Morris. *Reminiscences.* New York: Neale Publishing, c. 1908.

Taussig, F. W. *The Silver Situation in the United States.* New York: G. P. Putnam's Sons, c. 1893.

Temple, John. *Mining: An International History.* New York: Praeger, c. 1972.

Twain, Mark. *Roughing It.* 1872. Reprint. New York, Harper and Row, c. 1962.

Vanderberg, William O. *Placer Mining in Nevada.* Reno: University of Nevada, c. 1936.

Van Dyke, John C. *The Desert.* 1901. Reprint. Salt Lake City: Peregrine Smith, c. 1980.

Watkins, T. H. *Gold and Silver in the West.* New York: Bonanza Books, c. 1971.

White, Trumbull. *Silver and Gold on Both Sides of the Shield.* C. 1985.

Young, Otis E. *Western Mining.* University of Oklahoma, c. 1970.

Zanjani, Sally Springmeyer. *The Unspiked Rail.* Reno: University of Nevada, c. 1981.

Essays
(Quarterlies, Law Reviews, Research Studies, Reports, Anthologies, etc.)

"Banks and Banking in California in the Fifties: Early Legislative Prohibitions," *Mercantile Trust Review of the Pacific*, June 1924, pp. 118-28.

Becker, William H. "Imperialism," *Encyclopedia of American Economic History.* New York: Charles Scribner, c. 1980.

Chan, Loren B. "The Chinese in Nevada: An Historical Survey, 1856-1970," *Nevada Historical Society Quarterly*, Vol. XXV, Winter 1982, No. 4.

Colby, William E. "The Freedom of the Miner and Its Influence on Water Law," *Legal Essays.* Berkeley, Calif.: University of California, c. 1935, pp. 67-84.

"Eureka County Resuscitant." Mining and Other Resources of Eureka County, Nevada, presented to the American Mining Congress, Goldfield, Nevada, Sept. 27, 1909.

Emmons, S. F. "Geological Distribution of the Useful Metals in the United States," *Transactions*, A.I.M.E., Vol. XXII, 1893.

———— "The Mining Work of the U.S. Geological Survey," *Transactions*, A.I.M.E, 1881-1882.

Foreward Mining Development Co. (Suite 19, Toltec Block, Denver, Colo.) "Facts about Goldfield, Nevada," c. 1905.

Garside, Larry J., and John H. Schilling. "Thermal Waters of Nevada," Nevada Bureau of Mines and Geology, Bulletin 91, 1979.

"Gold-to-Silver Ratio Strategy," Research Study by North American Coin and Currency, Ltd., Chamber of Commerce Center, Phoenix, Ariz.

"Guidebook to the Geology of Four Tertiary Volcanic Centers in Central Nevada," Nevada Bureau of Mines and Geology Report 19, Mackay School of Mines, University of Nevada, c. 1974.

Hanson, Clinton J. "Why a Location System for Hard Minerals?" *Rocky Mountain Mineral Law Institute*, Vol. 13.

Israel, Daniel H. "The Emergency of Tribal Nationalism and Its Impact on Reservation Resource Development, *Colorado Law Review*, Vol. 47, 1976.

Jerome, S. E., and D. R. Cook. "Relation of Some Metal Mining Districts in the Western United States to Regional Tectonic Environment and Igneous Activity," Nevada Bureau of Mines, Bulletin 69, 1967.

"Joe Tognoni." Anthology of famous characters of Nevada mining districts, Nevada Historical Society Library. Referenced under Joe Tognoni.

Johnson, J. W. "Early Engineering Center in California," *California Historical Society Quarterly*, Vol. XXIX, 1950, p. 193.

Lehrman, Lewis E. "The Case for the Gold Standard," Morgan Stanley Investment Research, New York, c. 1981.

Lewin, Tobias. "The History of Government Property in Minerals in the United States," *St. Louis Law Review*, Vol. 16, 1930-31.

Martin, Albro. "Economy from Reconstruction to 1914," *Encyclopedia of American Economic History*, Vol. 1, c. 1980. New York: Charles Scribner.

Merrill, Charles W. "The Significance of the Mineral Industries in the Economy," *Economics of the Mineral Industries*, 1964.. Edited by Edward A. Robie. American Institute of Mining Engineers' Seeley Mudd Series of Articles by Specialists. Penn.: The Maple Press Co.

Paroni, Genevieve M. "A Brief History of Eureka, Nevada," Historical Society of Eureka.

Paul, Rodman. "The Beginning of Agriculture in California: Innovation Versus Continuity," *California History Reappraised*, California Historical Society, 1973.

Peck, Raymond A., Jr. "And Then There Were None," *Rocky Mountain Mineral Law Institute*, Vol. 25, Article 3.

Pound, Roscoe. "The Law of the Land," *Dakota Law Review*, October, 1927, Vol. 1, No. 4.

Powell, J. W. *Annual Report*, U.S. Geological Survey, 1880-81.

Raymond, R. W. "Biographical Notice of Clarence King," *Transactions*, A.I.M.E., Vol. XXXIII, 1903.

Raymond, Rossiter W. "The History of the Relative Values of Gold and Silver," *Transactions*, A.I.M.E., Vol. III, 1874-75.

Reich, Charles A. "Bureaucracy and the Forests," Center for the Study of Democratic Institutions, Santa Barbara, Calif., c. 1962.

Robinson, Florence B. "Tonopah Nevada, Mizpah, 1907," Union Plaza Hotel Public Relations Dept., Las Vegas, 1979.

Rocha, Guy Louis. "Nevada Mining Law, Eminent Domain, and Historic Preservation: A Study in Conflicting Public Use and Limitations of the Police Power," unpublished paper, University of Nevada, May 15, 1980.

Scheid, Vernon E. "Mineral and Water Resources in Nevada," Nevada Bureau of Mines, Bulletin 65, 1964.

Shannon, Charles W. "Geological Report on Cascabel Property, Arizona," April 1972.

Shutes, Milton H. "Abraham Lincoln and the New Almaden Mine," *California Historical Quarterly*, Vol. XV, March 1936.

Stephen, Charles. "Trying for a Change: Sixteen Years in the White River Valley, Nevada," *Nevada Historical Society Quarterly*, Vol. XXV, Summer 1982, No. 2.

Stewart, William Morris. "Analysis of the Functions of Money," Senate Document No. 336, 55th Congress, 2nd Session, July 6 , 1898, Vol. 26.

Taylor, Paul S. "Excess Land Law: Calculated Circumvention," Report by Special Advisor on Reclamation, Senate Document No. 92, 68th Congress, 1st Session, 1924.

Trescott, Paul. "Central Banking," *Encyclopedia of American Economic History*, Vol. 1, c. 1980. New York: Charles Scribner.

Walcott, Charles D. *Annual Report*, U.S. Geological Survey, 1884-85.

"W. F. Mendes," *Nevadians* (anthology), Nevada Historical Society Library, c. 1910.

Williams, C. C., Jr. "Conservation of Mineral Resources: A Brief Survey," *West Virginia Law Quarterly and The Bar*, Vol. XLVII, June 1941.

Young, Fred E. "Geological Report on Silverton Mining Property," 1920.

Periodicals

Courtland, Lee, and David Russell. "Federal Leasing: The Need for a Perspective," *Mining Engineering*, Vol. 29, No. 5, May 1977.

Davenport, John A. "The New Allure of the Gold Standard," *Fortune*, April 7, 1980.

Dvorchak, Bob. "Coal town's longtime eyesore may become magnet for jobs,"

Arizona Daily Star, March 27, 1983, Sec. B, p. 3.

"Hualapais Hire Mexican Oil Hunters," Denver AP, *Arizona Daily Star*, May 11, 1982, Sec. A, p. 2.

Lehrman, Lewis. "The Means to Establishing Financial Order," *Wall Street Journal*, Feb. 18, 1981.

Rickard, Thomas A. "Rich Ore and Its Moral Effects," *Mining & Scientific Press*, Vol. XCVI, 1908.

Salisbury, David F. "How a former Arizona strip mine was turned into valuable farm land," *Christian Science Monitor*, March 9, 1982.

Smith, Lee. "Armand Hammer and the Phosphate Puzzle," *Fortune*, April 7, 1980, pp. 48-51.

Stewart, William Morris, ed. *Silver Knight-Watchman*, August 15, 1895, first edition, p. 1.

Stout, Wesley. "High, Wide and Handsome," *Saturday Evening Post*, February 28, 1931, pp. 18-19, 82-87.

Symmes, Whitman. "Decline and Revival of Comstock Mining," *Mining & Scientific Press*, Vol. XCVII, Oct. 12 and 24, 1908, pp. 496-500 and 570-76.

Van Slambrouck, Paul. "First oil, now minerals—U.S. frets at import growth," *Christian Science Monitor*, Oct. 2, 1980, pp. 1, 6.

Wargo, Joseph G. "The Next Exploration Stage for Carlin-Type Gold Deposits," *Mining Engineering*, Vol. 31, No. 9, September 1979.

Western Rebel, first edition, Nevada, September 1980.

Winter, Wayne, ed. *Western Prospector & Miner*, March 1982, p. 8.

Other

California State Constitution, Article IV, Section 34.

Caminetti Act, "An Act to create the California Debris Commission and regulate hydraulic mining in the State of California," March 1, 1893, ch. 183, 27 Stat.L507; 6 Fed.Stat.

Castle vs. Womble, 19L.D.,455, 1894.

Clark vs. Nash, 198 U.S.361,370,25S.Ct.676, 49L.Ed.1085, 4 Ann. Cas. 1171, Justice Peckham.

Eureka Consolidated Mining Co. vs. Richmond Mining Co., Cir. Ct. for U.S. Dist. of Nevada, 1877. 4 Sawy.302, Fed. Cas. No. 4548.

Hearings, Senate Committee for Banks and Currency, Subcommittee on RFC, June 22, 23 and 30, 1949.

House Executive Document No. 46, 46th Congress, 2nd Session, 1880. Report of Public Lands Commission created by Act of March 3, 1879.

House Executive Document No. 730, 84th Congress, 1st Session 6, 1955. Outline of abuses prompting "common varieties act," 69 Stat.367.

House Report 5667, September 16, 1941.

Irwin vs. Tognoni, "Complaint," 5th Dist. Ct. of Nevada, 1901.

Irwin vs. Tognoni, et al. and Risch, et al., "Decree," 5th Dist. Ct. of Nevada, December 1, 1901, Judge Mark R. Averill.

Lux vs. Haggin, 69, California, 450, Justice Ross.

Multiple Use, Inc. vs. Rogers C. B. Morton, Secretary of the Interior, U.S. Court of Appeals for the Ninth Circuit, No. 73-1218, Opinion filed, October 2, 1974.

People vs. Association Oil Co., 211 Cal93, 294 Pac.717.

Public Law 46, February 25, 1920.

Report of the Committee on the Conservation and Administration of the Public Domain (Hoover Commission), Jan. 1, 1931. Transmitted to the U.S. President in pursuance of Act of April 10, 1930.

Senate Document No. 154, 58th Congress, 3rd Session, 1905. Report of Public Lands Commission of 1903.

Senate Document No. 188, 58th Congress, 2nd Session, 1904. Report of Public Lands Commission created in 1903.

Senate Report Nos. 1649 and 1650, 77th Congress, 2nd Session, October 20, 1942.

Stewart, William Morris. *Congressional Globe*, June 18, 1866. 39th Congress, 1st Session, pp. 3225-29.

Taylor Grazing Act, June 28, 1934, 48 Stat.1269 (1943) as amended 43 U.S.C., Sec.315, 3152-3154 (1952).

Tognoni vs. Irwin, et al. "Opening Brief for Plaintiff" and "Reply to Brief," P. E. Keeler, Thomas E. Kepner, Charles H. Burritt, 5th Dist. Ct. of Nevada, 1910.

29 Stat.526 (1897).

U.S. Constitution, clause I, section 10, article I, clause 5, section 8, article I.

U.S. vs. Desert Gold Mining Co., No. CIV-4883 Phx., November 1963.

U.S. vs. Haskins, Secretary of Interior's decision, April 22, 1935.

U.S. vs. Haskins. A-3037, December 19, 1966, Stipulation 23.20, Ninth Cir. Ct. of Appeals, app. October 3, 1969.

U.S. vs. Haskins, 505 F.2d, 246 (1974).

U.S. vs. Midwest Oil Co., 236 U.S.459 (1915) at 472-473.

Woodruff vs. North Bloomfield Gravel Mining Company, 16 Fed. Rep. 25, April 1883, "Debris Case."

Index

Agricola, ix, xv
Alaska, 8, 46, 136, 139, 140
Anaconda Copper Company, 36, 90, 153
Andesite, 67, 155
Antimony, 59, 75, 86, 87
Appalachian gold fields, 20
Arizona, 21, 64, 90, 131, 141, 142, 143, 144, 152, 155
Arkansas, 90
Assessible Stock Corporation, 32
Australia, ix, 8, 46, 81, 121, 151
Austria, 78

Bank of California, 24
Banking, 31, 81, 82, 96, 100, 114, 122, 153
Baruch, Bernard, 78
Basalt, 23, 65, 67
Basque, 36, 61
Bimetallism, 1, 29, 47, 75-78, 80, 81, 82, 96, 101, 121, 122
Britain, xiii, 22, 32, 45, 77, 80-82, 120-22, 152, 154, 155
Bryan, William Jennings, 80, 108, 149
Butler, Jim, 55, 56, 57
Butte, Montana, 90, 130, 152, 153

Caminetti Act, 5
Canada, 81, 144
Carbonari, 38, 41, 46, 47, 127
Carlin Mine, 32, 117
Carnegie Institute (Department of Terrestrial Magnetism), 111
Carson City Mint, 27, 35
Carson River, 94
Carson Valley, 62
Carson River, 94
Catholic Church, 4, 69, 125, 126
Charcoal, 38, 41, 65, 119, 126, 127
Cherokee, 12, 17, 23, 24
Chinese (China), ix, 20, 25, 36, 38, 46, 65, 102, 123, 125, 126
Cinnabar, 58
Civil War, xiii, 16, 20, 21, 62, 83, 87-89, 121, 125
Clay, 120, 133, 140, 141
Coal, 111, 129, 150

Colorado, 17, 46, 47, 104, 152
Como, 35, 36, 62
Comstock, 12, 16, 24, 27, 30-32, 35, 56, 61, 62, 98, 121, 137
Copper, 21, 36, 40, 64, 65, 66, 69, 78, 83, 86, 88, 90, 123, 141, 143, 145, 154
Cornwall, xi, 21, 65, 81, 129
Curtis, Joseph Story, 121
Cyaniding, 83, 89, 91, 132, 144
Cyprus Mines, 88

Dangberg, 94
Davis, Diamondfield Jack, 57, 139
"Debris Case," 5, 8, 12
Dredging, 15, 16, 23, 25, 144, 151
Duckwater, Nevada, 2, 3, 8, 39, 58, 63, 79, 88, 91, 93-100, 102, 103, 106-9, 117, 118, 135

Electrum, 120, 123
Elko, Nevada, 71
Ely, Nevada, 64, 117, 132
Emmons, S. F., 17
Eureka, Nevada, 63, 66, 78, 102, 109, 116, 117, 118-21, 125-30, 131, 132, 134, 135
Exxon Mineral Co., 145

Federal Reserve, 80
Field, Stephen Justice, 119
Fort Churchill, 35, 36
France, xiii, 75, 77, 119
Franklin, Benjamin, xiii
Fraternal Orders, 125
Freiburg, 12, 21
Fremont, John C., 3, 28

Germany, xiii, 12, 21, 30, 47, 82, 119, 126, 144
Gianella, Vincent, 8, 11-18, 19, 22, 23, 24, 25, 62, 90, 99
Gold, xi, xiii-xiv, xv, 6, 8, 12, 15, 16, 19-23, 28-31, 46, 56, 60, 63, 75, 76-78, 80-83, 90, 95, 104, 113, 114, 117, 120-24, 132-34, 136-39, 142, 144, 149, 150, 151, 152, 154
Goldfield, Nevada, 56, 57, 63, 67, 102, 106, 136-39, 145, 147-52, 155, 156, 157
Grangers, 113
Granite, 14, 16, 25, 27, 47, 67, 119, 150

Grass Valley, California, 10, 12-14
Gresham's Law, 77, 121-24
Guggenheims, 132

Hague, Arnold, 118
Hamilton, Alexander, 29
Hamilton, Nevada, 12, 88, 96, 134
Hammon, W. P., 23
Hammon, John Hays, 47
Harvey, William Hope, 80
High Grading, 150
Highways, 63, 64, 89, 138
Hoover, Herbert, ix
Houston Oil and Minerals Company, 31
Hydraulic Mining, 5, 8, 12, 13-15, 20, 23, 151,
    154

Incan Indians, 60
India, ix, 75, 121, 122
Indians, 28, 33, 35, 36, 38, 40, 42, 43, 56, 65, 66,
    71, 90, 99, 100, 102, 114, 115, 129, 142
Ireland, xiii, 46, 65
Iron, 15, 56, 67, 144, 155
Irrigation, 56, 71, 79, 100-104, 105, 106, 108, 112,
    113, 117, 118
Italians, 36-41, 62, 65, 102, 118, 119, 126-28, 138

Jackson, President Andrew, 82
Jefferson, Thomas, 29, 82, 83
Judson, Egbert, 23

King, Clarence, 60, 130
Kloez, Dr. Hans, 14

Labor, 81, 114, 149
Lake Lahontan, 36, 118
Lead, 36, 38, 40, 65, 75, 89, 120, 121, 128, 142,
    143
Leasing Minerals, 40-42, 112
Limestone, 47, 49-52, 65, 74, 75, 84, 90, 97, 119,
    120, 141
Lincoln, Abraham, 22, 82
Lindgren, Waldemar, 16, 144
Locke, John, 122
Locke, Madison, 87-88, 113

Mackay School of Mines, 12, 33, 58, 90
Malakoff Pit, 11, 15, 16
Marx, Karl, 76
McCarran, Senator Patrick, 64
McGill, Nevada, 78, 83, 84, 132
Mercury, 58, 153
Mexico, xiii, 30, 75, 82
Mining Laws, xii, xiii, 7, 16, 20, 21, 22, 40, 41, 52,
    53, 57, 103, 104, 105, 112, 119, 148, 152, 155
Mobil Oil, 142
Molybdenum, 86, 145

Money (paper), 20, 21, 29, 83, 84
Mormons, 30, 98

Nelson, Harry E., 90, 141
Nevada City, California, 4-7
Nevada State Legislature, 58, 151
New Almaden Quicksilver Mine, 22
New Idria Quicksilver Mine, 58
Newmont Mining Company, 4, 32, 143, 157
Newton, Sir Isaac, 121, 122
New York, 57, 64, 132
Nixon, George, 57, 78, 150
North Bloomfield Mining District, 15-16

Oddie, Tasker L., 57, 64, 70
Ophir, xiv, 6, 8
Ormsby Massacre, 28, 36
Oroville, California, 17, 19, 22, 23
Overland Trail, 3

Parks, William H., 104
Peterson, Bill, 96, 99
Phelps Dodge, 66, 86
Phillips Petroleum, 134
Pittman, Senator Key, 32, 64, 68, 71, 101, 151
Platinum, 60, 140, 141, 144
Polk, President, 40
Powell, Wesley, 30
Precious Minerals, 17, 32, 47, 56, 77, 81, 144
Public Lands, xv, 7, 21, 33, 40-42, 50, 52, 53, 90,
    105, 115

Quartz, 8, 13, 15, 16
Quicksilver, 22

Railroads, 62, 63, 64, 89, 102, 106, 117, 119, 127,
    138
Railroad Valley, 4, 63, 68, 71, 79, 86-91, 108, 110,
    135
Ralston, W. C., 24, 101
Ransome, Frederick, 155, 156
Reconstruction Finance Corp., 113, 114, 140,
    153
Reno, 6, 25, 27, 58, 59
Rhyolite, 46, 67, 86, 120
Rice, George Graham, 139, 149, 151
Richthofen, Baron, 30
Rickard, T. A., 150
Roman Mining Law, xii, 103
Roosevelt, Franklin, 16, 17, 21, 32, 51, 68, 82,
    101, 113, 123, 153
Roosevelt, Theodore, 149
Rothchild, 78
Russia, ix, xv, 11, 20, 139

Sadler, Reinhold, 125
Salt, 87, 129
Sargent, Aaron, 5, 7

Sawyer, Judge Lorenzo, 5. *See also* "Debris Case" and Hydraulic Mining
Searls Historical Library, 4, 5
Shale, 119, 129
Sherman Silver Purchase Act, 47
Shurz, 35, 39, 40
Silica, 59, 67, 78, 93, 132, 133
Silver, xiii, 29-33, 38, 47, 56, 64, 65, 68, 69, 73-79, 80-84, 86, 89, 90, 114, 120-22, 125, 128, 132, 142, 143, 144, 145
Slavic Miners, 119
South Africa, ix, 47, 81, 129
South America, 83, 126
South Dakota, 21, 138
Spain (Spanish), xi, xiii, 22, 36, 77, 80
Sparks (Nevada governor), 149
Spring Valley Mining Company, 12, 23
Stalin, 21
Steamboat Springs, 59, 61
Stewart, William Morris, xii, xiii, xiv, 5, 8, 32, 75, 76, 77, 78, 80, 88, 101, 148, 155
Stimler, Harry, 32, 58, 68, 114
Sutro, Aldolph, 31, 35, 96
Sutter (Sutter's Fort), 1-3, 6

Taft, President William, 149
Tax on Mines, 148, 154
Teapot Dome, 42
Thomas, Charles S. (Colorado governor), 152
Tin, 144
Tonopah, 1, 55-57, 63, 64, 101, 102, 131, 136-39
Troy, Nevada, 88-89
Tungsten, 144, 153
Twain, Mark, x, 43, 131, 148
Tybo, 65, 134

United States Government
    Atomic Energy Commission, 60, 61, 64
    Conservation and Administration of Public Lands, 42
    Defense Department, 43, 55
    Forest Service, Department of Agriculture, 21, 42, 50-53
    Geological Survey, 17, 30, 59-61, 94, 112, 118, 120, 121, 130, 143, 155
    Interior, Department of, 40, 41, 50, 113
    Land Management, Bureau of, xiii, 42
    Mines, Bureau of, 143, 147
    Reclamation, 42, 98, 102, 105, 106
    Securities Exchange Commission, 43, 140, 152, 153
    Treasury, 29, 77, 82, 114
Uranium, 47, 52, 60
Utility Companies, 5, 112

Vanadium, 47, 49, 50

Wales, xiii, 119
Walsh, James, 61
Water, 17, 56-58, 59, 62, 65, 67, 91, 94-98, 99, 102-8, 111, 112, 113, 116, 117, 120, 135, 144
Wilson, Woodrow, 82
Wingfield, George, 57, 58, 78, 101, 114, 115, 150
World War I, 16, 32, 81, 122
World War II, xv, 14, 16, 31, 55, 58, 64, 111, 119, 131, 140, 153
Wyoming, 41, 152

Zinc, 36, 75, 89, 90, 142, 153
Zirconium, 144

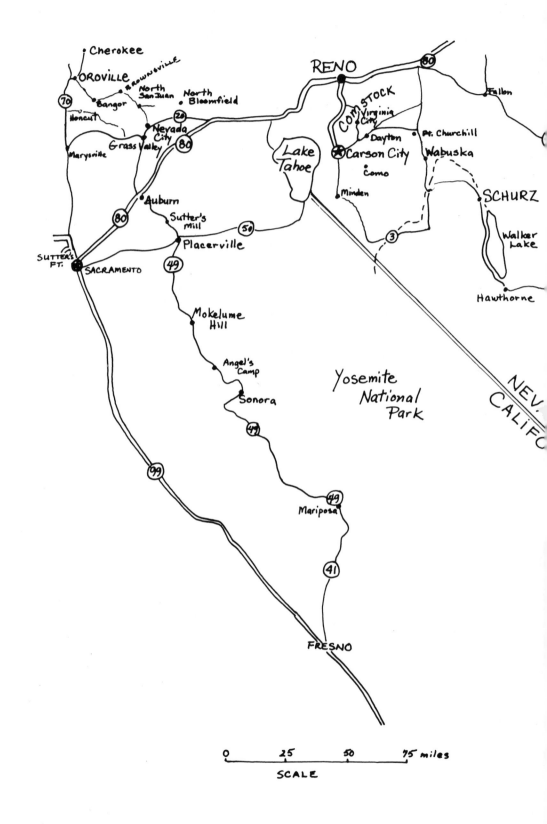